Miss. Griffiths

A LESSON FOR EVERY DAY

7–8 YEARS

MATHS

7–8 YEARS

A & C Black • London

Published 2010 by A & C Black Publishers Limited
36 Soho Square, London W1D 3QY
www.acblack.com
ISBN 978-1-4081-2548-9
Copyright text © Hilary Koll, Steve Mills, Caroline Clissold 2010
Editors: Dodi Beardshaw, Jane Klima, Marie Lister, Clare Robertson, Lynne Williamson
Compiled by Mary Nathan and Fakenham Photosetting

The authors and publishers would like to thank Ray Barker, Fleur Lawrence and Rifat Siddiqui for their advice in
producing this series of books.

A CIP catalogue record for this book is available from the British Library.

Printed and bound in Great Britain by Martins the Printers, Berwick-on-Tweed.

A & C Black uses paper produced with elemental chlorine-free pulp, harvested from managed sustainable forests.

Contents

Introduction

A Lesson for Every Day: Mathematics is a series of seven photocopiable activity books for the Foundation Stage and Key Stages 1 and 2, designed to be used during the daily maths lesson. The books focus on the skills and concepts outlined in the National Strategy's *Primary Framework for literacy and mathematics*. The activities are intended to be used in the time allocated to pupil activities; they aim to reinforce the knowledge and develop the facts, skills and understanding explored during the main part of the lesson and to provide practice and consolidation of the objectives contained in the Framework document.

A Lesson for Every Day: Mathematics Ages 7–8 supports the teaching of mathematics to children aged 7 to 8 by providing a series of activities to develop:

- processes for using and applying mathematics in real situations
- skills in talking about the mathematics in real situations
- essential skills in counting and recognising numbers
- the learning of simple number facts
- an understanding of ideas of addition, subtraction, multiplication and division
- spatial vocabulary in order to increase awareness of properties of shape and measurement concepts
- understanding of key concepts within the handling data cycle
- the skills of collecting, organising, presenting, analysing and interpreting data.

On the whole, the activities are designed for children to work on independently, although due to the young age of the children, the teacher may need to read the instructions with the children to ensure that they understand the activity before they begin working on it.

Extension

Many of the activity sheets end with a challenge (**Now try this!**), which reinforces and extend children's learning, and provides the teacher with an opportunity for assessment. These might include harder questions, with numbers from a higher range, than those in the main part of the activity sheet. Some extension activities are open-ended questions and provide opportunity for children to think mathematically for themselves. Occasionally the extension activity will require additional paper or that the children write on the reverse of the sheet itself. Many of the activities encourage children to generate their own questions or puzzles for a partner to solve.

Organisation

Very little equipment is needed, but it will be useful to have available: coloured pencils, counters, cubes, scissors, dice, glue, coins, squared paper, number lines, grids and tracks, 2D and 3D shapes, a variety of different classroom items.

Where possible, children's work should be supported by ICT equipment, such as data handling programmes on interactive whiteboards, or computer software for moving pictures or photographs to show similarities and differences between groups and also charting information. It is also vital that children's experiences are introduced in real-life contexts, such as those portrayed in home/role play areas and through practical activities and number or nursery rhymes that they know. The teachers' notes at the foot of each page and the more detailed notes on pages 6–23 suggest ways in which this can be done effectively.

To help teachers select appropriate learning experiences for the children, the activities are grouped into sections within the book. However, the activities are not expected to be used in this order unless stated otherwise. The sheets are intended to support, rather than direct, the teacher's planning.

Some activities can be made easier or more challenging by masking or substituting numbers. You may wish to re-use pages by copying them onto card and laminating them.

Teachers' notes

Brief notes are provided at the foot of each page, giving ideas and suggestions for maximising the effectiveness of the activity sheets. These can be masked before copying.

Solutions be found on pages 214–216.

Assessment

Use the completed activities as part of your day-to-day assessment to help you to build a picture of children's learning in order to plan future teaching and learning. Activities can also be used as examples of significant evidence for your periodic assessment. In order to help you to make reliable judgements about your pupils' attainment, the assessment focuses for each activity are given in the grids on pages 6–23.

Some of the activities provide opportunities for children to carry out self assessment. Encourage children to reflect on their learning and discuss with them whether there are areas that they feel they need to practise further.

The CD-ROM

All activity sheets can be found as PDF and Word versions on the accompanying CD-ROM. These can be printed or displayed on an interactive whiteboard. The Word versions can be customised in Microsoft Word in order to assist personalised learning.

They can be accessed through an interface that makes it easy to select worksheets and display them. You can also search for lessons that will meet a particular Assessment Focus for Assessing Pupils' Progress. For more information on system requirements, please see the inside front cover.

If you have any questions regarding the *A Lesson For Every Day* CD-ROM, please email us at the address below. We will get back to you as soon as possible.

educationalsales@acblack.com

Whole class warm-up activities

The following activities provide some practical ideas that can be used to introduce or reinforce the main teaching part of the lesson, or provide an interesting basis for discussion.

What's my number?

Write a number on a sticky note and stick it to a child's forehead so they are unable to read it. Ask other children to give clues about the identity of the number, for example 'It's less than 10,' 'It's more than 6,' 'It is a multiple of 3,' 'It is even'.

Guess my shape

Pick a shape from a bag of flat shapes but do not show it to the children. They can ask three questions, for example 'Does it have five corners?', to which you answer 'Yes' or 'No'. A more difficult version involves playing the game using 3-D shapes.

Odd, odd, odd

This activity encourages the children to work systematically. Write the number 15 on the board. Ask them to suggest ways of adding three odd numbers to make 15, for example 1 + 5 + 9, 11 + 3 + 1. Write correct suggestions in a list and prompt the children to look for more. 'How many threes have we written? How many nines? Are we missing any?' Begin to organise the list so all the number sentences beginning with 1 come together, for example 1 + 3 + 11, 1 + 5 + 9. Discuss whether a digit can be used more than once, such as 3 + 3 + 9.

Larger/smaller

With the class sitting in a circle, ask a child to say a number between 500 and 1000. The next child should say a number that is larger than this. The next child in the circle should say one that is smaller than the new number, working around in a circle, e.g. 705, 895, 894, 900, 300, 413, 324... To add an extra level of difficulty, explain that the children can only use the digits 4, 7 and 5 in their answers, e.g. 475, 754, 744, 755, 444, 557, 555, etc. Record the numbers on the board and see how many numbers can be written in this way using the digits without a number being repeated.

Crocodile

Invite two children to the front of the class with some place value cards. Give each child a three-digit number to make using the cards. Invite a third child to be the greedy crocodile and to come to the front and stand facing the child with the larger number, holding arms to represent the crocodile's mouth. Demonstrate how this can be recorded, e.g. 157 > 127 or 156 < 157. Point out that the mouth is always open towards the larger number.

Catch it

Throw a soft ball to children in turn asking questions such as, 'Three times four', 'Eight add nine' or 'Fifteen take away six'. Each child returns the ball as they answer. There could be a 'Catch it' focus on addition or the five times table etc.

Flash cards

Make sets of flash cards with a question on one side and the answer on the other. For example one set might focus on the division facts for the five times table. Children can work in pairs, with all the questions face up on the table. Each child takes a turn to point to a card and give an answer to the question. If correct, they keep the card. It can quickly be seen which questions children are unsure of as these will be left until last. An alternative game is for each child to point to a card for their partner to answer.

Twenty questions

Hide a 3-D shape in a bag and ask the children to find out which shape it is by asking questions. You can only answer 'yes' or 'no' to their questions. Challenge the children to guess the shape in twenty questions.

Make a metre

Call out lengths in centimetres that are less than a metre, for example 50 cm, 70 cm, 22 cm, and ask the children to give the length that would make this measurement up to 1 metre: 50 cm, 30 cm, 78cm. Hold up a metre stick and show the lengths to help the children to visualise the measurements. The same activity can be adapted for kilograms or litres, where measurements such as 350 g or 900 ml are given.

Block A Counting, partitioning and calculating – Unit 1

Activity name	Strand and learning objectives	Notes on the activities	Assessment Focus	Page number
Domino distractions: 1 and 2	**Using and applying mathematics** Describe and explain methods, choices and solutions to puzzles and problems, orally and in writing, using pictures and diagrams	**Domino distractions: 1 and 2** Processes: look for pattern, reason, test ideas, be systematic The second Domino sets sheet can be used to provide further opportunities for children to investigate this domino grid.	Communicating	24–5
Number cards	**Counting and understanding number** Read, write and order whole numbers to at least 1000 and position them on a number line; count on from and back to zero in single-digit steps or multiples of 10	**Number cards.** Different games and activities can be played. *Table subhead activities* 1) Pelmanism – place all the cards face down and turn over pairs (one of each shape). If the numbers match, keep them; if not, turn them back face down and continue. 2) Ordering – pick four cards and put them in order of size, smallest first. Record the numbers in words and in figures. *Games for two* 1) Pelmanism – as above. The player with the most pairs wins. 2) Snap – one child should have the number name cards and the other should have the number in figures. If two cards show the same value, the first to say 'Snap' wins the cards. 3) Snap variation – using only the cards showing numbers in figures, 'Snap' is called when two numbers in the pair show the same number of hundreds, tens or units, for example 118 and 538 both have eight ones. SUGGESTED QUESTIONS • Read this number to me. Is it more or less than five hundred? • How would this number be written in figures/using words? **Code breaker.** For this activity, it is important to clearly display somewhere in the classroom the correct spellings of the number names of numbers to 20, and multiples of 10 to 100, to which children can refer. SUGGESTED QUESTION • Look at the spelling on the board. Can you see any difference between my spelling and how you have spelt it? **More or less.** For this activity, ensure that the children are familiar with the 'greater than' and 'less than' symbols by revising them at the start of the lesson. Write a number and the 'less than' sign, for example 246 < ? and ask the children to state numbers that could go to its right. Discuss that there are hundreds and hundreds (an infinite number) of possibilities. Show how the number of possibilities could be narrowed by writing another sign to the right, for example 246 < ? < 300. Explain that the first part of the inequality (246) must be less than the new number, and the new number must be less than 300. Write further inequalities in the same way. Ask the children to describe the number range in words. **Animal antics.** Some children might find it easier to write multiples of 10 along each line to help them place the joining lines more carefully. Encourage the children to check each other's work once the lines have been placed. For the extension activity, ensure the children realise that there can be more than one acceptable answer for each and discuss their answers as a class at the end of the lesson. SUGGESTED QUESTIONS • Have you checked your answers? • Which number do you think this might be? **Monkey puzzles.** To provide further similar worksheets, the numbers could be altered on the CD. Watch out for children who think that 1010 is less than 910 as the sum of its digits is smaller. This common error demonstrates a lack of understanding of place value ideas. SUGGESTED QUESTIONS • Where on the line would you mark the number 652? • Between which two multiples of 10 does it lie?	Numbers and the number system	26
Code breaker				27
More or less				28
Animal antics				29
Monkey puzzles				30
Piggy in the middle		**Piggy in the middle.** Support the children who are finding this activity difficult by asking them to count up from the lower number to the higher and to write these numbers down, and then choose one of the numbers they have written. Alternatively, point to the sheep numbers on a number line to 1000, and ask the children to say the numbers in between. Hide the number line, and ask the children to pick one of the numbers that they had read. SUGGESTED QUESTIONS • Which number lies between these two? • Are there other numbers it could be? • What is the lowest/highest number it could be? **Swimming lanes.** Draw the children's attention to the fact that some sequences involve counting on and others involve counting back. SUGGESTED QUESTIONS/PROMPT • What is 10 more than 100? Find it on your sheet. • What is 10 less than 160? • What do you notice about the ones digits of the numbers in the sequence? • What if the sequence started on the number one, counting on in tens? **Mixed up, missed out!** When children begin counting on in steps that are multiples of 10, such as in steps of 20, 30 or 40, encourage them to use what they already know about counting on in twos, threes or fours. If they know 2, 4, 6, ... they should be encouraged to see the link with that and 20, 40, 60, ... SUGGESTED QUESTIONS • How many are we counting on each time in this sequence? • What is 20/30/40 more than 120? **Multiple octopus.** A multiple octopus can be a permanent feature on the wall of any classroom. It can serve as a useful focus for a mental/oral activity, where you call out a number and the children say whether this number is a multiple of 2, 3, 4, 5, 6, 7, 8 or 9 by looking at the legs of the octopus. It can help the children to see that some numbers are common to more than one set of multiples. Note that in the extension activity, the children are asked to say which octopus leg(s) the numbers appear in, rather than listing all the numbers that are factors, for example 36 is not on the twos or threes legs but yet are factors of 36. If appropriate, discuss how the legs could be extended to include further multiples. SUGGESTED QUESTIONS • Is this in the sevens octopus leg? • Does 23 appear in any of the legs? • Is 42 a multiple of 6? **Changing the guard.** This activity can be introduced practically. Ask the children to stand (or sit) in lines of ten, perhaps in the hall. Call out a multiple of 10 and ask the children in turn to count back in equal-sized steps, for example from 30 in threes. When the end of the line is reached, the front child should march to the back and a new multiple of 10 given. Continue in this way so that the children get a variety of questions of varying difficulty.		31
Swimming lanes				32
Mixed up, missed out!				33
Multiple octopus				34
Changing the guard				35

Activity name	Strand and learning objectives	Notes on the activities	Assessment Focus	Page number
Superheroes	**Counting and understanding number** Partition three-digit numbers into multiples of 100, 10 and 1 in different ways	**Superheroes.** This activity enables children to practise partitioning three-digit numbers. For children who find this difficult, you could provide place value cards and write H, T and U above the numbers on the sheet. Ask the children to say the number in words before they try to split it, for example 'two hundred and sixty-two'. As they say each part of the number, they can take the appropriate place value cards and place them on the table so that they can see how the number is made up. SUGGESTED QUESTIONS • What amount is Hundreds Man in charge of? • What do you notice about the amount Tens Girl is in charge of in the number 605?	Numbers and the number system	36
Slider sums	**Knowing and using number facts** Derive and recall all addition and subtraction facts for each number to 20, sums and differences of multiples of 10 and number pairs that total 100	**Slider sums.** This activity can be used to encourage the children to explore number patterns and to see relationships between sums. Children will require scissors and glue. The sheet could be photocopied onto A3 paper and used for display purposes. Ask the children who complete the extension activity what they notice about the sums they have written to reinforce that addition can be done in any order. SUGGESTED QUESTION/PROMPT: • Can you see patterns in the sums? • Tell me three things you notice about these patterns. **Bows and arrows.** A similar target board could be displayed on a large sheet of paper or on screen, and the activity introduced to the whole class as an oral activity. Arrows made out of thin card could be tacked onto the paper, or lines drawn onto an interactive whiteboard to provide the sums. Focus on those facts that children experience most difficulty with, such as 6 + 7, 8 + 5, 7 + 8, 7 + 4, 8 + 4 etc. and discuss how 9 can be added by adding 10 and subtracting 1. Ask the children to suggest other strategies that might be useful, for example using doubles, near doubles, and making 10 to derive facts quickly. SUGGESTED QUESTIONS • What total does this show? • How did you work this out? • Did you just know the fact or did you use a double or another act to help you work this out?	Mental methods	37
Bows and arrows				38

Block A Unit 2

Activity name	Strand and learning objectives	Notes on the activities	Assessment Focus	Page number
Noah's arcs (addition) Noah's arcs (subtraction)	**Using and applying mathematics** Describe and explain methods, choices and solutions to puzzles and problems, orally and in writing, using pictures and diagrams	**Noah's arcs (addition and subtraction)** Processes: explain, compare, reason Encourage the children to describe their strategies for working out the answer. Ask them to demonstrate this in different ways, for example using practical material, number lines, 100-squares, place value cards. The numbers can be altered before copying to provide differentiation. SUGGESTED QUESTIONS • What calculation do these arrows represent? • Which number is missing here? • Why? • How can you be sure? • Do you agree?	Communicating	39 40
Partition pots: 1 and 2 Matchmakers	**Counting and understanding number** Partition three-digit numbers into multiples of 100, 10 and 1 in different ways	**Partition pots: 1 and 2.** The cards could also be used for a variety of place value activities, such as finding two cards with the same tens digit, for example 743 and 841. SUGGESTED QUESTIONS/PROMPT • How many tens has this number? • Find me a card with two hundreds and two ones. What is the value of the tens digit? **Matchmakers.** The cards could be photocopied onto thin card and laminated to provide a more permanent classroom resource. SUGGESTED QUESTIONS/PROMPT • Have you sorted the cards into groups? Now arrange the cards in one group into an order. • What is the total of each card in this group? • How could you continue this pattern further?	Numbers and the number system	41–2 43
Lifebelts Rounders Whose dog?	**Counting and understanding number** Round two-digit or three-digit numbers to the nearest 10 or 100 and give estimates for their sums and differences	**Lifebelts.** Practise counting in tens from 0 to 100 and back again. Ask the children to say a number that is less/more than a given multiple of 10, and then move on to asking children to say which multiple of 10 a given number rounds to. SUGGESTED QUESTIONS • Can you find a number that ends in the digit 5 on your sheet? • Do numbers ending in the digit 5 round up or down? **Rounders.** Explain to the children that, although there are more squares than circles on the number line, there are no numbers that round down to 300, so there is an equal chance of squares or circles winning. Note that the sheet could be enlarged onto A3 and laminated to provide a more permanent resource. SUGGESTED QUESTION • What multiple of 10 is this nearest to? **Whose dog?** As a further extension, the children could draw more dogs on the sheet and write three-digit numbers between 350 and 949 on their sides. They should then join them to the appropriate owner by rounding the numbers to the nearest 100. SUGGESTED QUESTIONS • Do numbers ending in 50 round up or down? • Which multiple of 100 is this nearest to?	Numbers and the number system	44 45 46
Pigs on parade	**Knowing and using number facts** Derive and recall all addition and subtraction facts for each number to 20, sums and differences of multiples of 10 and number pairs that total 100	**Pigs on parade.** Watch out for the common error of writing a number that will add to 110 rather than 100. This is because children have learnt, for example, that 70 and 30 make 100 and therefore believe that 71 and 39 make 100. Demonstrate how the 1 and 9 add to make 10 so there only needs to be 90 made by the tens digits. Encourage the children to check their answers by adding them each time. SUGGESTED QUESTIONS • Have you checked your answers? • What is the total of the numbers in this pair?	Mental methods	47

Activity name	Strand and learning objectives	Notes on the activities	Assessment Focus	Page number
Counting sheep	**Knowing and using number facts** Derive and recall multiplication facts for the 2, 3, 4, 5, 6 and 10 times-tables and the corresponding division facts; recognise multiples of 2, 5 or 10 up to 1000	**Counting sheep.** This activity can be used as an introduction to the 4 times-table. Point out that all the answers are even and encourage the children to use this fact to check their answers. Also ask them to use a number line and count on in fours from zero to ensure that they have correctly noted all the answers. Children could also be given this sheet as cards to take and use at home.	Mental methods	48
		SUGGESTED QUESTIONS • What connection can you see between the 4 times-table and the 2 times-table? • Could you use facts in the 2 times-table to help you to work out facts in the 4 times-table?		
Genius gerbil	**Calculating** Multiply one-digit and two-digit numbers by 10 or 100, and describe the effect	**Genius gerbil.** At the start of the lesson, practise counting in tens from 0 to numbers over 100. Say the 10 times-table together, and ask for tables facts out of order. You could make paper '10 times machines' to demonstrate what is happening.	Mental methods Operations and relationships between them	49
		SUGGESTED PROMPT/QUESTION • Describe what happens to a number when it is multiplied by 10. • What happens to the digits of the number?		

Block A Unit 3

Activity name	Strand and learning objectives	Notes on the activities	Assessment Focus	Page number
At the ice rink	**Using and applying mathematics** Solve one-step and two-step problems involving numbers, money or measures, including time, choosing and carrying out appropriate calculations	**At the ice rink** *Processes: reason, make decisions, record* Children should work in pairs and record calculations for each problem to show what they think should be done. Remind them to use the correct unit in their answers where appropriate. Discuss differences in the calculations they write.	Problem solving	50
		SUGGESTED QUESTIONS • How did you find this solution? • Have you written the same number sentences as Jo?		
Round and about Rain rounding Have a good trip!	**Counting and understanding number** Round two-digit or three-digit numbers to the nearest 10 or 100 and give estimates for their sums and differences	**Round and about.** This activity involves approximating answers to two-digit addition and subtraction questions. The children should round the numbers to the nearest 10 and write them onto the teacups above, before adding the two multiples of 10 together to provide an approximation for the question. Introduce and use a range of vocabulary, for example: roughly, about, estimate, round, approximate. **SUGGESTED PROMPT** • Say roughly what the answer to this question would be. **Rain rounding.** Similarly, this activity involves rounding to the nearest 100 and using these approximations to estimate the answer to the	Numbers and the number system	51 52 53
		addition or subtraction. The children could find the exact answers, using a written method or a calculator, to see how close their estimates were. **Have a good trip!** This activity involves rounding distances to help when estimating a total. Discuss with the children why this sort of rounding and estimating is useful in everyday life, and ask them to give other examples of situations where the exact answer is not needed. **SUGGESTED QUESTION** • About how many kilometres have they travelled on this journey?		
Jack-in-the-box	**Knowing and using number facts** Derive and recall multiplication facts for the 2, 3, 4, 5, 6 and 10 times-tables and the corresponding division facts; recognise multiples of 2, 5 or 10 up to 1000	**Jack-in-the-box.** This activity tests the children's knowledge of facts in the 3 and 4 times-tables. You could use it when children have been learning these tables for a few weeks to test how well they remember which numbers are multiples of 3 or 4.	Mental methods	54
		SUGGESTED QUESTIONS • Is 18 an answer in the 3 or the 4 times-table? • Which of these numbers are answers in the 3 and the 4 times-tables?		
The value of words	**Calculating** Add or subtract mentally combinations of one-digit and two-digit numbers	**The value of words.** For this activity, the children should be using their knowledge of totals to 20 to help them, for example if they know that 8 + 7 = 15, they should know that 38 + 7 = 45. Discuss such approaches at the start of the lesson and provide number lines to 100 for those children who experience difficulty with this task.	Mental methods	55
		SUGGESTED QUESTIONS • How did you work out this answer? • Which fact did you use to help you?		

Activity name	Strand and learning objectives	Notes on the activities	Assessment Focus	Page number
Katie's kittens: 1 and 2	**Calculating** Develop and use written methods to record, support or explain addition and subtraction of two-digit and three-digit numbers	**Katie's kittens: 1.** This activity can be used for those children who are beginning to show competency in adding using a range of written methods and who can be introduced to a vertical method, using partitioning. See the Guidance Paper on Calculation for more information. SUGGESTED QUESTIONS • What known number fact did you use to work out 40 + 70? • Why can we write the addition 66 + 37 in this way? **Katie's kittens: 2.** This written method of subtraction mirrors the addition method on the previous page. It is a method which is based upon children's ability to partition two-digit numbers in different ways. See the Counting and Understanding Number strand of this series for more activities to develop this skill. SUGGESTED QUESTIONS • Why can we write the subtraction 85 – 29 in this way? • What did you do when you discovered that you could not take 9 away from 5? Why?	Written methods	56–7

Block B Securing number facts, understanding shapes – Unit 1

Activity name	Strand and learning objectives	Notes on the activities	Assessment Focus	Page number
Triangle tricks Question time Problem page	**Using and applying mathematics** Represent the information in a puzzle or problem using numbers, images or diagrams; use these to find a solution and present it in context, where appropriate using £.p notation or units of measure	**Triangle tricks** Processes: *visualise, be systematic, test ideas, trial and improvement* Encourage the children to begin the activity by making different triangles from the shapes and totalling the number of dots on each side. Ask them to record their results and then look at how to swap shapes around so as to have 12 dots on each side. SUGGESTED QUESTION • What strategies did you use? **Question time** Processes: *explain, reason, record* These questions can be copied onto thin card and laminated and used as a more permanent classroom resource. The cards could be picked at random and used for whole class problem-solving activities in spare moments.	Communicating	58 59 60
		SUGGESTED QUESTIONS • How did you find the answer? • How did you write this as a number sentence or number sentences? **Problem page** Processes: *reason, explain, record* Observe the methods children use to find the answers, for example noting which children use the picture, their fingers, equipment or a mental method. SUGGESTED QUESTIONS • How did you find the answer? • Which questions did you find the hardest? Why? • What method did you use to find the answer? • Did anyone write this as a number sentence?		
Bing, Bong, Bang Find my house Chair challenge	**Using and applying mathematics** Identify patterns and relationships involving numbers or shapes, and use these to solve problems	**Bing, Bong, Bang** Processes: *be systematic, look for pattern, compare, record, reason* Encourage the children to work systematically. Some children will begin to notice that, to an extent, they can use one set of answers to help them find the next (for example, by swapping over all the Bings with Bongs). SUGGESTED QUESTIONS • What patterns did you use to help you? • What patterns did you notice? • How do you know you have found all the solutions? **Find my house** Processes: *visualise, compare, test ideas, trial and improvement, be systematic, look for pattern* Once the children begin listing solutions they will notice patterns in the cards and realise that by making one substitution each time they will eventually find all the solutions.	Reasoning	61 62 63
		SUGGESTED QUESTIONS • How would you describe how to get to house number 7? • How is that set of instructions different from house number 5? **Chair challenge** Processes: *trial and improvement, test ideas, record, explain, reason* Encourage the children to notice patterns in the numbers, for example to realise that 3 rows of 5 will have the same number of chairs as 5 rows of 3 etc. Encourage them to work systematically. SUGGESTED QUESTIONS • What patterns did you use to help you? • What patterns did you notice? • How do you know you have found all the solutions?		
Easter-egg hunt Brain box	**Knowing and using number facts** Derive and recall all addition and subtraction facts for each number to 20, sums and differences of multiples of 10 and number pairs that total 100	**Easter-egg hunt.** For ease of marking, the only egg uncoloured should be that marked with a 2. SUGGESTED QUESTIONS • How quickly did you answer these? • How did you work out this subtraction? • Did you just know the fact or did you use a double or another fact to help you work this out? **Brain box.** This activity is useful for encouraging the children to use reasoning and trial and improvement. SUGGESTED QUESTIONS • How did you work out which number to write in that space? • The difference between two numbers is 11. What could the numbers be?	Mental methods	64 65
Funfair cards and Funfair game	**Knowing and using number facts** Derive and recall multiplication facts for the 2, 3, 4, 5, 6 and 10 times-tables and the corresponding division facts; recognise multiples of 2, 5 or 10 up to 1000	**Funfair cards and Funfair game.** This activity focuses on the 2, 5 and 10 times-tables. (It might be useful to copy the sheet onto A3 for easier use.) Explain to the children that they can hold onto the 'have another go' card and use it when they are not sure of the answer (and so pick another card to try), or use it when they want to have another turn. SUGGESTED QUESTIONS • What do you know about answers in the 10 times-table? • What digit do they always end with? • How can you use doubling to help you work out facts in the 2 times-table?	Mental methods	66–7

Activity name	Strand and learning objectives	Notes on the activities	Assessment Focus	Page number
Permission to land	**Knowing and using number facts** Use knowledge of number operations and corresponding inverses, including doubling and halving, to estimate and check calculations	**Permission to land.** These questions involve adding pairs of three-digit numbers. The children could use a written column method involving partitioning, or they could use more informal methods. SUGGESTED QUESTIONS/PROMPT • How did you estimate the total of 696 and 218? • Show me the method you used to find the actual total of 696 and 218. Why did you choose that method?	Mental methods Operations, relationships between them	68
Spot the difference	**Understanding shape** Relate 2-D shapes and 3-D solids to drawings of them; describe, visualise, classify, draw and make the shapes	**Spot the difference.** It is important that children begin to appreciate when two shapes have similarities and differences. The pairs of shapes on this worksheet are different because they have been enlarged (or reduced), reflected, stretched, or because one vertex has been moved. The children should be encouraged to develop the necessary vocabulary to describe such features and to identify aspects that have remained the same. Pairs could make jottings on the backs of the cards as a reminder for when whole-class discussion takes place. SUGGESTED QUESTIONS • How many sides/corners/angles does this shape have? • Are the sides/corners/angles of this shape the same or different?	Properties of shape	69
A sticky situation		**A sticky situation.** It is not expected that children will be able to name the four-sided shapes as a rhombus or a trapezium at this stage, but they should be learning that it is possible to make four-sided shapes other than rectangles or squares, and that all are known as quadrilaterals. Note that there are many different answers to this investigation, depending on the positioning of the sticks. SUGGESTED PROMPT/QUESTIONS • Do you know what this shape is called? • Describe the shape to me. What does it remind you of? • How many sides/corners/angles does it have?		70
Building work		**Building work.** Children often struggle to visualise a 3-D solid from a 2-D drawing. If the children find this activity difficult, colour the cubes on the worksheet and give them corresponding coloured cubes with which to build. When the children carry out the extension activity, encourage them to pick up the models they have made and twist them around to work out which of the shapes are the same. During the plenary, discuss whether the children think that the shapes are different or the same if they are positioned differently on a table. SUGGESTED QUESTIONS • How many cubes have you used to make this shape? • Can you colour the picture to match the colour of your cubes?		71
Traffic lights		**Traffic lights.** Revise the terms 'faces' and 'edges' and ensure that the children are familiar with the terms 'vertex' and 'vertices', meaning 'corner' and 'corners'. Provide each child with red, orange and green coloured pencils for this activity. SUGGESTED QUESTIONS • What shapes are the faces of a cube/cuboid/triangular prism? • Which shapes have one or more curved faces?		72

Block B Unit 2

Activity name	Strand and learning objectives	Notes on the activities	Assessment Focus	Page number
Two numbers	**Using and applying mathematics** Solve one-step and two-step problems involving numbers, money or measures, including time, choosing and carrying out appropriate calculations	**Two numbers** *Processes: look for pattern, reason, explain* Observe the methods children use to find the answers, for example noting which children use pictures, their fingers, equipment or a mental method. Revise the terms 'product' and 'total' and ask the children to work together to discuss their strategies. SUGGESTED QUESTIONS • How did you find this solution? • What does the word product mean? • How could you write these as two number sentences?	Problem solving	73
Spiders and flies		**Spiders and flies** *Processes: explain, ask own questions, reason* This activity can help the children to see how many different questions can be asked about a context and encourages them to make up their own questions. SUGGESTED QUESTIONS • How many different questions have we asked in our class? • How would you answer Jo's question?		74
Match it: 1 and 2	**Using and applying mathematics** Represent the information in a puzzle or problem using numbers, images or diagrams; use these to find a solution and present it in context, where appropriate using £.p notation or units of measure	**Match it: 1 and 2** *Processes: explain, record, reason* These two sheets provide the children with the opportunity to consider and identify which operations are necessary in solving each question. For these sheets, remind the children that 100p = £1 and 100 cm = 1 m. SUGGESTED QUESTION • Which calculation would you use?	Communicating	75-6
Sweet talk		**Sweet talk** *Processes: explain, look for pattern, record, test ideas, trial and improvement, make own decisions* This problem-solving activity requires children to understand the relationship between halving and doubling. Encourage the children to make their own decisions about how to tackle these problems and to record their workings. SUGGESTED QUESTIONS • What was difficult about this task? • How could you record what you did so that someone else would be able to work it out?		77

Activity name	Strand and learning objectives	Notes on the activities	Assessment Focus	Page number
Pattern maker Miss Moneybags	**Using and applying mathematics** Identify patterns and relationships involving numbers or shapes, and use these to solve problems	**Pattern maker** Processes: *look for pattern, compare, reason, predict, test ideas, explain* There are a wide variety of different patterns that the children could make with these cards. SUGGESTED QUESTIONS • Can you describe this pattern? • What do you predict? • How could you check? **Miss Moneybags** Processes: *look for pattern, test ideas, predict, reason* This activity encourages the children to see patterns in numbers that can be used to help them solve problems more quickly. Having completed the sheet, ask the children questions about the number of 10p, 1p or £1 coins that make different amounts. Encourage them to use the patterns they notice to explain how they answered them quickly. SUGGESTED QUESTION/PROMPT • Describe the relationship between the number of £1, 10p and 1p coins in each amount of money. • How could you use that to help you answer this question?	Reasoning	78 79
Toy sale Make one hundred: 1 and 2	**Knowing and using number facts** Derive and recall all addition and subtraction facts for each number to 20, sums and differences of multiples of 10 and number pairs that total 100	**Toy sale.** Again, watch out for the common error of writing a number that will add to 110 rather than 100. This is because children have learnt, for example, that 70 and 30 make 100 and therefore believe that 71 and 39 make 100. Demonstrate how the 1 and 9 add to make 10 so there only needs to be 90 made by the tens digits. The extension activity involves questions that test children's understanding of this idea. SUGGESTED QUESTION • Have you checked your answers? **Make one hundred: 1** and **2.** Children can work in small groups for this activity. To provide a more permanent resource, the cards could be copied onto thin card and laminated. Children could use a number line or 100-square to check their answers. SUGGESTED QUESTIONS • Have you got the number that adds to make 100? • Are you sure? • What if you count on from this number up to 100? • Could you use a number line to check?	Mental methods	80 81–2
Victorian classroom	**Knowing and using number facts** Derive and recall multiplication facts for the 2, 3, 4, 5, 6 and 10 times-tables and the corresponding division facts; recognise multiples of 2, 5 or 10 up to 1000	**Victorian classroom.** This activity can be used as an introduction to the 6 times-table. Point out that all the answers are even and encourage the children to use this fact to check their answers. For the initial questions, encourage the children to use their knowledge of the 2, 5, 10, 3 and 4 times-tables and reverse them, for example for the first four questions. SUGGESTED QUESTIONS • What connection can you see between the 3 times-table and the 6 times-table? • How could you use facts in the 3 times-table to help you to work out facts in the 6 times-table?	Mental methods	83
Draw and name game Shape all-sorts	**Understanding shape** Relate 2-D shapes and 3-D solids to drawings of them; describe, visualise, classify, draw and make the shapes	**Draw and name game.** The children need one worksheet per pair. A third child could act as adjudicator, if desired. At the start of the lesson, discuss some of the descriptions of the shapes on the worksheet and ask children to come to the front of the class to draw shapes to match. Revise the common shape names, including the term 'quadrilateral'. Encourage the children to use a ruler when drawing 2-D shapes. SUGGESTED QUESTIONS • Do you know the name of this shape? • How many sides/right angles/lines of symmetry has this shape? **Shape all-sorts.** At the start of the lesson, demonstrate how a Carroll diagram is used to show data, drawing attention to the fact that the headings along the top refer to the whole columns and that the other headings refer to the whole rows. If possible, display the shape names for the children to refer to when completing this activity. SUGGESTED QUESTIONS • Do you know the name of this shape? • How many faces/vertices has this shape? • Are its faces curved or straight?	Properties of shape	84 85
Symmetry Cemetery Shape symmetry Mosaic patterns	**Understanding shape** Draw and complete shapes with reflective symmetry; draw the reflection of a shape in a mirror line along one side	**Symmetry Cemetery.** Watch out for the following errors: line 1 shape 3 – children often mistake as symmetrical; line 2 shape 5 – children often miss the line of symmetry, as it is neither vertical nor horizontal; line 3 shape 3 – children often miss the horizontal line of symmetry. SUGGESTED QUESTIONS • Can you draw some more shapes that have one line of symmetry? • Is the line of symmetry vertical, horizontal or diagonal? **Shape symmetry.** At the start of the lesson, demonstrate how to place the mirror along the mirror line and lift and replace the mirror to see the reflection. Perspex equipment (such as a MIRA) that allows not only the reflection to be seen but also the drawing on the other side of the line can be a useful resource for those children who struggle with mirrors. **Mosaic patterns.** Encourage the children to use a mirror (or a MIRA) to check for the position of the mirror line in each pattern and then to work out where the tiles need to be shaded. Once the tiles have been shaded the children should hold the mirror along the mirror line and then lift it to check whether their answer underneath is correct. SUGGESTED QUESTIONS • Where do you think the mirror line must be? • Can you use the mirror to check?	Properties of position and movement	86 87 88

Block B Unit 3

Activity name	Strand and learning objectives	Notes on the activities	Assessment Focus	Page number
Express pizza Loop the loop	**Using and applying mathematics** Solve one-step and two-step problems involving numbers, money or measures, including time, choosing and carrying out appropriate calculations	**Express pizza** *Processes: reason, explain, record* Children could work together in pairs on this activity to promote discussion. Talk about strategies for answering each question, for example adding £5 and subtracting 1p when adding £4.99. SUGGESTED QUESTIONS • How did you find this solution? • What strategies did you use? **Loop the loop** *Processes: reason, make decisions* At the start of the lesson, remind the children about the notation kg and g and that 1000 g is the same as 1 kg. SUGGESTED QUESTIONS • How did you find this solution? • If you can't find the answer, is it because the answer is in grams rather than kilograms?	Problem solving	89 90
Sheep solutions Sensible statements Coin quiz	**Using and applying mathematics** Represent the information in a puzzle or problem using numbers, images or diagrams; use these to find a solution and present it in context, where appropriate using £.p notation or units of measure	**Sheep solutions** *Processes: visualise, make decisions, reason, be systematic, test ideas* Remind the children that they do not necessarily need to work through the clues in order. SUGGESTED QUESTIONS • How did you find this solution? • Have you checked each rule against your answers? **Sensible statements** *Processes: reason, record, explain* In this activity, the numbers can be changed before copying to provide further investigations. SUGGESTED QUESTIONS • How could you work this out? • Why did you decide to record it like this? **Coin quiz** *Processes: record, explain, reason* This activity provides the children with practice in using pounds/pence notation. Some children may benefit from being given coins to work with. Draw attention to the fact that some questions contain 10p coins and others contain 1p coins. SUGGESTED QUESTIONS • What does £4.02 mean? • How would you write 3 pounds and eleven pence?	Communicating	91 92 93
Right-angle wrangle Right-angle tangle Clock angles	**Using and applying mathematics** Identify patterns and relationships involving numbers or shapes, and use these to solve problems	**Right-angle wrangle** and **Right-angle tangle** *Processes: look for pattern, explain, reason, compare, record* Children can work in pairs or small groups to compare and discuss their answers. Ensure the children only count right angles that are inside the shapes, not those outside. SUGGESTED QUESTIONS • Do you know the name of this shape? • How many right angles has it? • Do you notice any patterns in the numbers of right angles? **Clock angles** *Processes: visualise, test ideas, look for pattern, record* These questions can be used as a lead-in to a wider investigation about the number of right angles turned by the minute hand between pairs of times. SUGGESTED QUESTIONS • How can you work out answers quickly? • What do you notice about these two times? • How many right angles does the minute hand turn in each hour?	Reasoning	94 95 96
Magic carpets Gee-up horse!	**Counting and understanding number** Read and write proper fractions (e.g. $\frac{3}{7}$, $\frac{9}{10}$), interpreting the denominator as the parts of a whole and the numerator as the number of parts; identify and estimate fractions of shapes; use diagrams to compare fractions and establish equivalents	**Magic carpets**. It is important that children appreciate that the number on the bottom of a fraction indicates the number of equal parts into which the whole has been split. The children could also play a memory pairs game where they place the cards face down and take it in turns to turn two over. If they match, the cards are won. The winner is the player with the most cards at the end. SUGGESTED QUESTIONS • How many equal parts are there altogether? • How many are shaded? **Gee-up horse!** As children's answers are estimates they will vary considerably. SUGGESTED QUESTION • Can the fraction be described in more than one way?	Numbers and the number system	97 98
Musical mental maths	**Knowing and using number facts** Derive and recall all addition and subtraction facts for each number to 20, sums and differences of multiples of 10 and number pairs that total 100	**Musical mental maths**. This could be used as an assessment activity to check speed of recall of the number facts expected to be learnt by this age. SUGGESTED QUESTION • Have you checked your answers?	Mental methods	99
Snap	**Knowing and using number facts** Derive and recall multiplication facts for the 2, 3, 4, 5, 6 and 10 times-tables and the corresponding division facts; recognise multiples of 2, 5 or 10 up to 1000	**Snap**. Remind children that division facts are the inverse of multiplication facts. Display tables facts for the 3, 4 and 6 times-tables for those who might need them to refer to. SUGGESTED QUESTIONS • Have you checked this answer? • How could you use the multiplication fact 3 × 6 = 18 to help you with this division question?	Mental methods	100

Activity name	Strand and learning objectives	Notes on the activities	Assessment Focus	Page number
The dabble birds	**Knowing and using number facts** Use knowledge of number operations and corresponding inverses, including doubling and halving, to estimate and check calculations	**The dabble birds.** Children often need convincing that the inverse cancels an operation out, particularly if a number of operations and their inverses are in a line. Encourage such children to use a calculator to key in the whole string and to notice that the first number is the answer. SUGGESTED QUESTIONS • What do you notice about the answer? • Why is this?	Mental methods Operations, relationships between them	101
Taboo or not taboo	**Understanding shape** Relate 2-D shapes and 3-D solids to drawings of them; describe, visualise, classify, draw and make the shapes	**Taboo or not taboo.** It is important that children have as much experience of describing 3-D shapes and their properties as possible. By making it 'illegal' to use the shape names, attention is focused on the nature of the properties of the shapes. SUGGESTED PROMPT/QUESTIONS • Look at the solid shapes. Which shapes have only one curved face? • How many edges has this cylinder?	Properties of shape	102
Learning about turning Angle art	**Understanding shape** Use a set-square to draw right angles and to identify right angles in 2-D shapes; compare angles with a right angle; recognise that a straight line is equivalent to two right angles	**Learning about turning.** The answers given on page 215 are those related to the angles up to 180°, i.e. they do not include reflex angles but the closest angle between the two letters (or 180° as in the case of HE). Children who find this work difficult could use a right angle tester (for example the corner of a sheet of paper or the right angle gobbler from page 170) to help them. SUGGESTED QUESTIONS • Is this angle smaller or larger than a right angle? • Which word involves a straight line that is the same as two right angles? **Angle art.** During the plenary, encourage the children to estimate the size of the smaller angles, for example: 'This looks about half a right angle' or 'This looks about one-third of a right angle'. SUGGESTED QUESTION • Is this angle smaller or larger than a right angle?	Properties of position and movement	103 104

Block C Handling data and measures – Unit 1

Activity name	Strand and learning objectives	Notes on the activities	Assessment Focus	Page number
Sorting coins	**Using and applying mathematics** Follow a line of enquiry by deciding what information is important; make and use lists, tables and graphs to organise and interpret the information	**Sorting coins** Processes: *visualise, compare, reason* This activity helps to appreciate how Venn diagrams can be used to represent information and how they can be used to show similarities and differences in a clear way. By introducing activities like this, children can begin to realise how such diagrams can be used when they are making and recording their own investigations. Provide sets of coins for children in pairs. SUGGESTED QUESTIONS • Why did you put the 5p coin there? • Why is the 50p coin outside both those rings?	Reasoning	105
Stream scheme Question time	**Measuring** Know the relationships between kilometres and metres, metres and centimetres, kilograms and grams, litres and millilitres; choose and use appropriate units to estimate, measure and record measurements	**Stream scheme.** At the start of the lesson, hold up a metre stick and discuss that there are 100 cm in one metre. Call out some multiples of one hundred as numbers of centimetres and ask the children to say how many metres these would be, showing the lengths both vertically and horizontally. SUGGESTED QUESTIONS • Do you think this is larger or smaller than 1m? • Can you show me with your hands how long you think this length is? • Can you think of something in the room that is about this length? Question time. These cards could be enlarged and laminated to create a more permanent classroom resource. SUGGESTED QUESTIONS • Which unit do you think would be best? • Does your partner agree?	Measures	106 107
Rulers rule	**Measuring** Read, to the nearest division and half-division, scales that are numbered or partially numbered; use the information to measure and draw to a suitable degree of accuracy	**Rulers rule.** Show the children a 30 cm ruler and explain that the worksheet shows pictures of rulers like this. SUGGESTED QUESTIONS • How long is this lizard? • Is it just over or just under 21 cm, or is it exactly 21 cm?	Measures	108
Vera's veggies Newspaper sales	**Handling data** Answer a question by collecting, organising and interpreting data; use tally charts, frequency tables, pictograms and bar charts to represent results and illustrate observations; use ICT to create a simple bar chart	**Vera's veggies** Encourage the children to look carefully at the lists and find and highlight which vegetable(s) each child likes. They need to remember that Vera wants to cook two vegetables so that everyone will like at least one. To simplify the activity, ask them to find the children who only like one vegetable first and then check that the others like one or both of these, too. SUGGESTED QUESTIONS: • How will you begin to sort out which vegetables Vera should cook? Why? • Who likes only one vegetable? • Which vegetables does Sammy like? Who else likes these vegetables? **Newspaper sales.** Before beginning the activity, remind the children of work they have done previously on frequency tables. Explain that frequency tables show how often something happened, in this case newspapers were sold. Ask the children which comics and magazines they read and draw a frequency table to show this information. You may need to suggest a few examples to help them. SUGGESTED QUESTIONS • What does this table need to tell us? • Is there another way you could show the information? • Which newspapers sold more than 2000 copies last week?	Processing and representing data Interpreting data	109 110

Activity name	Strand and learning objectives	Notes on the activities	Assessment Focus	Page number
Berries	**Handling data** Use Venn diagrams or Carroll diagrams to sort data and classify objects using more than one criterion	**Berries.** Before you begin, discuss the idea behind Venn diagrams: sorting according to two criteria, overlap indicates items within both criteria, any not belonging to either will be placed outside the rings. Link with any similar work covered previously where the children sorted into loops or rings. SUGGESTED QUESTIONS • What does this Venn diagram show? • What does this middle part show? • Where are you going to look to find out how many children like strawberries?	Processing and representing data	111
Multiples		**Multiples.** Before you begin this activity, ask the children to practise counting in multiples of 3 and 4. Use this as an opportunity to discuss multiples, factors and rehearse multiplication facts for the 3 and 4 times-tables.		112
Party food: 1 and 2		**Party food: 1 and 2.** Before you begin, discuss the children's favourite types of party food and make a list. Discuss ways of sorting these and together think of headings for a Venn diagram, for example meat, snacks. During the plenary, ask the children to explain why there are no foods outside the rings and within the rectangle. (A price can only be more than £1 or less than £2. To be outside both rings, a price would have to be less than £1 and more than £2, which is impossible.) SUGGESTED QUESTIONS • How will you decide which party foods to use? • Which party food will go in the middle? • Will there be any foods that don't fit inside the Venn diagram? Why not?		113–4

Block C Unit 2

Activity name	Strand and learning objectives	Notes on the activities	Assessment Focus	Page number
Someone said: 1 and 2	**Using and applying mathematics** Follow a line of enquiry by deciding what information is important; make and use lists, tables and graphs to organise and interpret the information	**Someone said: 1 and 2** *Processes: make decisions, record, co-operate, predict* These activity sheets encourage the children to make decisions and to plan how to follow lines of enquiry by collecting data. SUGGESTED QUESTION • How did you decide what to do? • What do you think the outcome might be?	Reasoning	115–6
How far? Woolly jumpers	**Measuring** Know the relationships between kilometres and metres, metres and centimetres, kilograms and grams, litres and millilitres; choose and use appropriate units to estimate, measure and record measurements	**How far?** This activity could be extended further by finding out how far the children in the class live from the school, and then a related map could be drawn and described. SUGGESTED QUESTIONS • How far away from the school do you think Ella lives? • Can you draw a house that is about 800 m from the school? **Woolly jumpers.** Provide each child with some string and a ruler. Encourage them to make an estimate of the length of the wool first before measuring with the string. SUGGESTED QUESTION/PROMPT • About how long do you think this piece of wool is? • Explain how the string and ruler can be used to help you check your estimate.	Measures	117 118
Kitchen scales	**Measuring** Read, to the nearest division and half-division, scales that are numbered or partially numbered; use the information to measure and draw to a suitable degree of accuracy	**Kitchen scales.** This worksheet requires the children to draw arrows onto each set of kitchen scales to match the mass given. Encourage the children to check each other's answers. SUGGESTED QUESTIONS • What does this scale show? • Where does the arrow go to show this weight?	Measures	119
Time interval loop cards	**Measuring** Read the time on a 12-hour digital clock and to the nearest 5 minutes on an analogue clock; calculate time intervals and find start or end times for a given time interval	**Time interval loop cards.** Provide clocks with movable geared hands to help the children with this activity. SUGGESTED QUESTIONS • What time does this clock show? • What time would it be 2 hours later/earlier?	Measures	120
At the laundry Birthday presents	**Handling data** Answer a question by collecting, organising and interpreting data; use tally charts, frequency tables, pictograms and bar charts to represent results and illustrate observations; use ICT to create a simple bar chart	**At the laundry.** During the plenary, give the children the opportunity to ask their questions and also to compare their lists, tables and pictograms and decide which of the three is the best way to show the information. They should give reasons why they think as they do. SUGGESTED QUESTIONS • How are you going to start to help Mrs Bubble? • What is wrong with her pictogram? **Birthday presents.** Begin by asking the children which birthday present they would like if given the choice. Make a frequency table to show this. This may be helpful in the extension activity. SUGGESTED QUESTIONS • How many children voted for table football? How did you work that out? • How many more voted for the keyboard? How do you know? • Which toys had fewer than 15 votes?	Processing and representing data Interpreting data	121 122

Activity name	Strand and learning objectives	Notes on the activities	Assessment Focus	Page number
Oranges and lemons Monkey business Symmetry: 1 and 2	**Handing data** Use Venn diagrams or Carroll diagrams to sort data and objects using more than one criterion	**Oranges and lemons.** Before beginning the activity, demonstrate how to make a Carroll diagram using the oranges/lemons criteria but ask the children what they like and input this information. During the plenary share the Venn diagrams from the extension activity. SUGGESTED QUESTIONS • What does this Carroll diagram tell you? • What does this part show you? • How many people like lemons? How do you know? **Monkey business.** Recap how to make a Carroll diagram using the banana/apple criteria asking the children which they like. Ensure that you create an opportunity to share the Venn diagrams from the extension activity and discuss which way they think is best and why. **Symmetry: 1 and 2.** This would fit well with a topic on 2D shape. Before you begin, briefly recap the properties of shapes including names, regularity, number of sides, types of angle, number of lines of symmetry. Remind them of the word quadrilateral and draw a few on the board. There is no need to name them. SUGGESTED QUESTIONS • Where will you put the irregular pentagon? • How many shapes are symmetrical and don't have four sides? • How else could you sort these shapes?	Processing and representing data	123 124 125–6

Block C Unit 3

Activity name	Strand and learning objectives	Notes on the activities	Assessment Focus	Page number
Lines of enquiry	**Using and applying mathematics** Follow a line of enquiry by deciding what information is important; make and use lists, tables and graphs to organise and interpret the information	**Lines of enquiry** *Processes: predict, test ideas, make decisions, trial and improvement, record* As an extension activity, encourage the children to find different ways of recording so that others can follow the instructions and repeat the steps. SUGGESTED QUESTION • How could you show this so that someone else could understand how you solved these problems?	Reasoning	127
Share and share alike Broken keys	**Using and applying mathematics** Describe and explain methods, choices and solutions to puzzles and problems, orally and in writing, using pictures and diagrams	**Share and share alike** *Processes: explain, reason, record, compare* This activity encourages the children to describe the strategies they would use to solve these problems and to consider the different ways that this could be done. You could give a time limit for children to make their predictions so that they do not write their calculated answer as a prediction. Calculations can be altered before copying. SUGGESTED QUESTIONS • What would you do? • What other ways could it be done? **Broken keys** *Processes: explain, reason, ask own questions* It is important that children are given the opportunity to consider different ways to answer calculations without using the keys on the calculators marked with a cross. Possible suggestions are given in the Answers, but children will find their own strategies and these should be discussed together as a class. SUGGESTED QUESTIONS • What would you do? • Is there another way?	Communicating	128 129
Milkshake mistakes Pyramid picture Game show	**Measuring** Know the relationships between kilometres and metres, metres and centimetres, kilograms and grams, litres and millilitres; choose and use appropriate units to estimate, measure and record measurements	**Milkshake mistakes.** At the start of the lesson, remind the children that 1000 ml is the same as 1 litre and pass round a container, bottle or carton that holds a litre of liquid. This will help the children to begin to develop a sense of how much 1 litre or 1000 ml is. Explain that 1 ml is the amount of water that would fit into a centimetre cube (if that were possible). SUGGESTED QUESTIONS • How did you know that 10 litres is not the same as 1000 ml? • How did you work out that 3000 ml is the same amount as 3 litres? **Pyramid picture.** At the start of the lesson, discuss the methods that the children use when estimating lengths and distances. Ask them to suggest things that they can compare lengths less than 1m to, for example a finger is about 1 cm wide, a hand is about 15 cm long. SUGGESTED QUESTION • How close was your estimate? **Game show.** This activity can be used as an assessment to see how comfortable the children are with the units of measurement, i.e. centimetres, metres, grams, kilograms, litres and millilitres. SUGGESTED QUESTION • Have you given the same answers as your partner?	Measures	130 131 132
Measuring jugs Thirsty work	**Measuring** Read, to the nearest division and half-division, scales that are numbered or partially numbered; use the information to measure and draw to a suitable degree of accuracy	**Measuring jugs.** Provide each child with a blue coloured pencil and hold up a jug that holds 1000 ml to give children experience of how much liquid is being described on the sheet. For the extension activity remind them that there are 1000 ml in 1 litre. SUGGESTED QUESTIONS • Where on this scale does 250 ml come? • Which two multiples of 100 does it lie between? • Is it half way between them? **Thirsty work.** These cards can be used for a range of games and activities. □ Game 1 The cards are placed face down on the table. The children, in pairs, pick two cards each and find the totals of the two amounts. The player with the larger amount of liquid scores a point. The cards are returned to the table and the game continues. □ Game 2 The cards are placed face down on the table. The children, in pairs, pick two cards each and find the differences between the two amounts. The player with the smaller difference scores a point. □ Game 3 The children, in pairs, pick a card each and say how much more or less than 1 litre their amount is. The player with the amount closest to 1 litre scores a point. □ Game 4 The cards are placed face down. A target amount is chosen and the children pick a card each and see who has the amount closest to the chosen target. – Individual children can pick two cards, read the scale and say which shows the largest amount and record them using the < or > signs. – More confident children can write the amounts in different ways, such as in litres, in millilitres, or in both. SUGGESTED QUESTIONS • How did you know that this jug holds 650 ml? • What method did you use to work out that 80 ml is 920 ml less than 1 litre?	Measures	133 134

Activity name	Strand and learning objectives	Notes on the activities	Assessment Focus	Page number
Hobbies: 1 and 2 The Basketeers Email The great library sort out: 1 and 2	**Handling data** Answer a question by collecting, organising and interpreting data; use tally charts, frequency tables, pictograms and bar charts to represent results and illustrate observations; use ICT to create a simple bar chart	**Hobbies: 1 and 2.** Before you begin, ask the children to think of their favourite hobbies and to make a tally. This could be used for the extension activity. During the plenary, ask them to share their questions for the rest of the class to answer. SUGGESTED QUESTIONS • Which is the most popular hobby? How can you tell without counting? • Which hobbies scored fewer than 8 votes? • Is this a helpful way to sort the information? Why/why not? **The Basketeers.** Discuss different types of sport that the children play and make a tally to show these. Discuss basketball and how it is played, inviting any child that knows about the game to share their knowledge. During the plenary, invite the children to share the statements they made up and ask the class to agree/disagree with them. SUGGESTED QUESTIONS • What has gone wrong with the tally? • How will you start to sort it out? • What will you expect it to look like when you have finished? **Email.** This activity asks the children to make up a bar chart from information given in a frequency table. Make previous examples of completed bar charts available for any who might benefit from that help. Discuss email and the types of folders that they are stored in, bringing in children's experiences whenever appropriate. SUGGESTED QUESTIONS • Which of Zak's folders has the most emails? • How many emails does he have on his account altogether? • Which folders have fewer than 10 emails in them? **The great library sort out: 1 and 2.** Before beginning this activity, discuss the types of book you would find in a library. Make a list, discussing the kinds of reading matter they would find in each type. Ensure you include the books on the Post-it notes on the activity sheet, for example geography: information about countries of the world, weather, landscapes, maps, rivers etc. To simplify the activity, mark the vertical axis in 1s before copying and ask the children to use the numbers from only one Post-it note per type of book. SUGGESTED QUESTIONS • How are you going to start making your bar chart? • What numbers will you need to go up the side? • Which will your highest column be? Why?	Processing and representing data Interpreting data	135–6 137 138 139–40

Block D Calculating, measuring and understanding shape – Unit 1

Activity name	Strand and learning objectives	Notes on the activities	Assessment Focus	Page number
Chocolate matters Fruit corner	**Using and applying mathematics** Solve one-step and two-step problems involving numbers, money or measures, including time, choosing and carrying out appropriate calculations	**Chocolate matters** *Processes: make decisions, record, reason, explain* These problems require the children to make their own decisions as to how to answer the questions. They should be encouraged to describe these methods and strategies and demonstrate how different equipment such as 100-squares, and number lines, could be used to help them reach answers. SUGGESTED QUESTIONS • How did you work out the answer to this question? • How did you know what to do? • Can you show me how you could use a number line to reach the answer? **Fruit corner** *Processes: reason, record, make decisions* Allow the children to make their own decisions about what to do and encourage them to use number sentences or pictorial methods to record their working. SUGGESTED QUESTIONS • How did you find this solution? • How could you write this as a number sentence?	Problem solving	141 142
What's the difference?	**Calculating** Add or subtract mentally combinations of one-digit and two-digit numbers	**What's the difference?** Children often make errors when finding the difference between numbers such as 28 and 19, giving the incorrect answer 11. This is because they are subtracting the smallest digit from the largest digit each time, regardless of which number comes first. Encourage children to check their work by adding, for example adding 19 and 11, to help them discover that the answer is 30 and not 28. SUGGESTED QUESTION/PROMPT • What number sentence could you show me for the three numbers along that rod? • Show me the method you used to work out the difference between those numbers.	Mental methods	143
Counter tracker	**Understanding shape** Read and record the vocabulary of position, direction and movement, using the four compass directions to describe movement about a grid	**Counter tracker.** Explain how positions can be found on a grid labelled with numbers and letters, like the grid shown on the worksheet. Draw a cross at C5, then draw an arrow to D5 and ask the children to say which direction they have moved in. Repeat for other positions, and then extend to moving in two directions, for example 3 squares West and 1 square South. SUGGESTED QUESTIONS • Can you follow this set of instructions? • Where would you end up?	Properties of position and movement	144
Ribbons Measure master	**Measuring** Know the relationships between kilometres and metres, metres and centimetres, kilograms and grams, litres and millilitres; choose and use appropriate units to estimate, measure and record measurements	**Ribbons.** Hold up a two-digit multiple of 10 and ask the children to hold up the complement to 100. Extend to holding up any two-digit number. Discuss the methods that the children used to work out the complements. SUGGESTED QUESTIONS • How many centimetres are there in a metre? • What method did you use to work out that answer? **Measure master.** Provide the children with a copy of the worksheet, a dice per pair, and counters in two colours. Show each of the pieces of measuring equipment to the children at the start of the lesson and discuss how they are used and for what purpose. Demonstrate how, for this game, they should roll the dice and look at the key to find out which piece of measuring equipment they must use, and then find a corresponding question that could be answered using that piece of equipment. SUGGESTED QUESTIONS • Which piece of equipment would be best for answering this question? • Why do you think that?	Measures	145 146

Activity name	Strand and learning objectives	Notes on the activities	Assessment Focus	Page number
Cookery class	**Measuring** Read, to the nearest division and half-division, scales that are numbered or partially numbered; use the information to measure and draw to a suitable degree of accuracy	**Cookery class.** Hold up a real kitchen timer and discuss what they are used for. Then look at the worksheet and point out that only every tenth division is numbered. SUGGESTED QUESTIONS • Does this timer show 21 minutes? • How many minutes does this timer show?	Measures	147
Time quiz Digital puzzles TV times: 1 and 2	**Measuring** Read the time on a 12-hour digital clock and to the nearest 5 minutes on an analogue clock; calculate time intervals and find start or end times for a given time interval	**Time quiz.** The time quiz game can be played as a whole class activity. Provide each child with a copy of the worksheet and call out clues for times on the worksheet. The children should identify which time you are describing. Clues can be as simple as saying the time in words, or can involve a time interval, for example 20 minutes after ten to five. SUGGESTED QUESTION/PROMPT • How did you know that the time I asked for was 11:20? • Tell me a way to describe 9.25. **Digital puzzles.** It is common for children to reverse times, showing ten past five as 10.5, as this matches more closely the way the time is spoken.	Measures	148 149 150–1

SUGGESTED QUESTIONS (for Time quiz column, cont.):
• How did you know that 8:40 is 20 minutes before 9 o'clock?
• Which of the times is 10 minutes before 5.05?
TV Times: 1 and 2. Provide clocks with movable geared hands to help the children with this activity. They should move the hands from one time to the other and work out how long has passed.
SUGGESTED QUESTIONS
• How long do you have to wait until the cartoons begin?
• How could you say that in a different way?
• How many minutes are between ten to two and half past 2?

Block D Unit 2

Activity name	Strand and learning objectives	Notes on the activities	Assessment Focus	Page number
Campsite capers	**Using and applying mathematics** Represent the information in a puzzle or problem using numbers, images or diagrams; use these to find a solution and present it in context, where appropriate using £.p notation or units of measure	**Campsite capers** *Processes: visualise, make decisions, reason, be systematic, test ideas* Remind the children that they do not necessarily need to work through the clues in order. SUGGESTED QUESTIONS • How did you find this solution? • Have you checked each rule against your answers? • If you were to do this again, would you try a different way?	Communicating	152
Ship ahoy!	**Calculating** Develop and use written methods to record, support or explain addition and subtraction of two-digit and three-digit numbers	**Ship ahoy!** The children's early written strategies of addition should be arranged horizontally where, as for mental methods, the most significant parts of the number are added first. For example when adding 27, the 20 is added first and then the 7. SUGGESTED PROMPT/QUESTION • Show me how you found the total of the two lengths. • How did you work out how much had to be sawed off?	Written methods	153
Odd one out	**Calculating** Find unit fractions of numbers and quantities (e.g. one-half, one-third, one-quarter and one-sixth of 12 litres)	**Odd one out.** Show visual representations of these questions to help the children to appreciate the nature of finding fractions of numbers, for example: *This rectangle represents the number 20.* *How much is one-fifth?* Show how each fifth must represent four so that five of them make 20. SUGGESTED QUESTIONS • What is one-third of 30? How could you find it out?	Fractions and decimals	154
Secret symmetry Dotty symmetry	**Understanding shape** Draw and complete shapes with reflective symmetry; draw the reflection of a shape in a mirror line along one side	**Secret symmetry.** This activity also addresses the objective 'Describing and locating regions in a grid', where children use letters to describe the column and numbers to describe the row, for example A4 or C2. SUGGESTED QUESTIONS • Is your pattern symmetrical? • Can you use a mirror to help you check? **Dotty symmetry.** The shapes can be altered to provide further differentiation. SUGGESTED QUESTIONS • How close to the mirror line is this vertex? • Is this vertex the same distance from the line?	Properties of position and movement	155 156
Map work	**Understanding shape** Read and record the vocabulary of position, direction and movement, using the four compass directions to describe movement about a grid	**Map work.** Encourage the children to measure the distances as accurately as they can. Most children will be able to measure to the nearest half-centimetre. SUGGESTED QUESTIONS • In which direction from the mosque is the café? • In which direction from the hotel is the hospital? • How far away is it?	Properties of position and movement	157

Activity name	Strand and learning objectives	Notes on the activities	Assessment Focus	Page number
Learner driver	**Understanding shape** Use a set-square to draw right angles and to identify right angles in 2-D shapes; compare angles with a right angle; recognise that a straight line is equivalent to two right angles	**Learner driver.** At the start of the lesson, ask the children to tell you everything they know about right angles and to identify examples of right angles in the classroom. Encourage the children to appreciate that right angles do not have to be made from vertical and horizontal lines – they can be diagonally orientated, for example those in the fence in the picture. **SUGGESTED PROMPT/QUESTIONS** • A right angle is a quarter turn. True or false? • Is this angle larger or smaller than a right angle? • How can you check?	Properties of position and movement	158
Weight lifters DIY tape measure	**Measuring** Know the relationships between kilometres and metres, metres and centimetres, kilograms and grams, litres and millilitres; choose and use appropriate units to estimate, measure and record measurements	**Weight lifters.** At the start of the lesson, remind the children that 1000 g is the same as 1 kg and pass round weights so that the children can begin to develop a sense of how heavy 1 kg or 1000 g is. Explain that 1 g is the weight of water that would fit into a centimetre cube (if that were possible). **SUGGESTED QUESTION** • How many grams is the same as 1 kilogram/ half a kilogram? **DIY tape measure.** It is important that children have plenty of experience in measuring with rulers, metre sticks and tape measures. They can	use their tape measures to find (and record) the lengths of a range of different things, for example parts of the body, plants, trees, vegetables in the school grounds, etc. **SUGGESTED QUESTIONS** • Is your wrist smaller than your ankle? • By how much? • How much less than 1 metre is the length around your head?	Measures	159 160

Unit 3

Activity name	Strand and learning objectives	Notes on the activities	Assessment Focus	Page number
Time for TV Record breakers Weekend bedtime	**Using and applying mathematics** Solve one-step and two-step problems involving numbers, money or measures, including time, choosing and carrying out appropriate calculations	**Time for TV** *Processes: reason, explain, record* For this activity, the children should be familiar with the p.m. notation and times written in digital form. Some children may benefit from being given geared clocks to help them work out durations and convert between digital time and analogue time. **SUGGESTED QUESTIONS:** • How many minutes in one hour? • Can you show me this time on a clock face? • How many minutes until the next hour? **Record breakers** *Processes: reason, make decisions, explain* These problems involve understanding units of length in context and appreciating the sizes of the world records. At the start of the lesson remind children about the notation mm, cm and m and that 10 mm = 1 cm and 100 cm = 1 m. **SUGGESTED QUESTIONS** • How many mm are the same as 1 cm? • How could you write this record in millimetres? **Weekend bedtime** As well as giving the opportunity to interpret data, this activity also provides the opportunity to rehearse elements of time. To begin, ask the children to find the different bedtimes on individual clocks. Ask questions such as who goes to bed the earliest/latest, who goes to bed earlier than Peter/later than Lily, how much earlier does Tim go to bed than Susie. Discuss the scenario facing Coco the clown and how his dilemma could be resolved. As an extension activity, ask the children to change the data so that it shows that Coco should cancel his weekend 6:30 show. You could also provide the opportunity for the children to make a table similar to this for their own class's weekend bedtime data. **SUGGESTED QUESTIONS:** • What headings did you choose for your table? Why? • How many children will be in bed during Coco's show? How do you know? • Is this a good way to help Coco make his decision? Why?	Problem solving	161 162 163
Racing cars	**Knowing and using number facts** Use knowledge of number operations and corresponding inverses, including doubling and halving, to estimate and check calculations	**Racing cars.** This activity provides an opportunity for the children to recognise multiples of 2, 5 or 10, and also to see that some numbers are multiples of more than one of those numbers. Before the children complete the activity you could practise saying the 2, 5 and 10 times-tables together. **SUGGESTED QUESTION** • Is it possible to have an answer that is a multiple of 10 but not a multiple of 2?	Mental methods	164
Strawberry picking A knight's challenge	**Calculating** Develop and use written methods to record, support or explain addition and subtraction of two-digit and three-digit numbers	**Strawberry picking.** Here, the children can find the sum or difference of pairs of two-digit numbers using any appropriate informal or written method. The children could also be given a calculator to help them check each other's answers. If neither player gets four counters in a row, the winner is the player with the most rows of three counters. **SUGGESTED PROMPT** • Explain how you worked out the answer. **A knight's challenge.** Here, the children can use any appropriate strategy for adding a two-digit number to a three-digit number, involving	crossing tens and hundreds boundaries. As an extension, the children could make up their own question with an answer that can be circled in the grid. **SUGGESTED QUESTIONS/PROMPT** • How could you work out this answer on paper? • Can you partition both numbers for me? Add the multiples of 10 first, then add the one-digit numbers. What is the total of your two answers?	Written methods	165 166

Activity name	Strand and learning objectives	Notes on the activities		Assessment Focus	Page number
Circuit training	**Calculating** Use practical and informal written methods to multiply and divide two-digit numbers (e.g. 13 × 3, 50 ÷ 4); round remainders up or down, depending on the context	**Circuit training.** Encourage the children to move the counters around the circuits to generate multiplication questions, for example to generate 74 × 5, and to answer them. The highest possible result is from multiplying 81 by 6, giving the answer 486.	**SUGGESTED QUESTIONS** • How did you work out this answer? Did you use partitioning?	Written methods Solving numerical problems	167
Triangular tiles	**Calculating** Understand that division is the inverse of multiplication and vice versa; use this to derive and record related multiplication and division number sentences	**Triangular tiles.** At the start of the lesson, practise saying different times-tables together. Discuss how the children can use multiplication facts to derive division facts.	**SUGGESTED QUESTIONS** • How did you know that you could write 70 ÷ 10 = 7? • What is the relationship between multiplication and division?	Operations, relationships between them Written methods	168
It's your turn! Birds' beaks	**Understanding shape** Use a set-square to draw right angles and to identify right angles in 2-D shapes; compare angles with a right angle; recognise that a straight line is equivalent to two right angles	**It's your turn!** At the start of the lesson, ask the children to stand up and face the front of the classroom. Give instructions for turns, for example: 'Turn one right angle anticlockwise'; 'Turn two half turns clockwise'. Encourage the children to turn slowly and not to look at others. During the plenary, ask the children to explain what they noticed about their answer to question 4. What size turn are two right angles equivalent to? **SUGGESTED PROMPT/QUESTIONS** • A right angle is a quarter turn. True or false? • What do you notice about two right angles? Is this the same as a half turn? • Is a half turn clockwise the same as a half turn anticlockwise? **Birds' beaks.** Here, the children must identify the approximate size of an angle in relation to a right angle, for example: 'This looks about half a right angle' or 'This looks about one-third of a right angle'. They should cut out and use the right angle gobbler to check their estimates. **SUGGESTED QUESTIONS** • Which of the beaks do you think shows an angle that is about half a right angle? • Which of the beaks do you think shows an angle that is about one-third of a right angle? • Which of the beaks do you think shows an angle that is just over a right angle?		Properties of position and movement	169 170
Crack the code: 1 and 2	**Measuring** Read, to the nearest division and half-division, scales that are numbered or partially numbered; use the information to measure and draw to a suitable degree of accuracy	**Crack the code: 1 and 2.** This activity provides opportunities for the children to read partially numbered scales. Before the children start on the activity, ask them to explain how they can work out what the unnumbered divisions must stand for on the first scale.	**SUGGESTED QUESTIONS** • What does this scale show? • What unit is this scale measuring? • Can you think of something that measures/weighs/holds about that amount?	Measures	171–2
At the airport The TV race	**Measuring** Read the time on a 12-hour digital clock and to the nearest 5 minutes on an analogue clock; calculate time intervals and find start or end times for a given time interval	**At the airport.** At the start of the lesson, show half past three on a teaching clock with an analogue face. Ask the children what time the clock would have shown 15 minutes before. Repeat for other time intervals. Provide clocks with movable geared hands to help the children with this worksheet. **SUGGESTED QUESTIONS** • What time does this clock show? • How long before it is quarter past three? **The TV race.** Provide the children with geared analogue clocks to help them work out or check their answers. **SUGGESTED QUESTIONS** • What time will the programme end? • How could you check your answer using this clock?		Measures	173 174

Block E Securing number facts, calculating, identifying relationships – Unit 1

Activity name	Strand and learning objectives	Notes on the activities		Assessment Focus	Page number
Centi-pods Flower totals: 1 and 2	**Using and applying mathematics** Follow a line of enquiry by deciding what information is important; make and use lists, tables and graphs to organise and interpret the information	**Centi-pods** *Processes: visualise, reason, trial and improvement, test ideas, compare* As children are investigating this context they may begin to notice patterns in the possibilities. Encourage them to look for reflections and rotations of the same shapes. **SUGGESTED QUESTIONS:** • What other shapes have you found? • How could you record this for someone else to understand? **Flower totals: 1 and 2** *Processes: be systematic, make decisions, look for pattern, record, compare*	Ensure that children understand the rules for the flower totals investigation, i.e. that each petal must have a number greater than zero and that the total of the petals is the number in the centre. Discuss when flowers are classed as the same, as in the example given. **SUGGESTED QUESTIONS** • How many different ways did you find? • How can you be sure that you have found them all? • Were you systematic?	Reasoning	175 176–7

Activity name	Strand and learning objectives	Notes on the activities	Assessment Focus	Page number
Ways to pay Patterns	**Using and applying mathematics** Identify patterns and relationships involving numbers or shapes, and use these to solve problems	**Ways to pay** *Processes: be systematic, compare, reason, record, look for pattern, explain* Encourage the children to describe any systematic strategies they used to help them find further solutions. SUGGESTED QUESTIONS • How many different ways did you find to pay 8p? • Are those all the ways? • What is the smallest number of coins you need? • What patterns do you notice? **Patterns** *Processes: look for pattern, compare, reason, predict, test ideas, explain* Encourage children to discuss the patterns in the numbers and to say whether it is the tens or units digit changing each time and which numbers in the calculations are increasing or decreasing. SUGGESTED QUESTIONS • Can you describe this pattern? • What do you predict? • How could you check?	Reasoning	178 179
Snail trail The great escape	**Knowing and using number facts** Derive and recall all addition and subtraction facts for each number to 20, sums and differences of multiples of 10 and number pairs that total 100	**Snail trail**. This sheet could be enlarged to A3 size to make it easier for young children to work with. Children require a dice and counter per pair and a coloured pencil each. At the start of the lesson discuss how multiples of 10 can be added in the same way as single-digit numbers, for example 3 + 4 = 7 so 30 + 40 = 70. SUGGESTED QUESTIONS • What is 40 + 70? How do you know? • Which fact did you use to help you? **The great escape**. Invite the children to answer all the questions quickly and then to find the 50 and 60 route through the maze from the dungeon cell to the unlocked door. SUGGESTED QUESTION • Can you make a puzzle like this where the route has different questions with the answer 80?	Mental methods	180 181
Cracking times	**Knowing and using number facts** Derive and recall multiplication facts for the 2, 3, 4, 5, 6 and 10 times-tables and the corresponding division facts; recognise multiples of 2, 5 or 10 up to 1000	**Cracking times.** This activity encourages the children to recall facts from the 3 times-table. Introduce the 'Look, cover, write, check' approach where children study the first row of answers, cover them with a hand/book, then try to write them in the next column. They should then check, before repeating the process two more times. Using the CD-ROM, you could change the 3 to another number to provide opportunities for children to revise other tables facts. SUGGESTED QUESTION • What helps you to remember this fact?	Mental methods	182
Tractor times	**Calculating** Use practical and informal written methods to multiply and divide two-digit numbers (e.g. 13 × 3, 50 ÷ 4); round remainders up or down, depending on the context	**Tractor times**. The numbers on this worksheet could be altered to provide differentiation, for example the numbers on the tractors could be three-digit or the single-digit numbers could be altered to include 'x 7', 'x 8' and 'x 9'. SUGGESTED QUESTIONS • How did you work out this answer? Did you use partitioning?	Written methods Solving numerical problems	183
Fraction stations	**Calculating** Find unit fractions of numbers and quantities (e.g. $\frac{1}{2}$, $\frac{1}{3}$, $\frac{1}{4}$ and $\frac{1}{6}$ of 12 litres)	**Fraction stations**. Children who find this activity difficult could use cubes, grouping them into quarters, sixths, etc. SUGGESTED QUESTIONS • What is one-quarter of 12? How could you find it out? • What other ways are there of dividing by four? • Could you use halving?	Fractions and decimals	184

Block E Unit 2

Activity name	Strand and learning objectives	Notes on the activities	Assessment Focus	Page number
The Street Pick 3 cards	**Using and applying mathematics** Solve one-step and two-step problems involving numbers, money or measures, including time, choosing and carrying out appropriate calculations	**The Street** *Processes: reason, make decisions, explain* Discuss strategies that the children chose to work out the answers, drawing attention to use of equipment such as number lines, 100-squares, materials or other methods or known number facts. SUGGESTED QUESTIONS • How did you find the answer? • What method did you use to find the answer? • Did you use the same method for each question or did you do anything different on this question? **Pick 3 cards** *Processes: record, make decisions, explain* Begin the lesson by reminding children of the pounds and pence notation and asking them to find the total of 35p and £1.28. Discuss different strategies and remind them that they should either work with both numbers in pounds or with both in pence. The prices on the sheet could be changed before copying. SUGGESTED QUESTIONS • How easy did you find this? • Did you find the answer straight away? • How did you work it out?	Problem solving	185 186

Activity name	Strand and learning objectives	Notes on the activities		Assessment Focus	Page number
Tile teasers Yo-ho-ho! Colourful kaleidoscopes	**Counting and understanding number** Read and write proper fractions (e.g. $\frac{3}{7}$, $\frac{9}{10}$), interpreting the denominator as the parts of a whole and the numerator as the number of parts; identify and estimate fractions of shapes; use diagrams to compare fractions and establish equivalents	**Tile teasers.** For the extension activity, provide the children with large isometric paper and ask them to cut out shapes made from triangles and shade them, writing what fraction of each shape is shaded. These help children to appreciate that the denominator shows how many triangles there are in the whole shape. **SUGGESTED QUESTION/PROMPTS** • Shade that tile. What fraction of the shape is shaded now? • Draw me a shape that has $\frac{2}{8}$ shaded. **Yo-ho-ho!** At the start of the lesson, write a range of unit fractions (those with the numerator 1) on the board. Call out a number and point to an appropriate fraction, for example $\frac{1}{2}$ and $\frac{1}{4}$, and ask the children to find one-quarter of 12. Demonstrate how this can be done practically, by sharing 12 counters into four equal groups. Point out that it can also be done mentally by dividing 12 by 4.	**SUGGESTED QUESTIONS/PROMPT** • What is one-quarter of 12? • Find one-sixth of 60 by dividing 60 by 6. What is the answer? **Colourful kaleidoscopes.** Many children find shading fractions as areas of a shape very difficult when the number of sections that the shape has been split into does not match the denominator of the shape. For example, when a shape has ten equal parts, they cannot find one-third. Show children how to find how many sections to colour. For example, to find $\frac{1}{3}$ of 12 sections count the total number of sections into which the whole has been split (12) and then divide this by the denominator (4). Another method is to use equivalent fractions, for example appreciating that $\frac{1}{3}$ is equivalent to $\frac{4}{12}$. **SUGGESTED QUESTIONS** • How can you find one-sixth of 12 pieces? • What is $\frac{1}{2}$ equivalent to?	Numbers and the number system	187 188 189
Motorcycle race	**Knowing and using number facts** Derive and recall multiplication facts for the 2, 3, 4, 5, 6 and 10 times-tables and the corresponding division facts; recognise multiples of 2, 5 or 10 up to 1000	**Motorcycle race.** This sheet could be enlarged to A3 on a copier to make it easier for children to work in pairs. Remind the children that division facts are the inverse of multiplication facts and encourage them to halve when dividing by two. Display the 2, 5 and 10 times-tables facts for children to refer to.	**SUGGESTED QUESTIONS** • How could you work out 16 ÷ 2? • Do you notice a link between 16 ÷ 2 and half of 16?	Mental methods	190
The Meddler	**Calculating** Multiply one-digit and two-digit numbers by 10 or 100, and describe the effect	**The Meddler.** You could use this activity to assess the children's understanding of what happens when numbers are multiplied by 100. Change the 100 to 10 and reduce each of the answers by a factor of 10 or change the 100 to 1000 and increase each answer by a factor of 10 to assess the children's ability to multiply by 10 or 1000.	**SUGGESTED PROMPT** • Describe what happens to a number when it is multiplied by 100.	Mental methods Operations and relationships between them	191
Cruncher: 1 and 2 Lost and found	**Calculating** Use practical and informal written methods to multiply and divide two-digit numbers (e.g. 13 × 3, 50 ÷ 4); round remainders up or down, depending on the context	**Cruncher: 1.** At the start of the lesson, say the 10 times-table together, and then ask the children to give facts from the times-table out of order. Discuss how the answers in the times-table are related to the numbers being multiplied by 10. The children could write the numbers and their multiples of 10 in a place value table and compare them: 	Hundreds	Tens	Units
---	---	---
	3	0
	3	3 | **SUGGESTED PROMPT/QUESTION** • Describe what happens to a number when it is divided by 10. • What happens to the digits of the number? **Cruncher: 2.** Children who are having difficulties with this activity could use place value materials to help them work out what 500 ÷ 100 is (i.e.	how many hundreds are in 500) and count up in hundreds to 500, keeping track on their fingers of the number of hundreds that they say. Link this to the numbers on a place value chart. **SUGGESTED PROMPT/QUESTION** • Describe what happens to a number when it is divided by 100. • What happens to the digits of the number? **Lost and found.** Alfie has lost his underpants. Encourage the children to work out all the multiplications before using the key to find the letters. **SUGGESTED QUESTIONS** • Why did you choose that multiplication method? • Would you use the same method to multiply 32 and 10 as you would for 32 × 4? Why not?	Written methods Solving numerical problems	192–3 194
Help! Mummy!	**Calculating** Understand that division is the inverse of multiplication and vice versa; use this to derive and record related multiplication and division number sentences	**Help! Mummy!** This activity provides an opportunity for the children to appreciate the usefulness of the inverse relationship between multiplication and division: it can help them to generate number facts that it would be difficult to work out.	**SUGGESTED PROMPT** • Draw a picture that shows me how 13 × 5 and 65 ÷ 13 are related.	Operations and relations between them	195
Teddy and Eddy	**Calculating** Find unit fractions of numbers and quantities (e.g. $\frac{1}{2}$, $\frac{1}{3}$, $\frac{1}{4}$ and $\frac{1}{6}$ of 12 litres)	**Teddy and Eddy.** This activity provides an opportunity for the children to find fractions of different masses. Encourage them to use the times-tables facts that they know to help them.	**SUGGESTED QUESTIONS** • Which times-table fact can you use to help you to work out $\frac{1}{3}$ of 18? • How did you work out the answer to the question in the extension activity?	Fractions and decimals	196

Block E Unit 3

Activity name	Strand and learning objectives	Notes on the activities	Assessment Focus	Page number
Parcel problems: 1 and 2	**Using and applying mathematics** Solve one-step and two-step problems involving numbers, money or measures, including time, choosing and carrying out appropriate calculations	**Parcel problems: 1 and 2** *Processes: reason, make own decisions, explain* These activities provide opportunity for children to determine which calculation is necessary to solve problems involving mass. The problems are varied and require considerable thought and the children should discuss in pairs their thoughts and reasoning. When children are recording number sentences they could be shown how to write each situation using a missing number rather than the last number always being the answer. Some situations may require more than one calculation. SUGGESTED QUESTIONS • How did you find the answer? • How did you write this as a number sentence or number sentences? • What method did you use to find the answer?	Problem solving	197–8
Dice: 1 and 2	**Using and applying mathematics** Follow a line of enquiry by deciding what information is important; make and use lists, tables and graphs to organise and interpret the information	**Dice: 1 and 2** *Processes: be systematic, make decisions, look for pattern, record, compare, reason* Encourage the children to compare their solutions and to work systematically to check whether they have found all the possibilities. SUGGESTED QUESTIONS • How many different ways did you find? • How can you be sure that you have found them all? • Were you systematic?	Reasoning	199–200
True or false	**Using and applying mathematics** Identify patterns and relationships involving numbers or shapes, and use these to solve problems	**True or false?** *Processes: look for pattern, test ideas, predict, reason* Ensure the children provide sufficient answers to prove or disprove each statement. SUGGESTED QUESTIONS • What examples can you give me? • Is this true or false? • How can you be sure? • Why?	Reasoning	201
Partition patterns Hedgehog numbers Going crackers!	**Counting and understanding number** Partition three-digit numbers into multiples of 100, 10 and 1 in different ways	**Partition patterns.** Partitioning in different ways, using multiples of 100, 10 and 1, underpins the most commonly used method of subtraction, known as decomposition. When subtracting 159 from 381 using a written method, the 381 can be changed to 3 hundreds, 7 tens and 11 ones so that the 9 ones in 159 can be subtracted. SUGGESTED QUESTION/PROMPT: • The pattern is moving ten across each time. What will the next number in the pattern be? **Hedgehog numbers.** Again, this activity encourages the children to develop confidence in partitioning numbers into multiples of 100, 10 and 1 in different ways. SUGGESTED QUESTIONS • How did you work out which number goes in the hedgehog? • How else could you split that number? **Going crackers!** This activity can be used throughout the year for checking children's understanding of the number system. As a further extension, the children could make up their own 'cracker' puzzles with suggested answers for someone else to try. SUGGESTED QUESTIONS/PROMPT • Which digit has changed between these two numbers? • Add 1 to this number to check your answer. • How many more is 583 than 183? How can you tell?	Numbers and the number system	202 203 204
Fraction wall Fit and tidy Clever cylinders Equivalent cards	**Counting and understanding number** Read and write proper fractions (e.g. $\frac{3}{7}$, $\frac{9}{10}$), interpreting the denominator as the parts of a whole and the numerator as the number of parts; identify and estimate fractions of shapes; use diagrams to compare fractions and establish equivalents	**Fraction wall.** Ensure the children appreciate that the number on the top of the fraction, the numerator, tells them how many of the pieces to count along from the left, for example $\frac{3}{8}$ means 3 of the eighths-rods. Also ensure that they are confident with the > and < signs. SUGGESTED QUESTION/PROMPT • Find another fraction that is equivalent. • Which is larger? How can you tell? **Fit and tidy.** Ask the children whether they consider themselves to be fit and tidy. Make a Venn diagram to show this. This will be a helpful reminder for the extension activity. SUGGESTED QUESTIONS: • Can you explain what the Carroll diagram will tell us when it is finished? • Where will you look to find out who is tidy? • Where will you look to find out who is not tidy? **Clever cylinders.** To give further practice to children who are finding this concept difficult, reproduce several copies of the cylinder diagrams and provide different-coloured pencils. The children could colour equivalent fractions the same, for example $\frac{2}{10}$, $\frac{1}{5}$ and $\frac{4}{20}$ could all be coloured red; $\frac{3}{6}$, $\frac{1}{2}$ and $\frac{4}{8}$ could all be coloured green. SUGGESTED QUESTION • Can you find another fraction that is equivalent/worth the same? **Equivalent cards.** The cards can be used to play different games and activities. *Individual activity* Place all the cards face down and turn over pairs. If the fractions are equivalent, keep the cards, if not turn them face down. The winner is the player with the most pairs at the end. *Pair games* 1) One child takes the cards with the diagrams to the right of the fractions and the other takes the cards with the diagrams to the left. If two cards are equivalent, the first to say 'snap!' wins the cards. 2) Place all the cards face down and take turns to turn over pairs. If the fractions are equivalent, keep the cards, if not turn them face down. The winner is the player with the most pairs. SUGGESTED QUESTION • Can you say another fraction that is equivalent/worth the same?	Numbers and the number system	205 206 207 208

Activity name	Strand and learning objectives	Notes on the activities	Assessment Focus	Page number
Different search Wind farm	**Calculating** Develop and use written methods to record, support or explain addition and subtraction of two-digit and three-digit numbers	**Difference search.** This activity involves finding the difference between pairs of numbers. The children could use a written column method involving partitioning, or they could use more informal methods. The children may need another sheet of paper for their workings. SUGGESTED QUESTION/PROMPT • How could you work out the difference between 106 and 79? • Show me how you could use an empty number line to work out the difference between 145 and 108. **Wind farm.** The numbers on this worksheet could be altered to provide more variety or differentiation, as required. SUGGESTED PROMPT • Explain to me how you worked out the difference between these two numbers.	Written methods	209 210
Peas please, Louise Post Office Pam	**Calculating** Use practical and informal written methods to multiply and divide two-digit numbers (e.g. 13 × 3, 50 ÷ 4); round remainders up or down, depending on the context	**Peas please, Louise.** Children who find the concept of remainders difficult could begin by using counters and grouping them. They could then record what they have done on a number line. SUGGESTED QUESTIONS • Why did you use that method for that division? • Do you think that there will be a remainder when 40 peas are shared between 10 friends? Why not? **Post Office Pam.** These cards could be laminated to form a more permanent classroom resource. As an extension, the children could make up their own questions for a partner to solve. SUGGESTED QUESTIONS • Did you round the answer up or down? Why?	Written methods Solving numerical problems	211 212
Smoothies	**Calculating** Find unit fractions of numbers and quantities (e.g. $\frac{1}{2}$, $\frac{1}{3}$, $\frac{1}{4}$ and $\frac{1}{6}$ of 12 litres)	**Smoothies.** At the start of the lesson, discuss how the children can find $\frac{1}{4}$ of an amount if they know what $\frac{1}{2}$ is. (Halve again.) Similarly, how can they find $\frac{1}{5}$ from $\frac{1}{10}$ of an amount, or $\frac{1}{6}$ from $\frac{1}{3}$ of an amount? SUGGESTED QUESTIONS • What method did you use to work out that $\frac{1}{4}$ of 60 is 15? • How did you work out that $\frac{1}{3}$ of 150 ml is 50 ml?	Fractions and decimals	213

Domino distractions: 1

- **Cut out the dominoes at the bottom of the sheet.**
- **Arrange the dominoes so that the totals along each side are the same.**

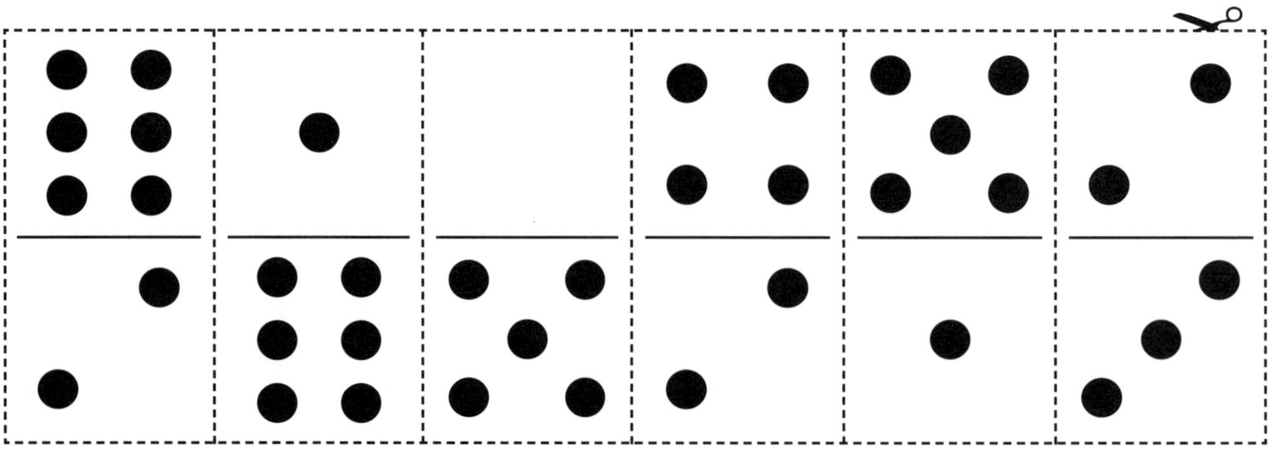

=

=

=

=

Teachers' note Ask the children to compare their answers and to find out whether there is more than one solution. Other sets of six dominoes, such as those on 'Domino distractions: 2', can be provided for further experience of this type.

A Lesson for Every Day
Maths
7-8 Years
© **A&C Black**

• **Use each set to solve the problem.**

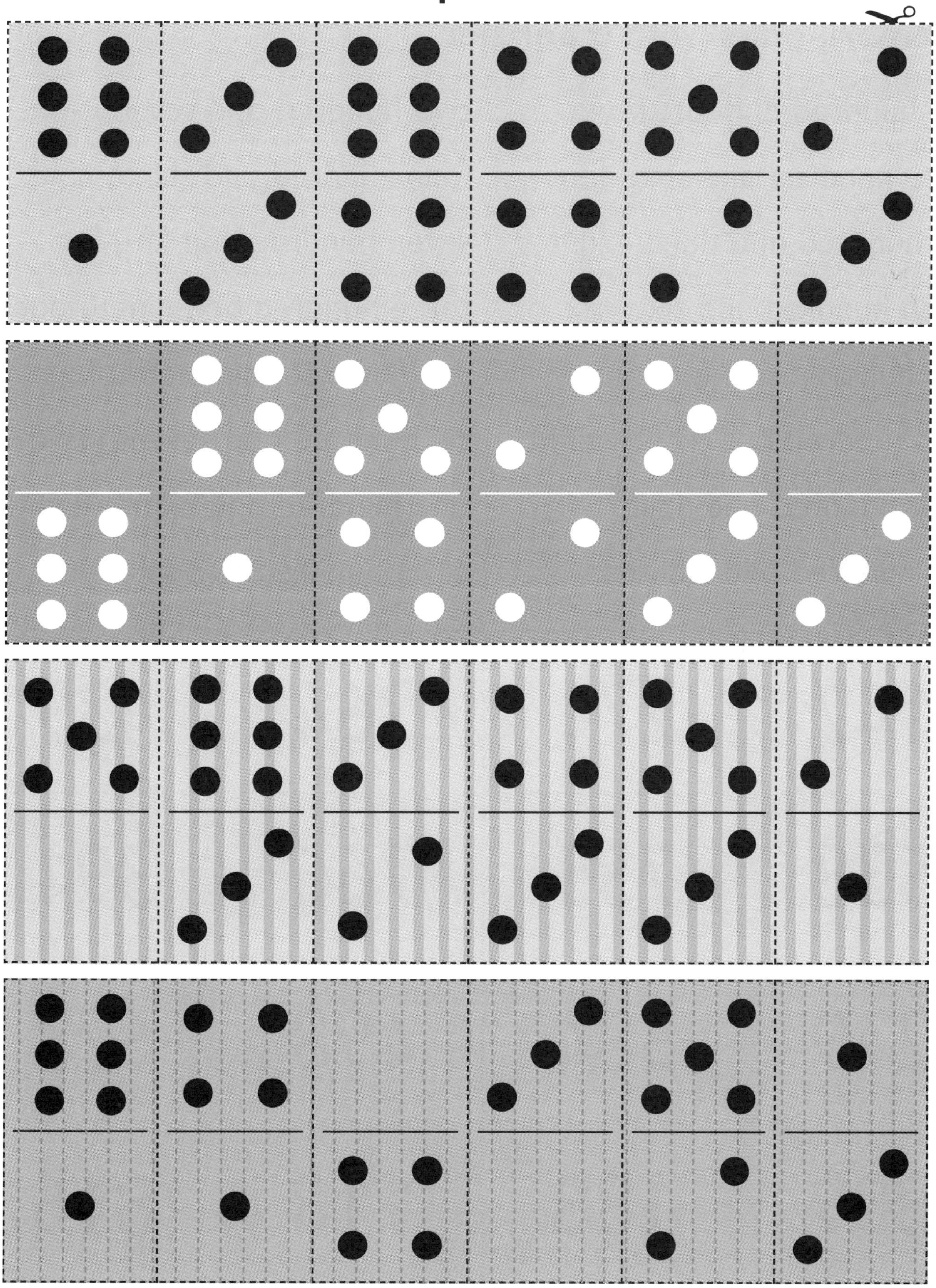

A Lesson for Every Day
Maths
7–8 Years
© A&C Black

Teachers' note Use this sheet in conjunction with 'Domino distractions: 1'.

Number cards

- **Cut out the cards and play 'Memory pairs' with a partner.**

one hundred and forty-two	two hundred and seventy-one
three hundred and sixty-four	four hundred and thirty-nine
five hundred and thirty-eight	seven hundred and fifty-five
seven hundred and sixty-six	three hundred and ninety-one
two hundred and forty-nine	five hundred and eighty-four
four hundred and ninety-eight	six hundred and seventy-two
eight hundred and nine	one hundred and eighty-eight
one hundred and eighteen	eight hundred and sixteen

142	271	364	439
538	755	766	391
249	584	498	672
809	188	118	816

Code breaker

- **Write these numbers with one letter in each box.**

200 | t w o | h u n d r e d

511

650

906

580

430

702

116

301

810

NOW TRY THIS!

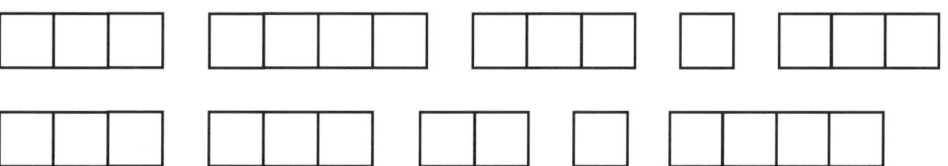

- **Write the letters marked with arrows to spell a sentence.**

- **Make up a similar puzzle of your own.**

Teachers' note This page contains numbers that contain zero as a place holder and children sometimes experience difficulty in saying the matching number names. Practise these numbers before the children start this activity. Ensure that the children have spellings to refer to.

A Lesson for Every Day
Maths
7-8 Years
© A&C Black

More or less

- **Use the clues to help you fill in one digit in each square.**

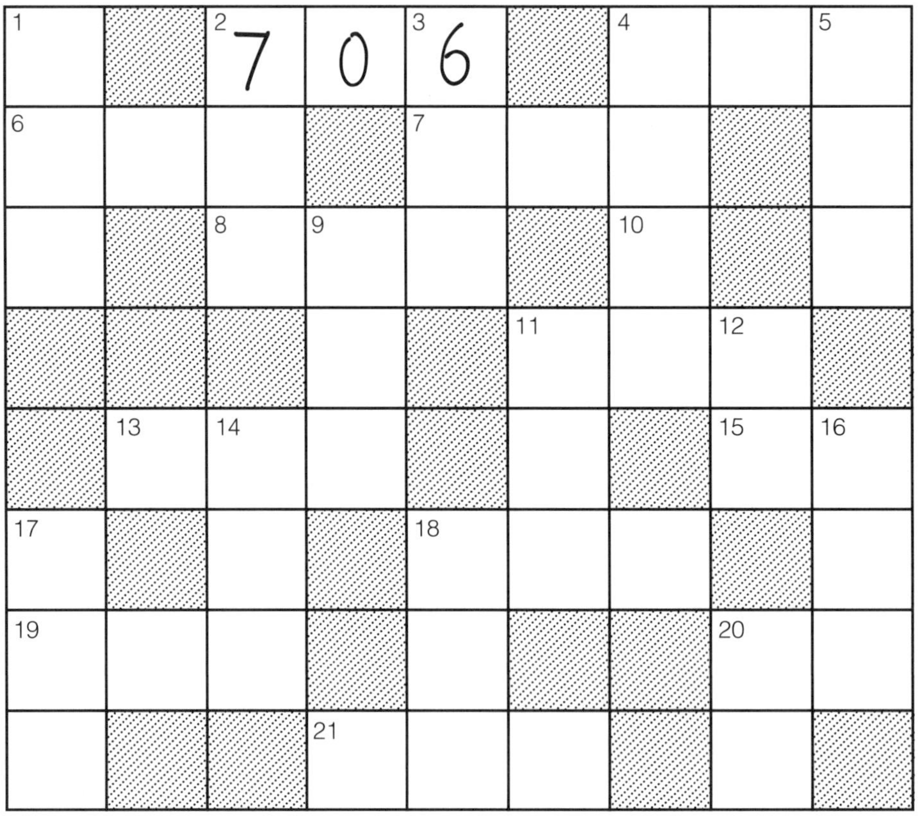

Across

2. Greater than 705, less than 707
4. □ > 157 and □ < 159
6. One less than 530
7. Ten more than a multiple of 100
8. 940 < □ < 942
11. One less than 610
13. One less than 700
15. 90 < □ < 100
18. A multiple of one hundred
19. 940 < □ < 945
20. A multiple of ten
21. 578 < □ < 580

Down

1. One more than 849
2. One less than 800
3. 640 < □ < 650
4. One more than 999
5. One less than 900
9. One less than 480
11. 650 > □ > 630
12. One less than 100
14. One more than 900
16. Ten more than 660
17. One less than 600
18. 275 < □ < 280
20. 56 > □ > 54

Teachers' note At the start of the lesson introduce the 'greater than' and 'less than' signs and show the different ways that a number range can be represented, e.g. □ > 157 and □ < 159 or 640 < □ < 650 or 56 > □ > 54. Ensure the children understand that the number range can refer to either one whole number or a set of possible whole numbers.

Animal antics

- **Draw a line from each animal to show its position on the number line.**

114 150 185 201 250 264 296

100   200   300

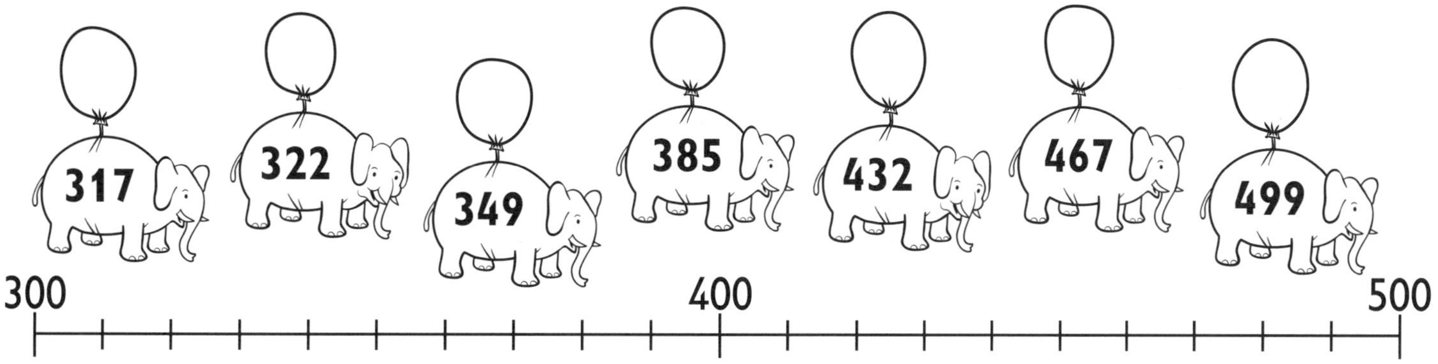

317 322 349 385 432 467 499

300   400   500

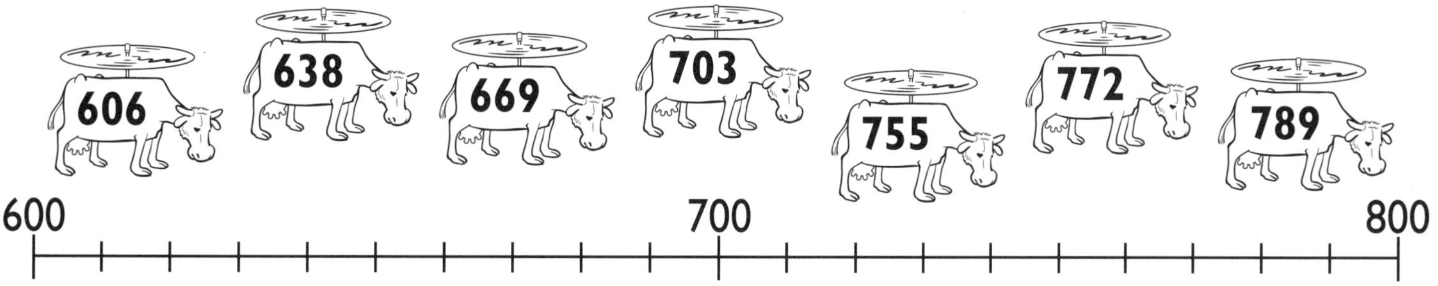

606 638 669 703 755 772 789

600   700   800

NOW TRY THIS!

- **Fill in numbers on the mice.**

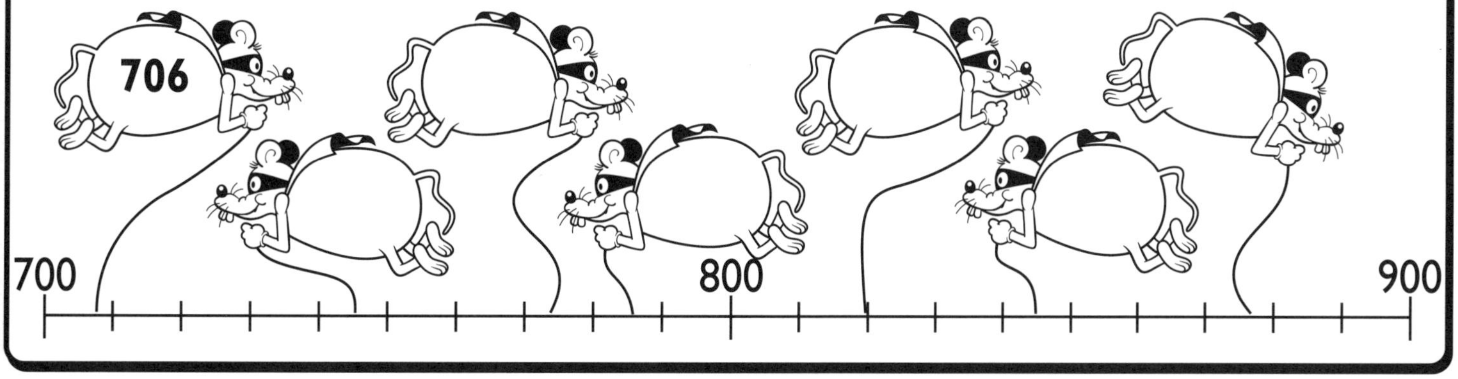

706

700   800   900

Teachers' note At the start of the lesson revise counting in tens from a multiple of one hundred, for example 700, 710, 720, 730... Encourage the children to draw their lines as accurately as they can.

A Lesson for Every Day
Maths
7–8 Years
© A&C Black

29

Monkey puzzles

• **The monkeys have been mixing up the numbers.**

  1 Write them in order, smallest first, on the dotted line.

  2 Draw arrows on the number line to show the numbers.

652	325	352	635	456

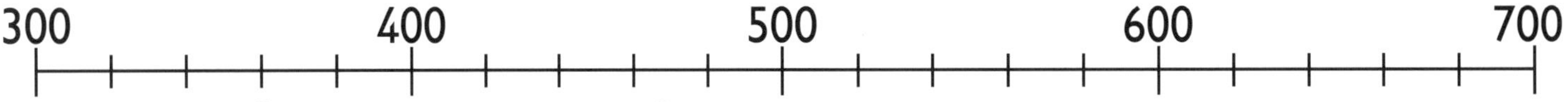

300   400   500   600   700

1010	1001	910	981	808

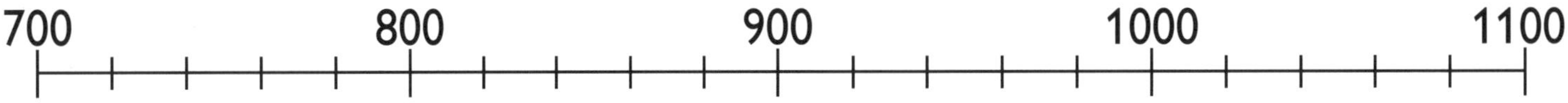

700   800   900   1000   1100

1050	1020	1120	1011	1210

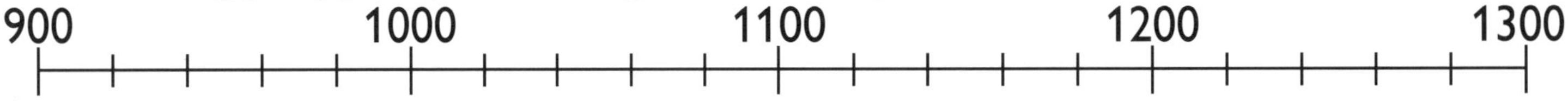

900   1000   1100   1200   1300

NOW TRY THIS!

• **Put these numbers in order, largest first.**

987	897	1001	1542	1190

_____

1006	1060	1016	1600	610

_____

2843	2483	8243	8342	4283

_____

30

Teachers' note At the start of the lesson revise counting in twenties from a multiple of 100, for example: 700, 720, 740, 760. Show how the marks on the number lines above can be labelled by counting in twenties and ask the children to estimate where particular numbers lie on such lines. Encourage the children to draw their lines as accurately as they can.

A Lesson for Every Day
Maths
7–8 Years
© A&C Black

Piggy in the middle

- **On each pig, write a number that lies between the two sheep numbers.**

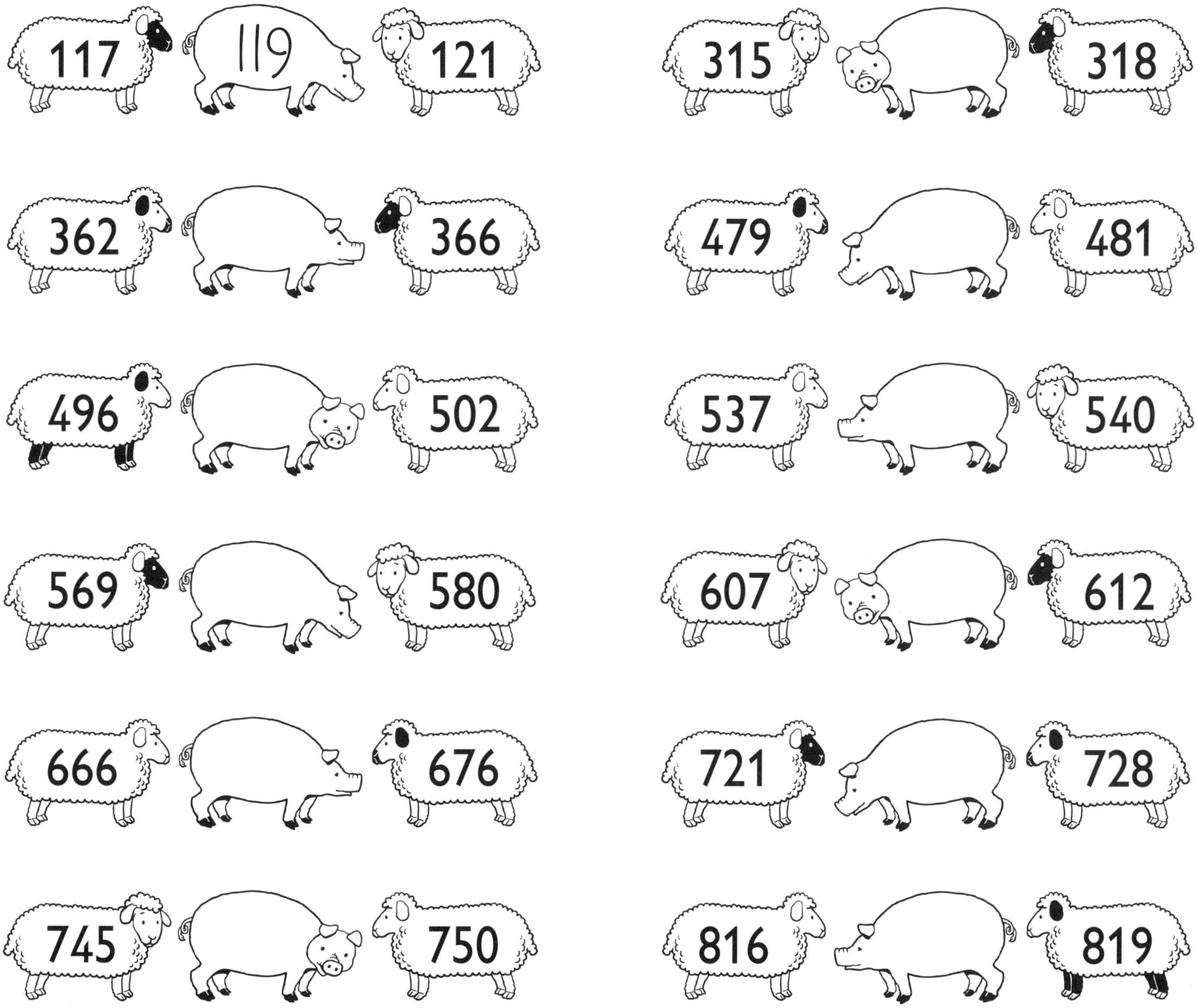

117   119   121

315   ⬡   318

362   ⬡   366

479   ⬡   481

496   ⬡   502

537   ⬡   540

569   ⬡   580

607   ⬡   612

666   ⬡   676

721   ⬡   728

745   ⬡   750

816   ⬡   819

NOW TRY THIS!

- **Write two sheep numbers that have a difference of 20 and lie either side of the pig number.**

787

Teachers' note At the start of the lesson, encourage the children to give numbers that lie between two others. Draw attention to the fact that there can be several numbers that lie between the sheep numbers, or in some cases only one whole number.

A Lesson for Every Day
Maths
7–8 Years
© A&C Black

31

Swimming lanes

- **Count on or back in** tens **.**
- **Write a number on each float.**

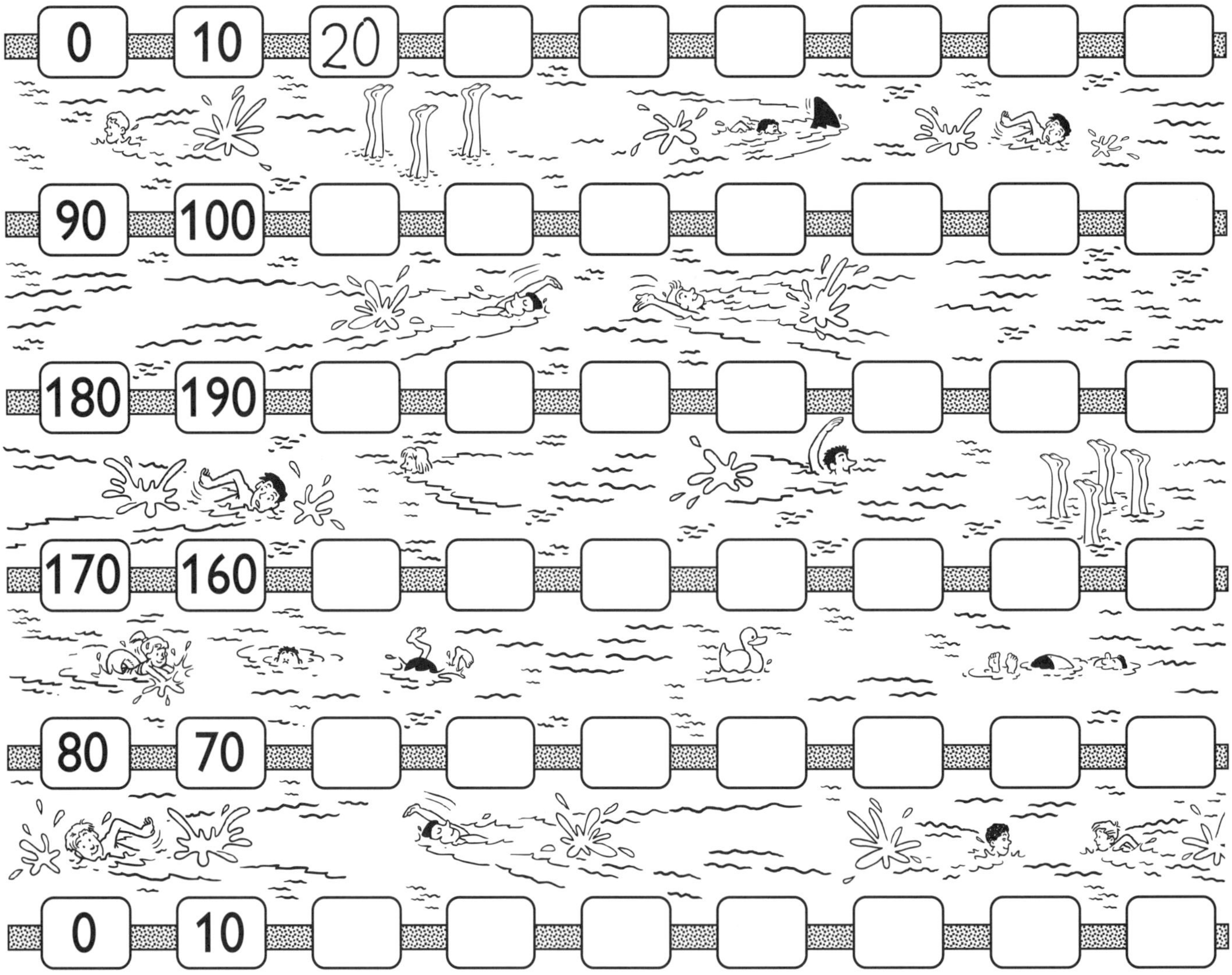

| 0 | 10 | 20 | | | | | | |

| 90 | 100 | | | | | | | |

| 180 | 190 | | | | | | | |

| 170 | 160 | | | | | | | |

| 80 | 70 | | | | | | | |

| 0 | 10 | | | | | | | |

NOW TRY THIS!

- **Count on in** tens **.**

| 37 | 47 | | | | | | | |

| 48 | 58 | | | | | | | |

Teachers' note Practise counting on and back in tens at the start of the lesson. Draw attention to the fact that the units/ones digit remains the same in any sequence, whatever the start number.

A Lesson for Every Day
Maths
7–8 Years
© A&C Black

Mixed up, missed out!

- **Two numbers in each sequence have been** | mixed up | .

1 Circle the two numbers.

| 0 | 10 | 20 | 30 | 40 | 50 | (70) | (60) | 80 | 90 | 100 | 110 |

| 0 | 50 | 100 | 150 | 200 | 250 | 300 | 350 | 450 | 400 | 500 | 550 |

| 0 | 20 | 40 | 60 | 80 | 100 | 120 | 160 | 140 | 180 | 200 | 220 |

| 0 | 30 | 60 | 90 | 120 | 150 | 180 | 210 | 240 | 300 | 270 | 330 |

| 0 | 40 | 80 | 120 | 160 | 240 | 200 | 280 | 320 | 360 | 400 | 440 |

- **Two numbers in each sequence have been** | missed out | .

2 Write the two numbers.

| 100 | 90 | 80 | _70_ | 60 | 50 | _40_ | 30 | 20 | 10 | 0 |

| 650 | 600 | 550 | 500 | 450 | 400 | 350 | 300 | ___ | ___ | 150 |

| 220 | 200 | 180 | 160 | ___ | 120 | 100 | 80 | ___ | 40 | 20 |

| 300 | 270 | 240 | 210 | ___ | 150 | 120 | ___ | 60 | 30 | 0 |

| 440 | 400 | ___ | ___ | 280 | 240 | 200 | 160 | 120 | 80 | 40 |

NOW TRY THIS!

- **Talk to a partner about patterns in these two sequences.**

| 0 | 20 | 40 | 60 | 80 | 100 | 120 | 140 | 160 | 180 | 200 | 220 |

| 0 | 40 | 80 | 120 | 160 | 200 | 240 | 280 | 320 | 360 | 400 | 440 |

Teachers' note This activity can follow on from work on counting in 2s, 3s, 4s and 5s. Encourage the children to notice patterns in the digits when they begin to count on in 20s, 30s, 40s and 50s.

A Lesson for Every Day
Maths
7-8 Years
© A&C Black

Multiple octopus

- **Start at 'zero' in the centre of the octopus.**
- **Count on along each leg.**

One leg has been done for you.

in 9s

in 2s

9 zero 14 16 18 20
12
10
8
6
4
2
8 7 6 5 4 3
in 3s

in 8s

in 7s

in 6s

in 5s

in 4s

NOW TRY THIS!

- **On which octopus leg or legs are these numbers?**

25	in 5s	81		6	in 2s, 3s and 6s
8		9		49	
35		28		36	

Teachers' note These octopus sheets make interesting displays. The children could use coloured paper to make their own large multiple octopuses for the classroom wall. Encourage them to look for particular numbers and to say on which leg or legs the number appears.

34

A Lesson for Every Day
Maths
7–8 Years
© A&C Black

Changing the guard

• **Fill in the missing numbers in each sequence.**

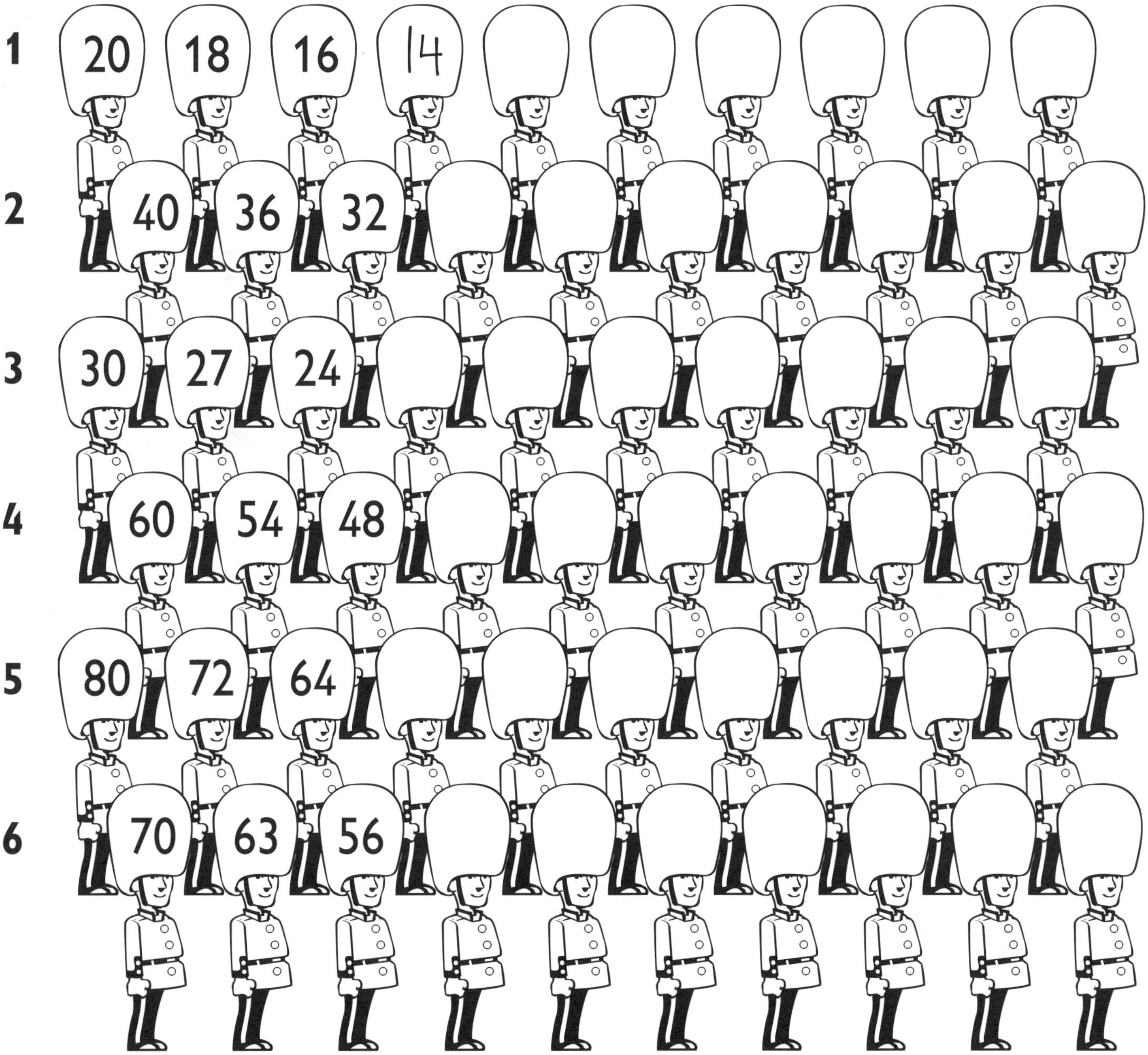

1 20 18 16 14

2 40 36 32

3 30 27 24

4 60 54 48

5 80 72 64

6 70 63 56

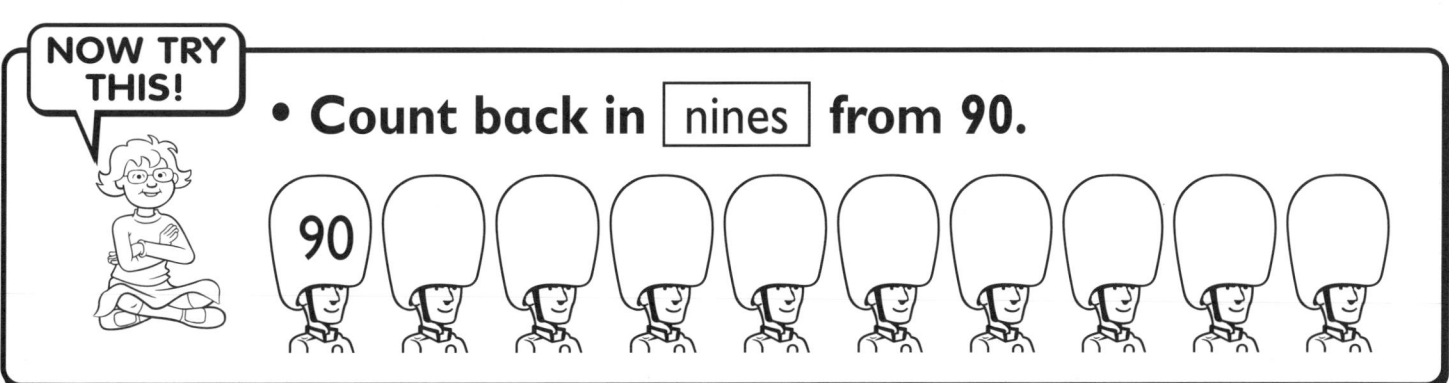

NOW TRY THIS!

• **Count back in** `nines` **from 90.**

90

Teachers' note This activity can be introduced practically (see page 6). As many children find
counting backwards difficult, provide them with a 0–100 number line and encourage them to mark
on the numbers to determine the pattern. For the extension activity, encourage the children to notice
patterns in the digits of the numbers created.

A Lesson for Every Day
Maths
7–8 Years
© A&C Black

Superheroes

Hundreds Man is in charge of the **hundreds**

Tens Girl is in charge of the **tens**

Ones Boy is in charge of the **ones** (or units)

- **Partition these numbers to show the amount each superhero is in charge of.**

1

2   6   2

200 + 60 + 2

2

4   5   7

_____

3

9   3   1

_____

4

8   4   4

_____

5

6   0   5

_____

6

2   7   8

_____

7

1   3   7

_____

8

5   0   9

_____

9

8   8   8

_____

NOW TRY THIS!

- **Find two numbers from above with:**

3 tens _____ _____   2 hundreds _____ _____

7 ones _____ _____   no tens _____ _____

Teachers' note Children love the place value superheroes. Begin by choosing three children to represent the hundreds, tens and ones superheroes. Call out a number and ask the children to say how much each superhero is in charge of. Encourage children to notice that *Hundreds Man's* amount is always larger than *Tens Girl's* amount, whatever the digit (greater than 0).

A Lesson for Every Day
Maths
7–8 Years
© A&C Black

Slider sums

☆ Cut out the sliders at the bottom.

☆ For each puzzle, slide them into position so that all additions are true. Glue them in place.

☆ Fill in any missing numbers.

6 +		= 19
☐ +		= 19
8 +		= ☐
9 +		= 19
10 +		= 19
☐ +		= 19
12 +		= ☐

☐ +		= 17
6 +		= 17
7 +		= ☐
☐ +		= 17
9 +		= 17
☐ +		= 17
11 +		= 17

4 +		= 15
5 +		= 15
6 +		= 15
☐ +		= 15
8 +		= 15
9 +		= ☐
10 +		= 15

3 +		= 16
4 +		= 16
5 +		= 16
☐ +		= 16
7 +		= 16
8 +		= ☐
9 +		= 16

☐ +		= 18
6 +		= 18
7 +		= ☐
☐ +		= 18
9 +		= 18
☐ +		= 18
11 +		= 18

sliders ✂

13	13	13	13	13
12	12	12	12	12
11	11	11	11	11
10	10	10	10	10
9	9	9	9	9
8	8	8	8	8
7	7	7	7	7
6	6	6	6	6
5	5	5	5	5

Bows and arrows

- **If the arrows add to the target shown, write** $\boxed{\text{hit}}$.
- **If it is a** $\boxed{\text{miss}}$, **write the actual total.**

1. Target 14

miss   12

2. Target 13

3. Target 18

4. Target 15

5. Target 12

6. Target 16

7. Target 16

8. Target 17

NOW TRY THIS!

- **Draw three arrows to make each target.**

23    **24**    **25**

Teachers' note Encourage the children to recall or derive the number facts quickly. They can be asked to record each target as an addition sum on paper, for example 6 + 7 = 13 and then to test each other at recalling the sums quickly.

A Lesson for Every Day
Maths
7–8 Years
© A&C Black

Noah's arcs (addition)

- **Fill in the missing numbers on each diagram to show how Noah answered each question.**

38 + 7	$+2$ ... $+5$ ... 38 ...

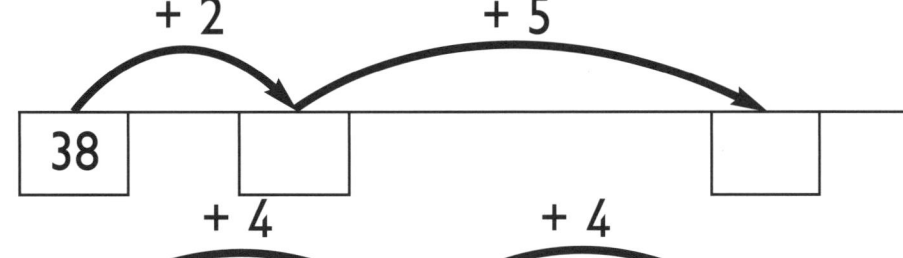

38 + 7   38 (+2) (+5)

46 + 8   +4 ... +4 ... 46

65 + 7   +5 ... +2 ... 65

58 + 6   +2 ... +4 ... 58

79 + 8   +1 ... +7 ... 79

47 + 8   +3 ... +5 ... 47

56 + 7   +4 ... +3 ... 56

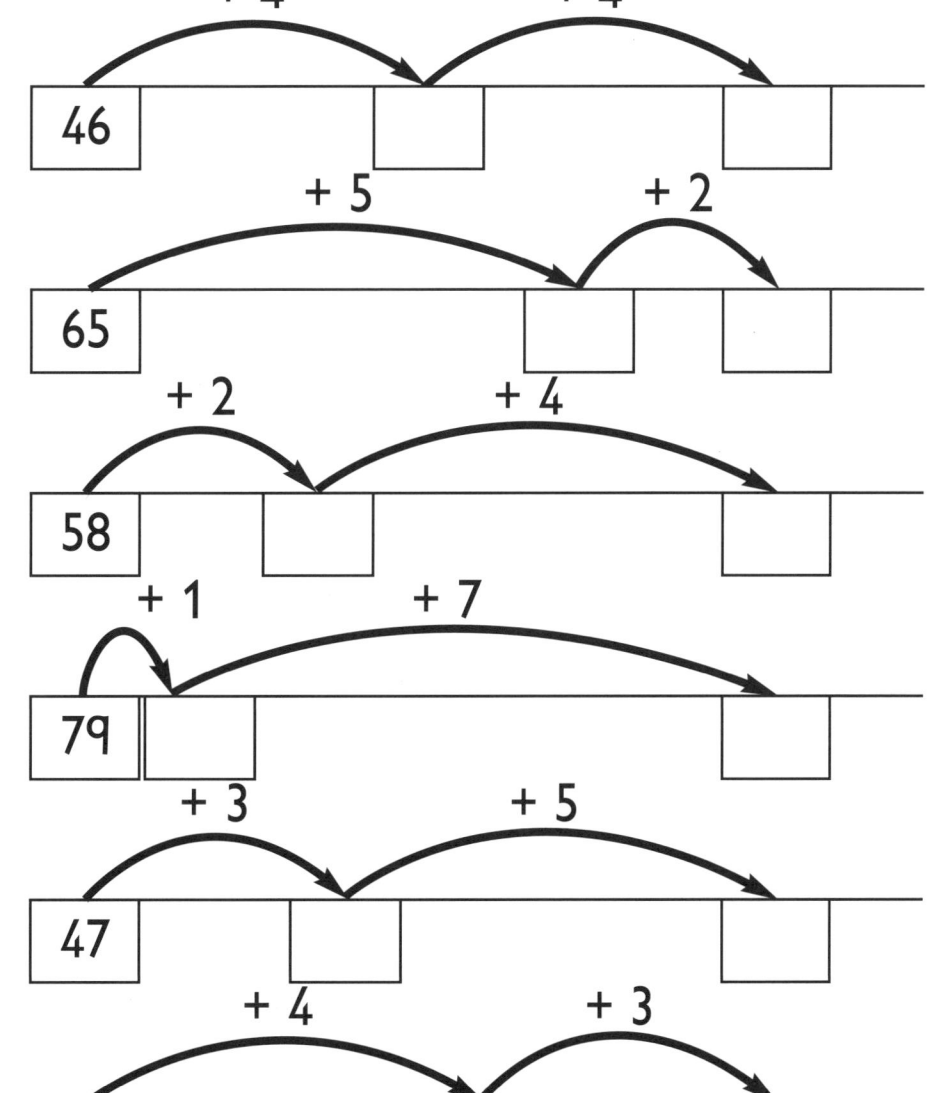

- **Talk to a partner about the patterns you notice in the calculations above.**

Teachers' note Encourage the children to observe how the number being added is split (partitioned) into parts to make the next multiple of 10 and that the remaining part forms the unit digit of the answer. The numbers can be masked and altered before copying to provide more variety. 'Noah's arcs (subtraction)' can also be used to provide practice of subtractions of this type.

A Lesson for Every Day
Maths
7–8 Years
© A&C Black

39

Noah's arcs (subtraction)

- Fill in the missing numbers on each diagram to show how Noah answered each question.

65 – 8

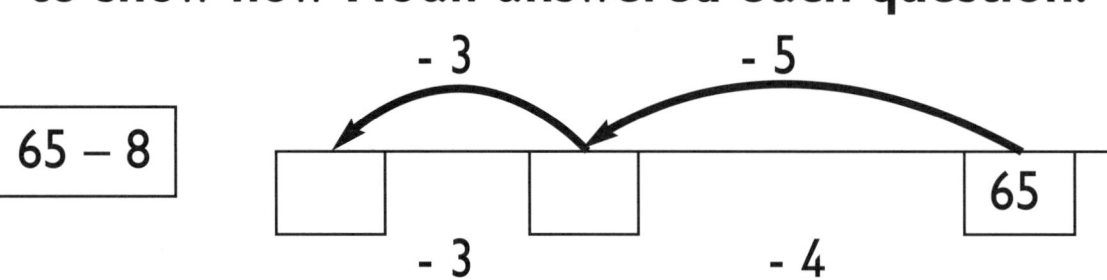

34 – 7

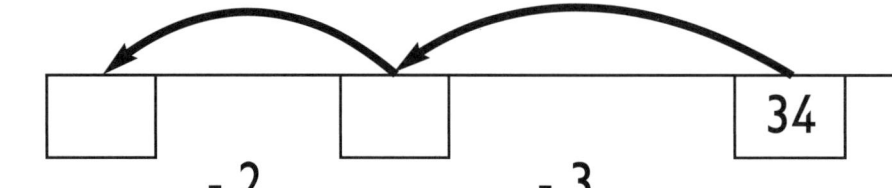

53 – 5

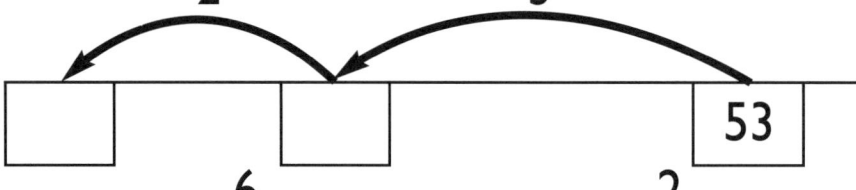

42 – 8

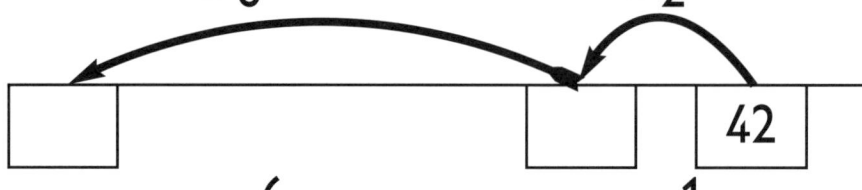

71 – 7

66 – 8

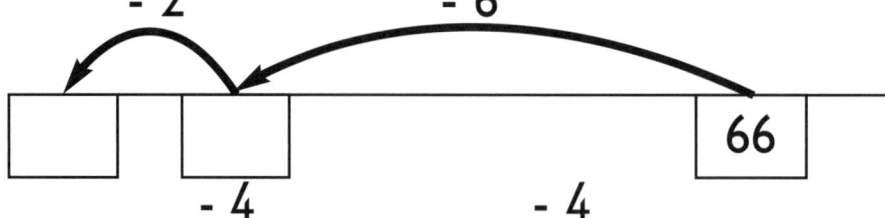

54 – 8

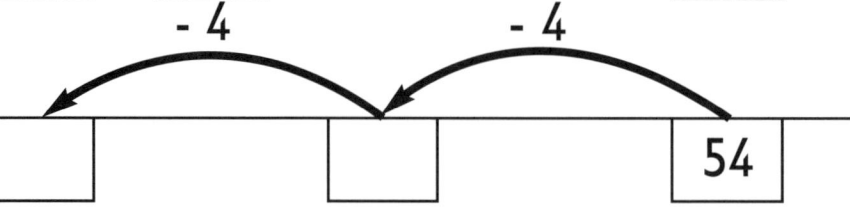

- Talk to a partner about the patterns you notice in the calculations above.

Teachers' note Encourage the children to observe how the number being subtracted is split (partitioned) into parts to make the previous multiple of 10. The numbers can be masked and altered before copying to provide more variety.

A Lesson for Every Day
Maths
7-8 Years
© A&C Black

Partition pots: 1

You need
Partition pots: 2

- **Play this game with a partner.**
- **Cut out the cards and the gameboard.**

Gameboard for player 1

hundreds digit	tens digit	ones digit
		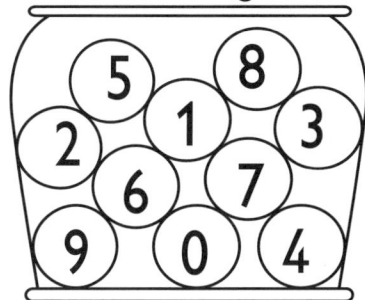

114	516	694	985
807	768	377	226
523	252	743	155
931	462	370	408
99	689	30	841

Teachers' note Use this sheet in conjunction with 'Partition pots: 2'. The children work in pairs, each child choosing the player 1 or player 2 gameboard. The cards from both sheets are placed face down on the table. The children take turns to pick a card, choose one of its digits and colour that digit in the correct pot on their gameboard. The winner is the first player to colour all the digits in their pots.

A Lesson for Every Day
Maths
7-8 Years
© A&C Black

Partition pots: 2

You need
Partition pots: 1

- **Play this game with a partner.**
- **Cut out the cards and the gameboard.**

Gameboard for player 2

hundreds digit	tens digit	ones digit

562	609	919	980
131	828	732	841
53	493	87	775
519	624	394	165
400	357	246	276

Teachers' note Use this sheet in conjunction with 'Partition pots: 1'.

A Lesson for Every Day
Maths
7–8 Years
© A&C Black

Matchmakers

- **Cut out the cards.**
- **Sort them into groups with the same total.**

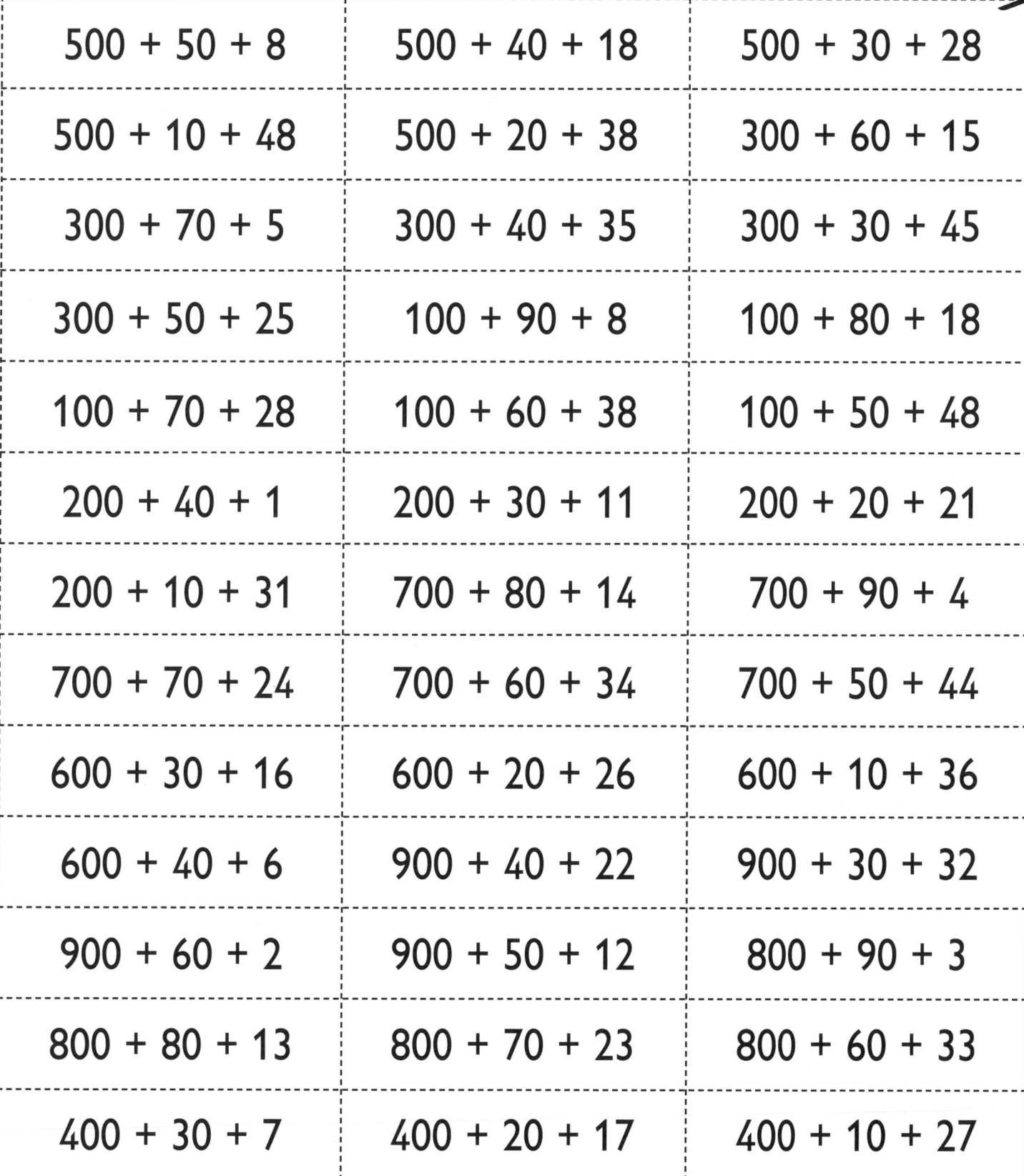

500 + 50 + 8	500 + 40 + 18	500 + 30 + 28
500 + 10 + 48	500 + 20 + 38	300 + 60 + 15
300 + 70 + 5	300 + 40 + 35	300 + 30 + 45
300 + 50 + 25	100 + 90 + 8	100 + 80 + 18
100 + 70 + 28	100 + 60 + 38	100 + 50 + 48
200 + 40 + 1	200 + 30 + 11	200 + 20 + 21
200 + 10 + 31	700 + 80 + 14	700 + 90 + 4
700 + 70 + 24	700 + 60 + 34	700 + 50 + 44
600 + 30 + 16	600 + 20 + 26	600 + 10 + 36
600 + 40 + 6	900 + 40 + 22	900 + 30 + 32
900 + 60 + 2	900 + 50 + 12	800 + 90 + 3
800 + 80 + 13	800 + 70 + 23	800 + 60 + 33
400 + 30 + 7	400 + 20 + 17	400 + 10 + 27

Teachers' note This activity encourages children to begin to realise how numbers can be partitioned into multiples of 100, 10 and 1 in different ways. If children are experiencing difficulty in sorting the cards into sets, ask them to take each card in turn and find the total. The cards can then be grouped according to totals and each set arranged to show partition patterns.

A Lesson for Every Day
Maths
7–8 Years
© A&C Black

43

Lifebelts

- **Round the number on the swimmer to the** `nearest 10` **.**
- **Draw a line from the swimmer to the correct lifebelt.**

1

2

3

4

5

6

7

8

9

10

NOW TRY THIS!

- **Write nine numbers that, when rounded to the** `nearest 10` **, give the answer** `100` **.**

_____ _____ _____ _____ _____ _____ _____ _____ _____

Teachers' note Provide the children with a number line to help them with this activity. Ensure they understand that a number with a units digit of 5 rounds up to the nearest 10. At the end of the activity, call out two-digit numbers and ask the children to round them to the nearest 10.

A Lesson for Every Day
Maths
7–8 Years
© A&C Black

Rounders

- **Play this game with a partner.**

☆ Player 1 is 'squares' and player 2 is 'circles'.

You need one counter and a dice.

☆ Take turns to roll the dice and move the counter around the pitch. Round the number to the **nearest 10**. If the answer is in a square, player 1 scores a point. If it is in a circle, player 2 scores a point.

300 (310) 320 (330) 340 (350) 360 (370) 380 (390) 400

312
396   328
369   334
338   392
349   358
364   316
319   361
356   353
305   309
331   323
389
379 371 337 345 378 **Start**

Teachers' note Encourage the children to move around the board many times and to continue to keep score. They can record their scores on scrap paper. The winner can be the first player to score 15 points.

A Lesson for Every Day
Maths
7-8 Years
© A&C Black

Whose dog?

- **Round each number to the** nearest 100 .
- **Draw a line to join the dog to its owner.**

547

849

945

459

851

638

500

800

900

461

501

400

600

700

652

794

408

645

712

350

NOW TRY THIS!

- **On the dog, write the highest possible number that rounds to** 400 .

Teachers' note Ensure the children understand that numbers ending in 50 round up to the nearest 100. At the end of the activity, call out three-digit numbers and ask the children to round them to the nearest 100.

A Lesson for Every Day
Maths
7–8 Years
© A&C Black

Pigs on parade

The numbers on each pig's body have a total of $\boxed{100}$.

• Fill in the missing numbers.

1.
100
35   65

2.
100
70

3.
100
45

4.
100
75

5.
100
5

6.
100
94

7.
100
84

8.
100
51

9.
100
15

10.
100
2

11.
100
57

12.
100
19

13.
100
34

14.
100
72

15.
100
63

16.
100
29

NOW TRY THIS!

• **Use these four digits to make different sums with a total of** $\boxed{100}$. $\boxed{2}$ $\boxed{7}$ $\boxed{4}$ $\boxed{6}$

Teachers' note Children of this age should be beginning to learn pairs of numbers with the total 100 by heart, including all whole number pairs, for example 36 + 64, 82 + 18. The numbers on this sheet can be masked and altered before copying to provide further practice in deriving and recalling these facts.

A Lesson for Every Day
Maths
7-8 Years
© A&C Black

Counting sheep

- **Write the number of sheep in each field.**
- **Cut out the cards and match the questions with the answers.**

🐑🐑🐑🐑 🐑🐑🐑🐑 🐑🐑🐑🐑 ⬜	🐑🐑🐑🐑 🐑🐑🐑🐑 🐑🐑🐑🐑 🐑🐑🐑🐑 ⬜	🐑🐑🐑🐑 🐑🐑🐑🐑 ⬜

$1 \times 4 =$	$2 \times 4 =$
$3 \times 4 =$	$4 \times 4 =$	$5 \times 4 =$
$6 \times 4 =$	$7 \times 4 =$	$8 \times 4 =$
$9 \times 4 =$	$10 \times 4 =$	$0 \times 4 =$

Teachers' note This activity can be given to children as a homework activity to familiarise them with the multiples of 4 and to help them practise learning and matching the questions in the 4 times-table to the correct multiples of 4. The question cards can also be used as flashcards, with the answers written on the reverse for further practice.

A Lesson for Every Day
Maths
7-8 Years
© A&C Black

Genius gerbil

This gerbil can multiply numbers by 10 by pulling strips of paper.

Example:

$24 \times 10 = 240$

- **Write the answers to these questions.**

1.

$35 \times 10 = $ _____

2.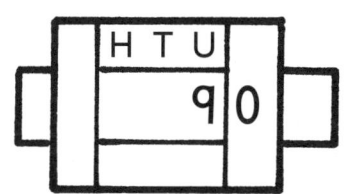

$9 \times 10 = $ _____

3.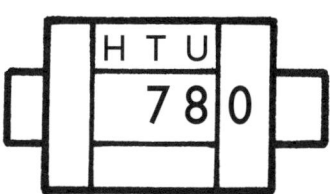

$78 \times 10 = $ _____

4.

$59 \times 10 = $ _____

5.

$8 \times 10 = $ _____

6.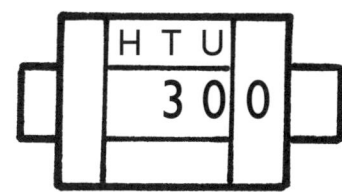

$30 \times 10 = $ _____

7.

$60 \times 10 = $ _____

8.

$47 \times 10 = $ _____

9.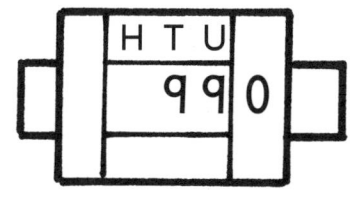

$99 \times 10 = $ _____

NOW TRY THIS!

- **Answer these questions.**

(a) ▢ $\times 10 = 70$ (b) ▢ $\times 10 = 520$

(c) ▢ $\times 10 = 800$ (d) ▢ $\times 10 = 180$

(e) ▢ $\times 10 = 4870$ (f) ▢ $\times 10 = 3600$

Teachers' note Use a strip of paper like the one shown to illustrate the effect of multiplying by 10. Encourage the children to appreciate the movement of the digits rather than focusing on 'putting a zero on the end', as this will cause them difficulties when multiplying decimals in the future, for example 3.5 × 10 = 35, not 3.50.

A Lesson for Every Day
Maths
7–8 Years
© A&C Black

49

At the ice rink

- **Cut out the cards.**
- **What calculations are needed?**
- **How did you decide?**

Work with a partner to solve these problems.

1 Jasmine skated round the rink 26 times and then 7 more times. How many times did she skate round in total?

2 Chloe went to the ice rink 8 times in February and 13 times in March. How many times did she go altogether?

3 Urvi went to the ice rink every day for 3 weeks. How many times did she go to the rink?

4 It costs £3.70 for a child and £5.80 for an adult to go into the ice rink. How much does it cost for 2 children and an adult?

5 Skate hire costs £2.10 for a pair of skates. How much does it cost for 5 pairs of skates?

6 It costs £5.80 for each child to skate (including skate hire). A group of children pay £23.20. How many children are there?

7 It costs £7.90 for each adult to skate (including skate hire). Some adults pay £23.70. How many adults are there?

8 There were 34 people on the ice. 26 come off and 17 more go on. How many are there now?

9 There were 27 people on the ice. 12 more go on and 15 come off. How many are there now?

10 Josh skated round 45 times. This was 8 times fewer than Fay. How many times did Fay skate round?

Teachers' note Some of these problems contain distracting words such as 'times' (as in the second question) or 'more' when multiplication or addition respectively is not the operation required. It is important that children interpret questions correctly rather than looking for trigger words to tell them what to do. They could record their calculations on the back of each card.

A Lesson for Every Day
Maths
7–8 Years
© A&C Black

Round and about

- **Round the numbers to the** nearest 10 **to help you estimate the answer.**

1

51 + 32 is about ☐

2

43 + 27 is about ☐

3

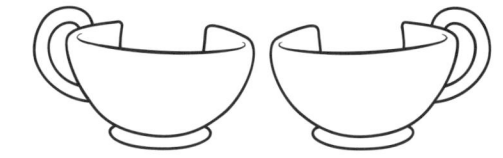

28 + 36 is about ☐

4

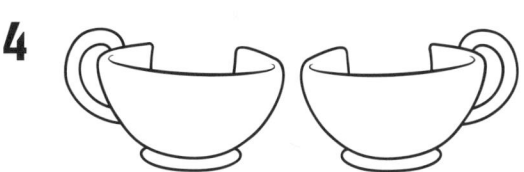

67 + 28 is about ☐

5

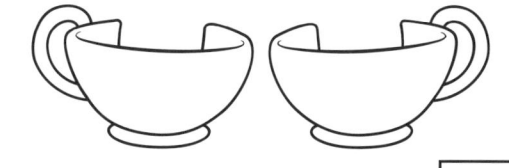

45 + 54 is about ☐

6

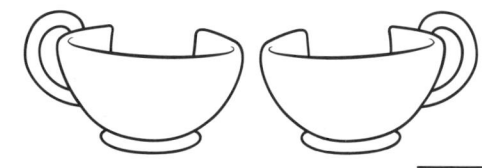

47 – 19 is about ☐

7

62 – 38 is about ☐

8

71 – 56 is about ☐

NOW TRY THIS!

The answer to an addition question is about 150 **.**

- **Write four questions that could give this answer.**

_____ _____ _____ _____

Teachers' note Ensure the children notice that some questions on the page are additions and some are subtractions. At the start of the lesson, revise rounding numbers to the nearest 10 and show how this can help you make an estimate for a calculation.

A Lesson for Every Day
Maths
7–8 Years
© A&C Black

51

Rain rounding

- **Round the numbers to the** nearest 100 **to help you estimate the answers.**

1

134 + 291 is about ▢

2

361 + 117 is about ▢

3

451 + 268 is about ▢

4

312 + 658 is about ▢

5

275 + 539 is about ▢

6

674 − 352 is about ▢

7

631 − 492 is about ▢

8

855 − 545 is about ▢

9

953 − 448 is about ▢

10

928 − 674 is about ▢

NOW TRY THIS!

The answer to an addition question is about 1200 .

- **Write four questions that could give this answer.**

_____ _____ _____ _____

Teachers' note Ensure the children notice that some questions on the page are additions and some are subtractions. At the start of the lesson, revise rounding numbers to the nearest hundred and show how this can help you make an estimate for a calculation.

A Lesson for Every Day
Maths
7-8 Years
© A&C Black

Have a good trip!

These families go on a day trip. The distances show how far they travelled, before and after a stop.

- Round the numbers to the nearest 100 to help you estimate the total distance travelled.

1
322 km
158 km

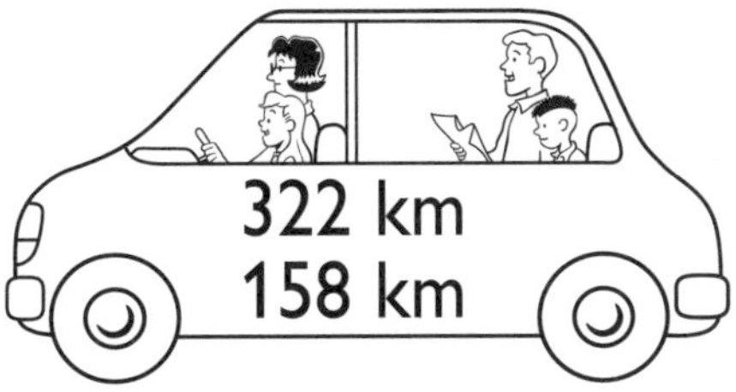

about _____ km

2
248 km
274 km

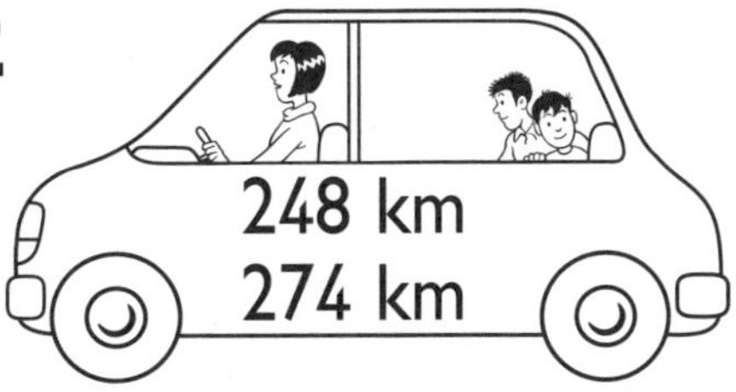

about _____ km

3
369 km
231 km

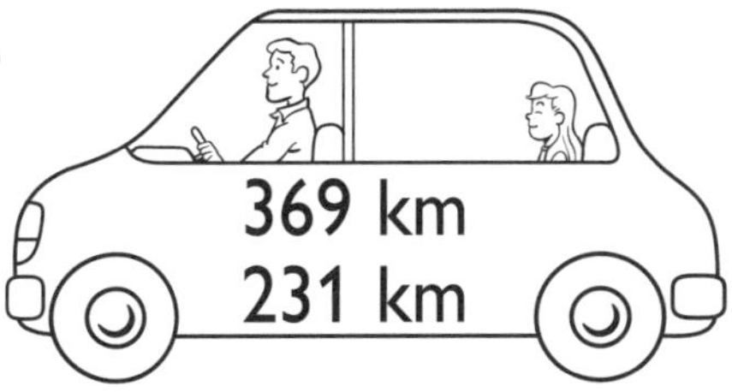

about _____ km

4
482 km
351 km

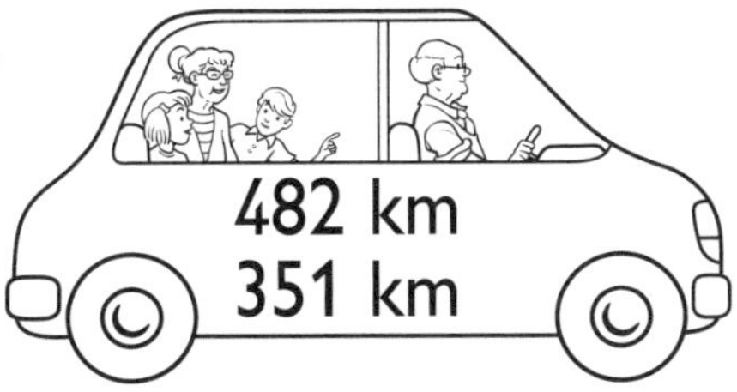

about _____ km

5
307 km
586 km

about _____ km

6
467 km
342 km

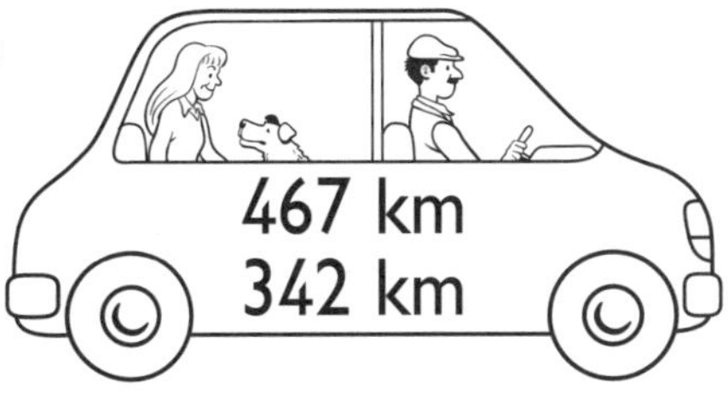

about _____ km

7
626 km
278 km

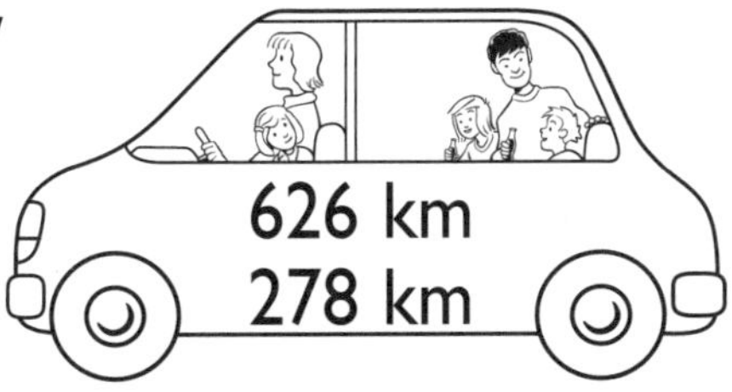

about _____ km

8
247 km
581 km

about _____ km

9
523 km
333 km

about _____ km

NOW TRY THIS!

- **Make estimates for these journeys.**

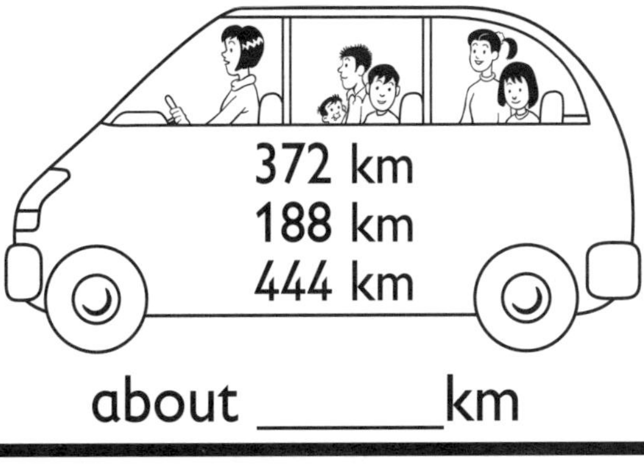

372 km
188 km
444 km

about _____ km

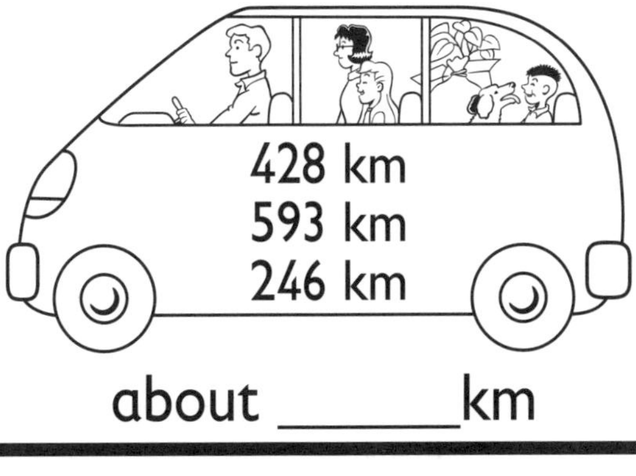

428 km
593 km
246 km

about _____ km

Teachers' note At the start of the lesson, revise rounding numbers to the nearest hundred and show how this can help you make an estimate for a calculation. Some children may find it easier to write the two rounded numbers first and then to add them. More confident children could round the numbers to the nearest 10.

A Lesson for Every Day
Maths
7–8 Years
© A&C Black

- **Fill in the answer boxes to make each statement correct.**
- **You can only use the numbers on the jack-in-the-boxes.**

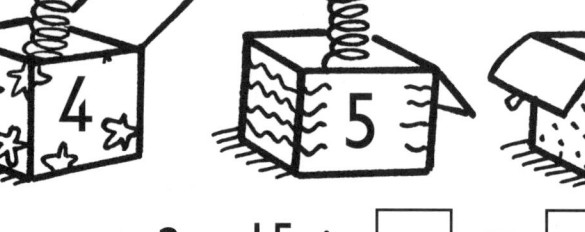

1. 20 ÷ ☐ = ☐   2. 15 ÷ ☐ = ☐

3. 12 ÷ ☐ = ☐   4. 24 ÷ ☐ = ☐

5. 18 ÷ ☐ = ☐   6. 21 ÷ ☐ = ☐

7. 28 ÷ ☐ = ☐   8. 35 ÷ ☐ = ☐

- **Now use the numbers on these jack-in-the-boxes.**

9. 40 ÷ ☐ = ☐   10. 24 ÷ ☐ = ☐

11. 36 ÷ ☐ = ☐   12. 27 ÷ ☐ = ☐

13. 45 ÷ ☐ = ☐   14. 32 ÷ ☐ = ☐

Teachers' note Encourage the children to make the link between multiplication tables facts and division facts. For this activity, it could be useful to have the tables facts displayed on the classroom wall for children to refer to. As an extension activity, ask the children to make up some jack-in-the-box puzzle questions of their own for a partner to solve.

A Lesson for Every Day
Maths
7–8 Years
© A&C Black

The value of words

a	b	c	d	e	f	g	h	i	j	k	l	m
8	24	37	51	7	62	83	77	9	39	43	74	35

n	o	p	q	r	s	t	u	v	w	x	y	z
66	4	91	56	48	37	29	6	61	52	94	5	47

- **Use the key to find the value of each letter.**
  Add the numbers to find the value of the word.

he ☐   so ☐   be ☐   ox ☐

to ☐   ma ☐   at ☐   us ☐

up ☐   pa ☐   is ☐   we ☐

it ☐   as ☐   of ☐   am ☐

an ☐   by ☐   or ☐   my ☐

NOW TRY THIS!

- **Find the** | difference | **between the two numbers.**

he ☐   so ☐   be ☐   ox ☐

to ☐   ma ☐   at ☐   us ☐

up ☐   pa ☐   is ☐   we ☐

it ☐   as ☐   of ☐   am ☐

an ☐   by ☐   or ☐   my ☐

Teachers' note For the extension activity encourage the children to realise that the difference can be found by counting back from the larger number, for example the difference between 54 and 7 can be found by counting back 7 from 54.

A Lesson for Every Day
Maths
7-8 Years
© A&C Black

Katie's kittens: 1

Katie's kittens have walked all over her homework.
- Fill in the hidden numbers.

1. 55 + 38

$$50 + 5$$
$$+ 30 + 8$$

80 + 13 = 93

2. 68 + 27

$$60 + 8$$
$$+ 20 + 7$$

__ + __ = __

3. 49 + 27

$$40 + 9$$
$$+ 20 + 7$$

__ + __ = __

4. 68 + 56

$$60 + 8$$
$$+ 50 + 6$$

__ + __ = __

5. 74 + 48

$$70 + 4$$
$$+ 40 + 8$$

__ + __ = __

6. 66 + 37

$$60 + 6$$
$$+ 30 + 7$$

__ + __ = __

NOW TRY THIS!

- **Answer these in the same way.**

Show your workings on a separate piece of paper.

(a) 59 + 47 = __

(b) 37 + 76 = __

(c) 66 + 56 = __

(d) 78 + 46 = __

Teachers' note The children will need to be familiar with partitioning for this activity. At the start of the lesson, demonstrate this method of addition. It might be useful to display the number facts to 20 on the classroom wall to help those children who have yet to memorise all the facts to work quickly and easily as they learn this written method.

A Lesson for Every Day
Maths
7–8 Years
© A&C Black

Katie's kittens: 2

Katie's kittens have walked all over her homework again!
- **Fill in the hidden numbers.**

1. 51 – 38

$$
\begin{array}{c}
\overset{40}{\cancel{50}} + \overset{11}{\cancel{1}} \\
- \ 30 \ + \ 8 \\
\hline
\end{array}
$$

10 + 3 = 13

2. 74 – 27

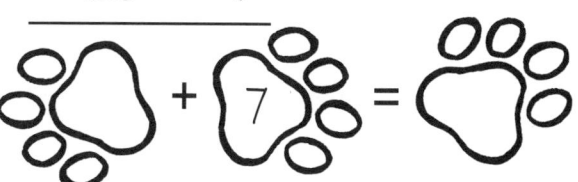

$$
\begin{array}{c}
\overset{60}{\cancel{70}} + \overset{14}{\cancel{4}} \\
- \ 20 \ + \ 7 \\
\hline
\end{array}
$$

+ 7 =

3. 62 – 35

$$
\begin{array}{c}
60 \ + \ 2 \\
- \ 30 \ + \ 5 \\
\hline
\end{array}
$$

+ =

4. 67 – 28

$$
\begin{array}{c}
60 \ + \ 7 \\
- \ 20 \ + \ 8 \\
\hline
\end{array}
$$

+ =

5. 85 – 29

$$
\begin{array}{c}
80 \ + \ 5 \\
- \ 20 \ + \ 9 \\
\hline
\end{array}
$$

+ =

6. 96 – 39

$$
\begin{array}{c}
90 \ + \ 6 \\
- \ 30 \ + \ 9 \\
\hline
\end{array}
$$

+ =

NOW TRY THIS!

- **Answer these in the same way.**

Show your workings on a separate piece of paper.

(a) 83 – 37 = 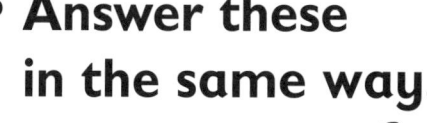 **(b)** 91 – 42 =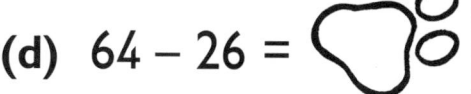

(c) 62 – 44 =  **(d)** 64 – 26 =

Teachers' note The children will need to be familiar with changing numbers such as '50 + 4' to '40 + 14' for this activity. At the start of the lesson, demonstrate this method of subtraction and emphasise how this enables the numbers to be subtracted more easily.

A Lesson for Every Day
Maths
7-8 Years
© A&C Black

Triangle tricks

- **Cut out the pieces. Arrange them to make a large triangle. Each side of the triangle must have** 12 **dots.**

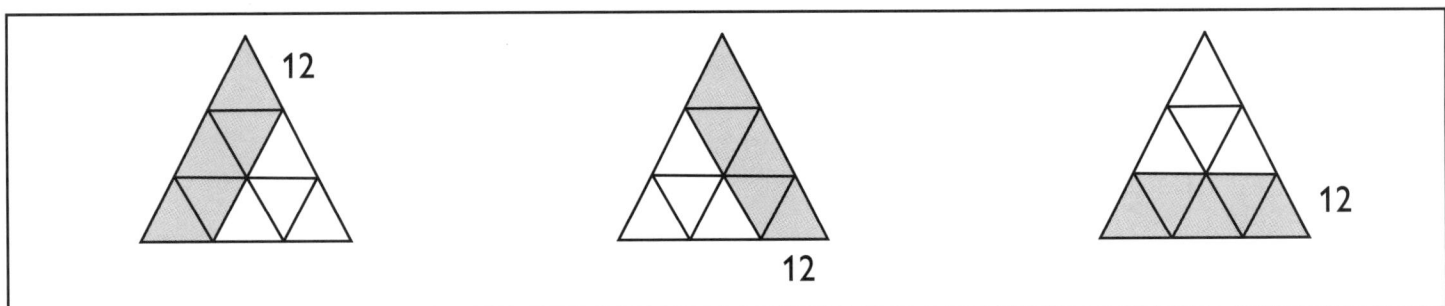

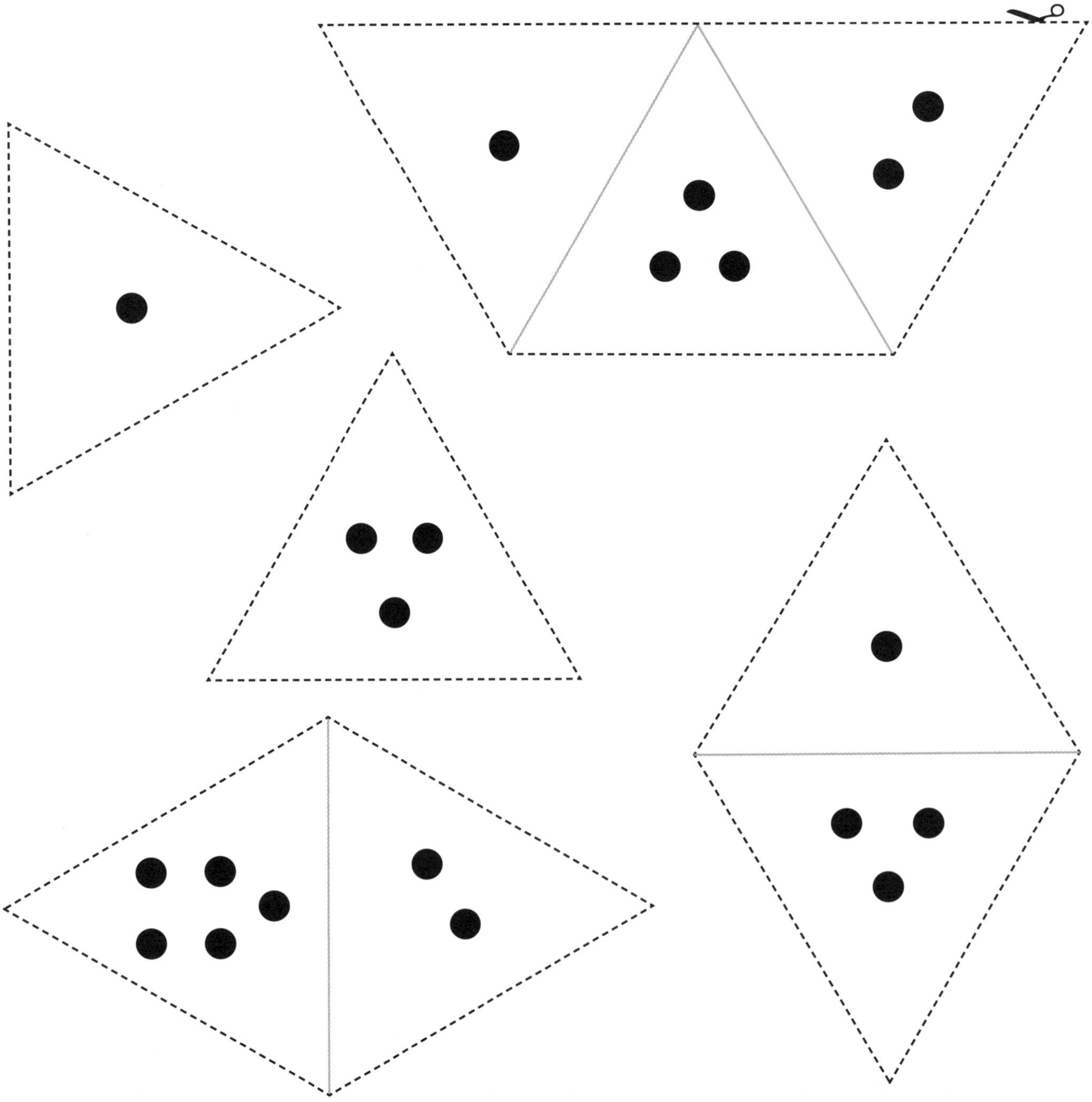

Teachers' note This puzzle requires perseverance and trial and improvement strategies. Note which children use reasoning strategies and those who give up quickly. See notes on the activity on page 9 for further hints that can be given to help children find a solution.

A Lesson for Every Day
Maths
7-8 Years
© A&C Black

Question time

- **For each question, write a calculation and work out the answer.**

I think of a number and add 12 to it. My total is 28. What is my number?

I think of a number and subtract it from 40. The answer is 17. What is my number?

I think of a number and multiply it by 3. The product is 18. What is my number?

I think of a number. My number is 24 less than 50. What is my number?

I think of a number and divide it by 5. The answer is 10. What is my number?

I think of a number and subtract 30 from it. The answer is 60. What is my number?

I think of a number. My number is 24 greater than 17. What is my number?

There are 4 of a number in 24. What is the number?

NOW TRY THIS!

- **Make up** 2 **of your own for a partner to solve.**

Teachers' note Note that different calculations could be written for each question. Ask the children to show how they might solve each question on a number line or 100-square. Encourage them to describe the strategies they used and to compare differences in the calculations suggested for each question, for example [ ] + 12 = 28 or 28 – 12 = [ ].

A Lesson for Every Day
Maths
7-8 Years
© A&C Black

Problem page

• **Write** | calculations | **for each problem to show how you might work out the answer.**

Work in pairs.

3 drinks cost 24p. What is the cost of 2 drinks? 	4 stickers cost 9p. How many stickers can be bought for 36p? 
Jo bought 10 pencils for 70p. How much would it have cost if she had bought 15 pencils? 	4 cakes cost 20p. What is the cost of 5 cakes? 
3 stickers cost 15p. How much would it cost to buy 9 stickers? 	A 20p tube of sweets contains 8 sweets. How many sweets could I buy with 60p?
5 fruit bars cost 25p. How many bars could I buy with 75p? 	3 buns cost 18p. What is the cost of 4 buns? 
Sam bought 6 pens for 24p. How much would it cost to buy 9 pens? 	4 stamps cost £1. How many stamps could I buy with £1.50? 

Teachers' note Ask the children to work together in pairs and to discuss how each problem could be solved. Discuss the problems together as a class at the end of the lesson and talk about ways of representing each problem as a calculation.

A Lesson for Every Day
Maths
7–8 Years
© A&C Black

Bing, Bong, Bang

- **The words Bing, Bong and Bang can be said in different orders. Write them here.**

   Bong Bing Bang

   _____

   _____

   _____

   _____

   _____

- **Use the words Bing, Bang, Bong, Bung.**
- **Find all the different ways that the words can be said.**

1 Start with Bing.

   Bing _____   Bing _____

   Bing _____   Bing _____

   Bing _____   Bing _____

2 Start with Bong.

   Bong _____   Bong _____

   Bong _____   Bong _____

   Bong _____   Bong _____

3 Start with Bang.

   Bang _____   Bang _____

   Bang _____   Bang _____

   Bang _____   Bang _____

4 Start with Bung.

   Bung _____   Bung _____

   Bung _____   Bung _____

   Bung _____   Bung _____

Teachers' note This activity encourages the children to tackle an investigation systematically, by asking them to work starting with each word in turn. The Spike Milligan poem 'On the Ning, Nang, Nong' could be used as an introduction to this activity.

A Lesson for Every Day
Maths
7-8 Years
© A&C Black

Find my house

- **Cut out the cards below.**
- **Pick an A card, a B card and a C card.**
- **Find which house you reach.**
- **Record your route and house number on paper.**
- **Try this several times. Can every house be reached?**

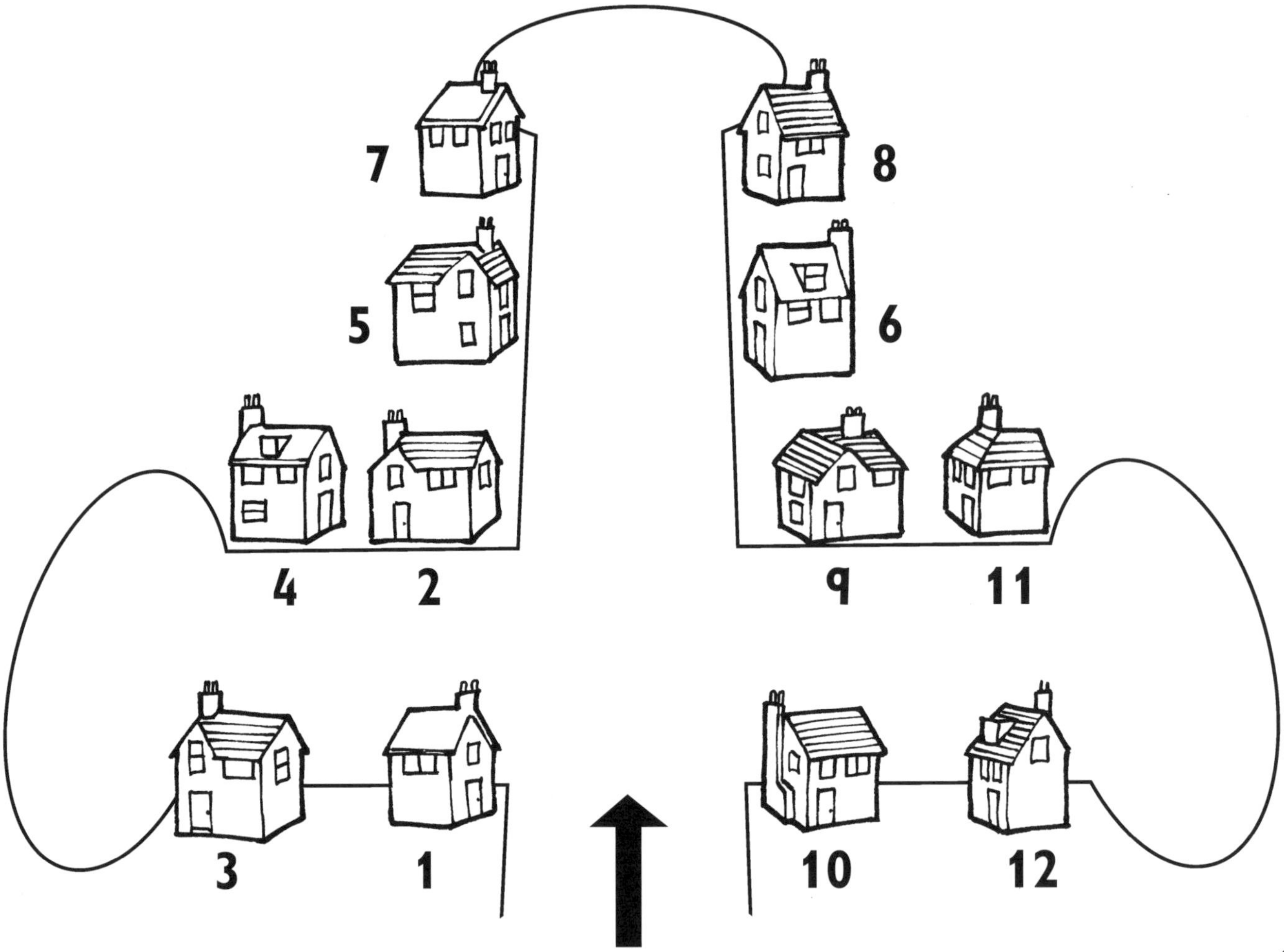

A	B	C
Turn right	first house	on the right
Turn left		
	B	**C**
Go straight on	second house	on the left

Teachers' note Once the children have begun to investigate the combinations of cards, explain that you would like them to record their findings and results as a poster for someone else to understand. This encourages children to be systematic and to consider how best to show the different combinations of cards and the related house numbers.

A Lesson for Every Day
Maths
7-8 Years
© **A&C Black**

Chair challenge

- **Cut out the** number cards **and place them in the boxes.**
- **How many different questions and answers can you find?**

Chairs are arranged in ☐ rows with ☐ chairs in each

row. People arrive and sit on the chairs. There are ☐ empty

chairs. How many people are there?

- **Write your calculations and answers here.**

NOW TRY THIS!

- **How many more answers are possible if you also had a 7 card?** 5 3 6 4

Teachers' note Encourage the children to notice patterns in the numbers, for example to realise that 3 rows of 5 will have the same number of chairs as 5 rows of 3 etc. Encourage children to work systematically.

Easter-egg hunt

The answers to these subtractions
are on the eggs.

- Colour the egg as you answer the question.
- Which egg is not coloured at the end? ____

18 − 9 = 9	13 − 9 = ☐	12 − 5 = ☐	15 − 8 = ☐
12 − 11 = ☐	19 − 7 = ☐	14 − 11 = ☐	17 − 13 = ☐
19 − 13 = ☐	17 − 9 = ☐	11 − 5 = ☐	20 − 12 = ☐
16 − 9 = ☐	19 − 8 = ☐	14 − 5 = ☐	15 − 7 = ☐
16 − 7 = ☐	20 − 14 = ☐	14 − 8 = ☐	13 − 6 = ☐
11 − 7 = ☐	18 − 10 = ☐	17 − 8 = ☐	

NOW TRY THIS!

- Make up an egg hunt of your own.
  The answers must be between 3 and 15.

Teachers' note Encourage the children to answer each question, one at a time, and then find the answer on the egg and colour it. There should be one egg uncoloured at the end of the activity.

A Lesson for Every Day
Maths
7–8 Years
© A&C Black

Brain box

The differences between the numbers in each row and column are shown.

- Fill in numbers with the correct differences to complete each square.

1.

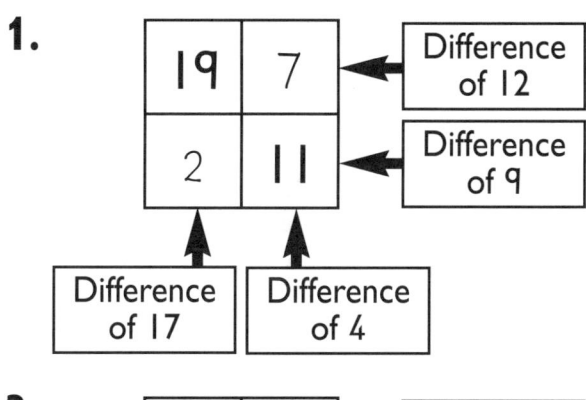

| 19 | 7 | ← Difference of 12 |
| 2 | 11 | ← Difference of 9 |

Difference of 17 — Difference of 4

2.

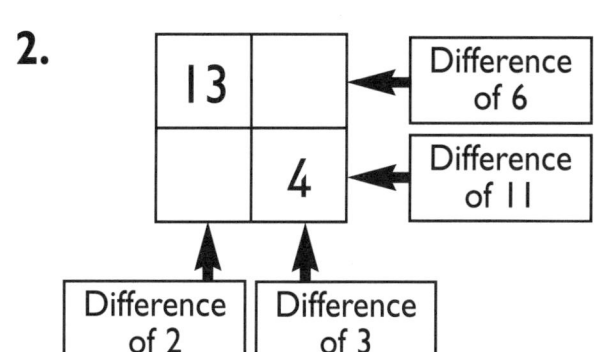

| 13 | | ← Difference of 6 |
| | 4 | ← Difference of 11 |

Difference of 2 — Difference of 3

3.

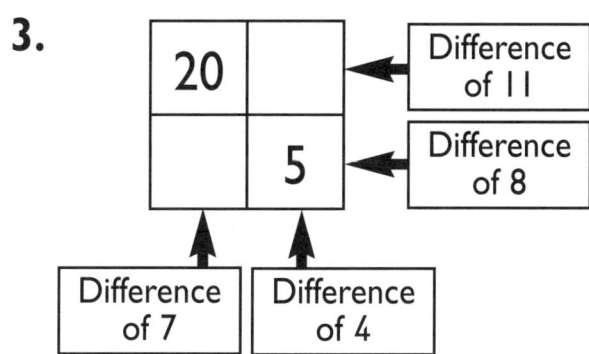

| 20 | | ← Difference of 11 |
| | 5 | ← Difference of 8 |

Difference of 7 — Difference of 4

4.

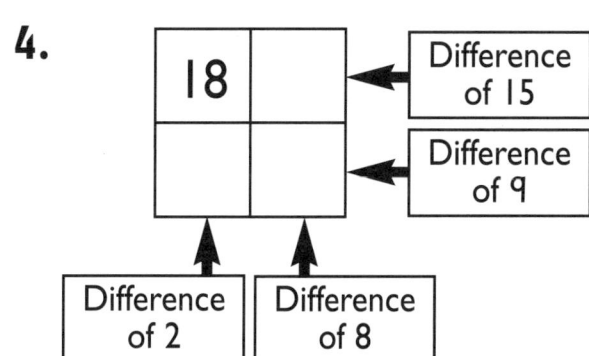

| 18 | | ← Difference of 15 |
| | | ← Difference of 9 |

Difference of 2 — Difference of 8

5.

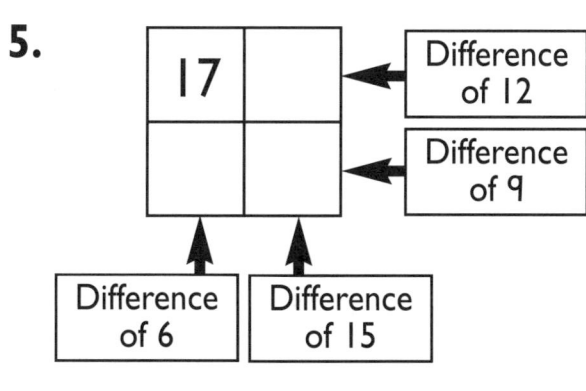

| 17 | | ← Difference of 12 |
| | | ← Difference of 9 |

Difference of 6 — Difference of 15

6.

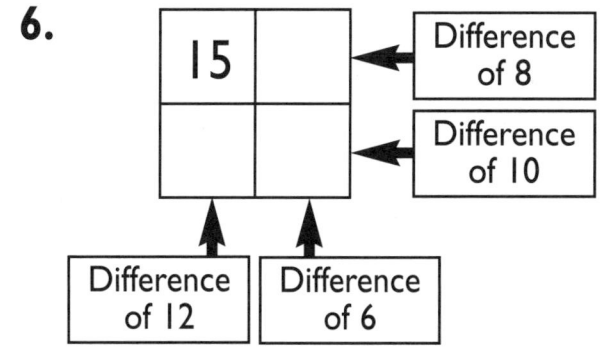

| 15 | | ← Difference of 8 |
| | | ← Difference of 10 |

Difference of 12 — Difference of 6

7.

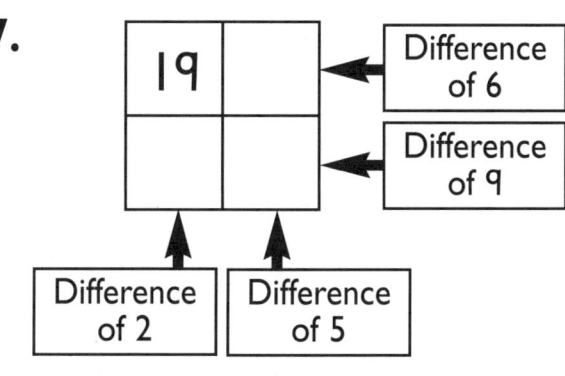

| 19 | | ← Difference of 6 |
| | | ← Difference of 9 |

Difference of 2 — Difference of 5

8.

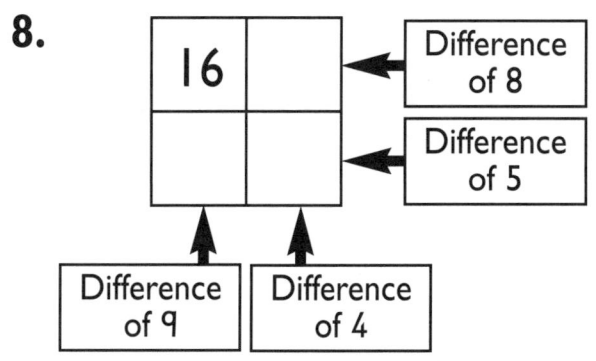

| 16 | | ← Difference of 8 |
| | | ← Difference of 5 |

Difference of 9 — Difference of 4

Teachers' note Encourage the children to write in pencil and try different answers, checking to see whether all of the differences are true each time. As an extension activity ask the children to make up some square puzzles for a partner to solve.

A Lesson for Every Day
Maths
7-8 Years
© A&C Black

Funfair cards

• **Cut out the cards and play the funfair game.**

0 × 2	9 × 2	7 × 5	6 × 10
1 × 2	10 × 2	8 × 5	7 × 10
2 × 2	0 × 5	9 × 5	8 × 10
3 × 2	1 × 5	10 × 5	9 × 10
4 × 2	2 × 5	0 × 10	10 × 10
5 × 2	3 × 5	1 × 10	Miss a turn
6 × 2	4 × 5	2 × 10	Have another go
7 × 2	5 × 5	3 × 10	Miss a turn
8 × 2	6 × 5	4 × 10	Have another go
1 × 2	1 × 5	5 × 10	Have another go

Teachers' note Use this sheet in conjunction with 'Funfair game'. The funfair cards could also be used generally in the class as flashcards or testing cards. The children could also be given this sheet as cards to take and use at home.

A Lesson for Every Day
Maths
7-8 Years
© A&C Black

Funfair game

- **Play this game with a partner. Your teacher will tell you how to play the game.**

Teachers' note Provide children with timers. Instructions: Place the funfair cards face down in a pile. Take turns to pick a card and answer the question within 5 seconds. If the answer is correct, place one of your counters on a ride. If the answer is incorrect place the card at the bottom of the pile. The winner is the first player to put a counter on all of the rides.

A Lesson for Every Day
Maths
7–8 Years
© A&C Black

67

Permission to land

- **Two spaceships can land on each planet, but their total must match the target on that planet.**

☆ For each planet, **estimate** which two spaceships will be able to land.

☆ Then add the spaceship numbers and show your workings.

Was your estimate correct?

Your answers may be different from your friend's.

537 358 127 696 162 479 218

1. workings	2. workings
 About 700	 About 400
3.  Under 300	4.  Over 900
5.  About 800	6.  About 600

A Lesson for Every Day
Maths
7–8 Years
© A&C Black

Spot the difference

- **Cut out the cards.**

Work with a partner.

- **Discuss each pair of shapes and say what is** similar **about them and what is** different .

Look at the length of sides and size of angles.

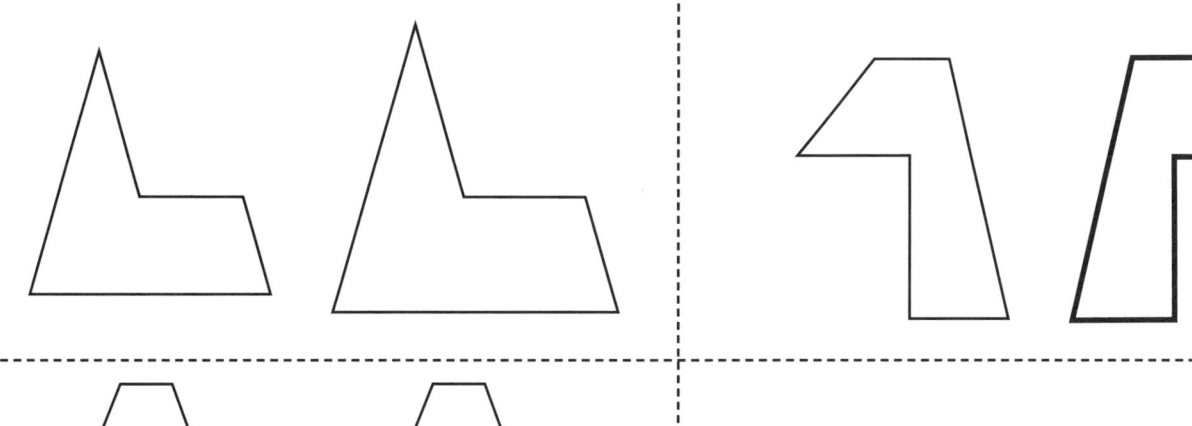

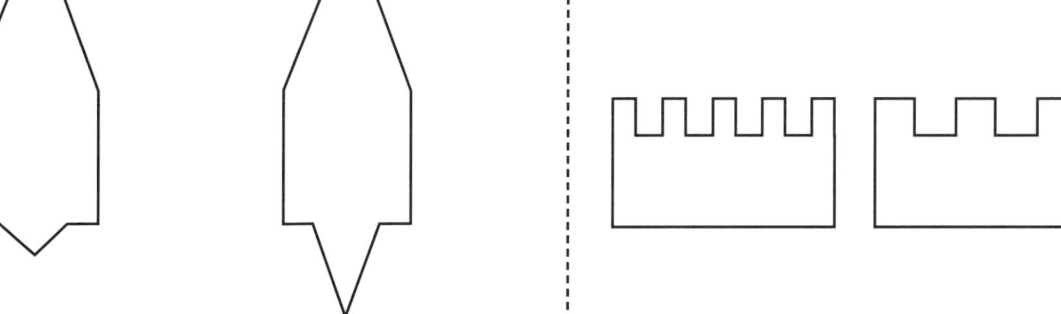

 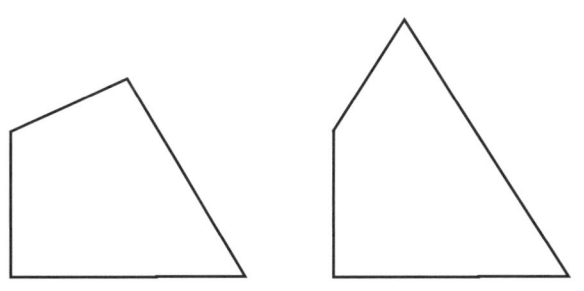

NOW TRY THIS!

- **On a piece of paper, draw four pairs of shapes that are different in some way.**
- **Swap with your partner.**
- **Write what is similar and what is different.**

Teachers' note The children should concentrate on one pair of shapes at a time. Encourage them to look at whether the shape has been reflected, enlarged, reduced or stretched in one direction, or whether one vertex has been moved. Ask them to describe the shapes in each pair, looking to see when corresponding sides and angles are the same and when they are different.

A Lesson for Every Day
Maths
7–8 Years
© A&C Black

A sticky situation

1. Arrange three sticks to make a shape.  You need matchsticks.

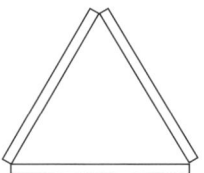

Name the shape.

_____

2. Add two more sticks, without moving the first three.

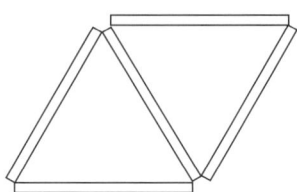

(a) How many sides? _____

(b) Name the shape.

_____

3. Add two more sticks, without moving the others.
Draw the shape.

(a) How many sides? _____

(b) Name the shape.

_____

4. Add two more sticks, without moving the others.
Draw the shape.

(a) How many sides? _____

(b) Name the shape.

_____

5. Add two more sticks, without moving the others.
Draw the shape.

(a) How many sides? _____

(b) Name the shape.

_____

70

Teachers' note The children do not need to consider the sticks in the centre of the shape when counting sides or naming the shape. Ensure that all shapes are closed and that sticks join end to end without gaps. Ask the children to compare their work with others, as different shapes are possible. They could continue adding two sticks at a time, recording on the back of the sheet.

A Lesson for Every Day
Maths
7–8 Years
© A&C Black

Building work

- **Build each shape.**
- **Write how many cubes you used for each shape.**

> **You need** interlocking cubes.

1.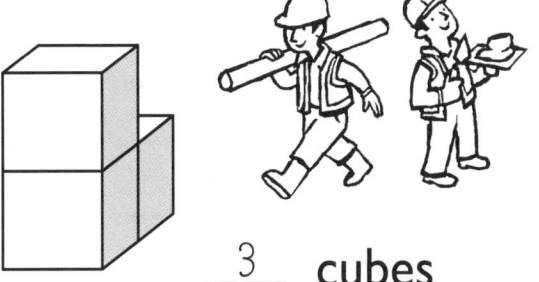

_3_ cubes

2.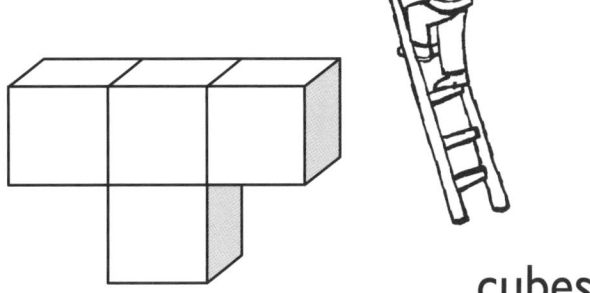

___ cubes

3.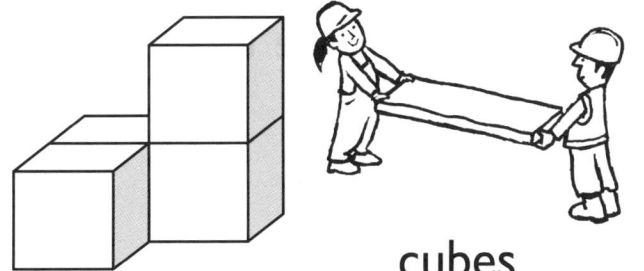

___ cubes

4.

___ cubes

5.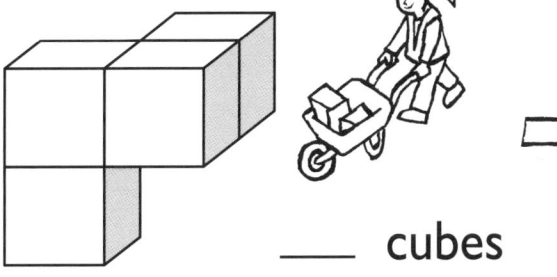

___ cubes

6.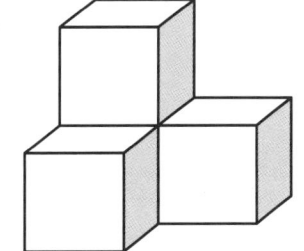

___ cubes

7.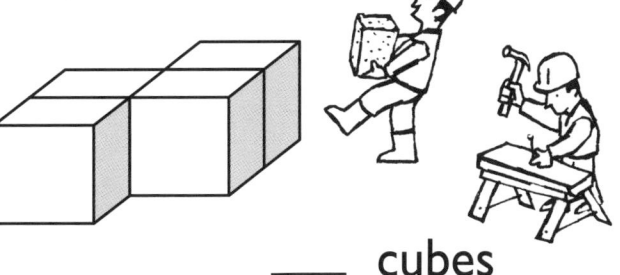

___ cubes

8.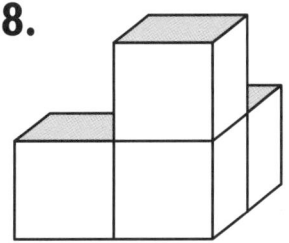

___ cubes

NOW TRY THIS!

- **Talk to a partner about which of the shapes above are the same.**

Teachers' note As a further extension, the children could colour the shapes on the worksheet to match the models they have made. This can help them to appreciate where some cubes are not seen at all or where only one or two of their faces are visible.

A Lesson for Every Day
Maths
7-8 Years
© A&C Black

Traffic lights

- **Colour the three sets of traffic lights, like this:**

  You need red, orange and green coloured pencils.

- **Now find the shape that matches each description.**
- **Colour the solid shape to match the traffic light.**

1.

It has a square face.

It has six vertices.

It has a curved face.

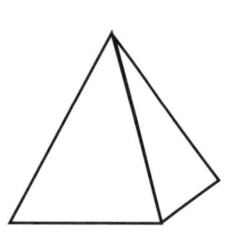 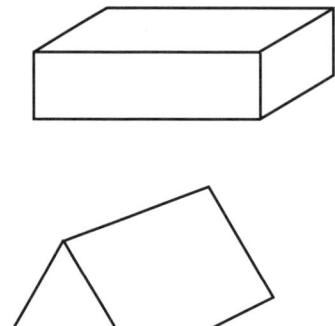 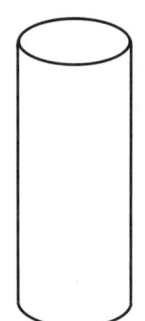

2.

It has a circular face.

It has eight vertices.

It has nine edges.

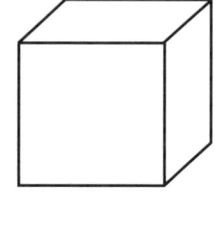 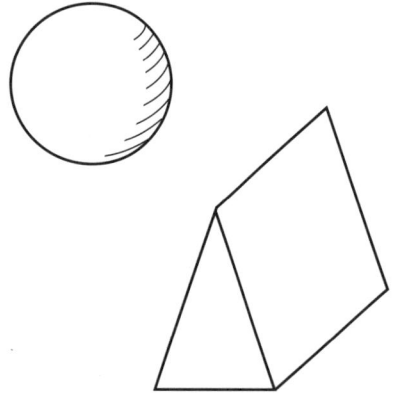 

3.

It has two circular faces.

It has one vertex.

It has no flat faces.

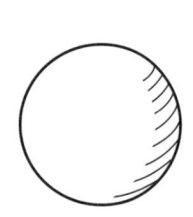 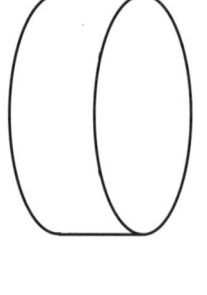  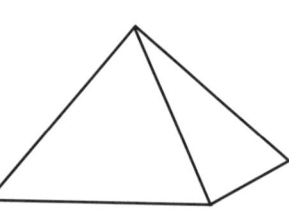

Teachers' note Before the children begin the activity, ensure that they have coloured each set of traffic lights correctly (you could colour the example at the top of the sheet before giving it to the children). Provide the children with matching solid shapes to enable them to count and examine the properties. As an extension, ask the children to name the three red shapes.

A Lesson for Every Day
Maths
7–8 Years
© A&C Black

Two numbers

• **Find the two missing numbers on each card.**

Two numbers ⟨2⟩ ⟨5⟩

Their total is 7.
Their product is 10.

Two numbers ☐ ☐

Their total is 5.
Their product is 6.

Two numbers ☐ ☐

Their total is 14.
Their product is 40.

Two numbers ☐ ☐

Their total is 10.
Their product is 25.

Two numbers ☐ ☐

Their total is 12.
Their product is 20.

Two numbers ☐ ☐

Their total is 11.
Their product is 10.

Two numbers ☐ ☐

Their total is 12.
Their product is 35.

Two numbers ☐ ☐

Their total is 19.
Their product is 90.

NOW TRY THIS!

• **Make up ⟨2⟩ of your own for a partner to solve.**

Two numbers ☐ ☐

Their total is _____.
Their product is _____.

Two numbers ☐ ☐

Their total is _____.
Their product is _____.

Teachers' note The children should be reminded of the words 'total' and 'product'. Encourage them to begin to generalise about how to work out the two numbers in each case. Ask them to say what strategies they used to help them work out the two numbers. Did they find the total clue or the product clue most useful initially?

A Lesson for Every Day
Maths
7–8 Years
© A&C Black

Spiders and flies

Here is some information.

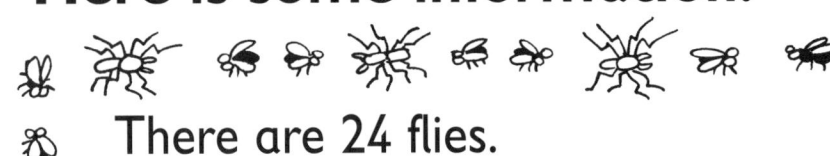

There are 24 flies.

There are 17 more flies than spiders.

Each fly has 6 legs.

Each spider has 8 legs.

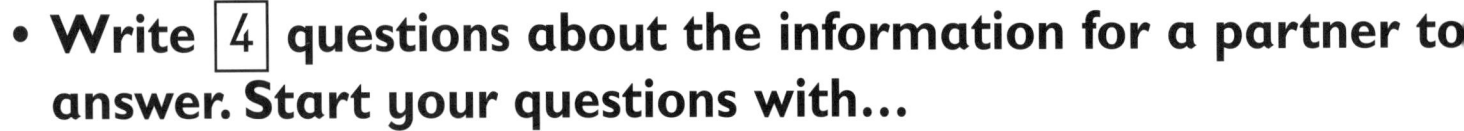

- **Write** 4 **questions about the information for a partner to answer. Start your questions with...**

How many...?   How many more...?   How many fewer...?

NOW TRY THIS!

- **Swap sheets with a partner and answer their questions.**

Teachers' note This activity encourages children to make up their own questions using appropriate vocabulary. When children exchange sheets for the extension activity, encourage them to describe how they decided what to do and encourage them to use number sentences to show the operation used. Adjust numbers to make them appropriate for the children's abilities.

A Lesson for Every Day
Maths
7–8 Years
© A&C Black

Match it: 1

- **Work with a partner.**
- Match **each question with a** number sentence **.**
- **Some number sentences can be used more than once.**

Two tables have a difference in length of 15 cm. The shorter table is 90 cm long. What is the length of the longer table?

$15 \times 90 = [\quad]$

A notebook and pencil cost 90p. The pencil cost 15p. How much did the notebook cost?

$90 + 15 = [\quad]$

£90 is shared between some people. Each person gets £15. How many people are there?

$90 - [\quad] = 15$

A ticket costs 90p. What is the price of 15 tickets?

$[\quad] - 15 = 90$

Ben has 90p. He buys a magazine and is left with 15p. How much did the magazine cost?

$[\quad] \times 15 = 90$

Pens come in packs of 15. How many packs would you need to have 90 pens?

$90 \div [\quad] = 15$

90 people travelled to a football match. 15 people went in each minibus. How many minibuses were needed?

$15 + [\quad] = 90$

A plant that was 15 cm tall grew to be 90 cm. How much had it grown?

$90 \div 15 = [\quad]$

NOW TRY THIS!

- **Make up a new story to match each number sentence.**

Teachers' note More than one possible answer is acceptable in most cases, for example the calculation 15 + [ ] = 90 or 90 – [ ] = 15 could refer to the same situation. Some children may find it easier to work out the answer to help them recognise which number sentence is the correct one.

A Lesson for Every Day
Maths
7–8 Years
© A&C Black

Match it: 2

- **Work with a partner.**
- Match **each question with a** number sentence .
- **Some number sentences can be used more than once.**

Two pieces of string are cut from a 1 m ball. One piece is 25 cm long. How long is the other piece if only 8 cm is left on the ball

$1 + 25 + 8 = [\quad]$

Into a fishtank Jo pours 1 litre, then 8 litres and then some more until she has 25 litres. How much more did she add?

$100 - 25 - [\quad] = 8$

Josh shares out £1 equally between 25 people. He then gives each person 8p more. How much do they each have now?

$100 \div 25 \times [\quad] = 8$

Tickets cost £1. Sam buys 8 and pays a 25p booking charge. How much does he pay?

$(1 + 8) \times 25 = [\quad]$

Al has a 1 metre plank of wood. He saws it into 25 cm lengths. How many 1 m planks does he need to have 8 pieces like this?

$100 \times 8 \div 25 = [\quad]$

Beth is given £1 each week for 8 weeks. How many 25p stickers can she buy with the money?

$(100 \times 8) + 25 = [\quad]$

A milkshake is made from 1 egg-cup of juice and 8 egg-cups of milk. Li makes 25 milkshakes. How many egg-cups of drink is this altogether?

$1 + 8 + [\quad] = 25$

A tree that was 1 m tall grew to be 8 times taller. It then grew a further 25 cm. How tall is it now?

$(100 \div 25) + 8 = [\quad]$

NOW TRY THIS!

- **Make up a story to match this number sentence.**

$100 + [\quad] - 25 = 8$

Teachers' note The questions are two-step calculations and children should work together in pairs to discuss them. Some children may find it easier to work out the answer to help them recognise which number sentence is the correct one.

A Lesson for Every Day
Maths
7-8 Years
© A&C Black

Sweet talk

There were some sweets in a bowl.

☆ First, Andy ate | half | the sweets.

☆ Then Mandy ate | half | the sweets that were left.

☆ Finally, Sandy ate | half | the sweets that were left after Mandy had had hers.

☆ | 5 | sweets were left in the bowl at the end.

- **How many sweets were in the bowl at the start?**
- **Show your working here.**

NOW TRY THIS!

- **Can you solve this problem in a similar way?**

☆ First, Andy ate | half | the sweets in a bowl.

☆ Then Mandy ate | half | the sweets left.

☆ Finally, Sandy ate a | quarter | of the sweets left.

☆ | 3 | sweets were left in the bowl at the end.

- **How many sweets were in the bowl at the start?** _____

Teachers' note Ensure that children understand the problem and encourage them to show their working in the box, whether pictorial or numerical. Numbers can be changed before copying, for example change the final 'half' to a 'a third of' and make the final number an even number.

A Lesson for Every Day
Maths
7–8 Years
© A&C Black

Pattern maker

- **Cut out the cards. Pick cards to make patterns with. Stick them onto paper and write the answers. If you need other numbers, write them onto the** blank **cards.**

600 + 50 + 7	600 + 40 + 17	600 + 30 + 27
600 + 10 + 47	600 + 20 + 37	700 + 50 + 17
800 + 50 + 7	900 + 50 + 7	600 + 30 + 7
600 + 30 + 17	600 + 30 + 37	600 + 30 + 47
500 + 10 + 47	400 + 10 + 47	300 + 10 + 47
200 + 10 + 47	100 + 10 + 47	900 + 40 + 7
900 + 30 + 7	900 + 20 + 7	900 + 10 + 7
700 + 40 + 27	700 + 30 + 37	700 + 20 + 47
700 + 10 + 57	300 + 10 + 57	300 + 20 + 47
300 + 30 + 37	300 + 40 + 27	300 + 50 + 17

78

Teachers' note This activity encourages the children to begin to realise how numbers can be partitioned into multiples of 100, tens and ones in different ways. If they are experiencing difficulty in sorting the cards into sets, ask them to take each card in turn and find the total. The cards can then be grouped according to totals and then each set arranged to show partition patterns.

A Lesson for Every Day
Maths
7-8 Years
© A&C Black

- **Complete this table to show how many of each coin makes the amount in the bag.**

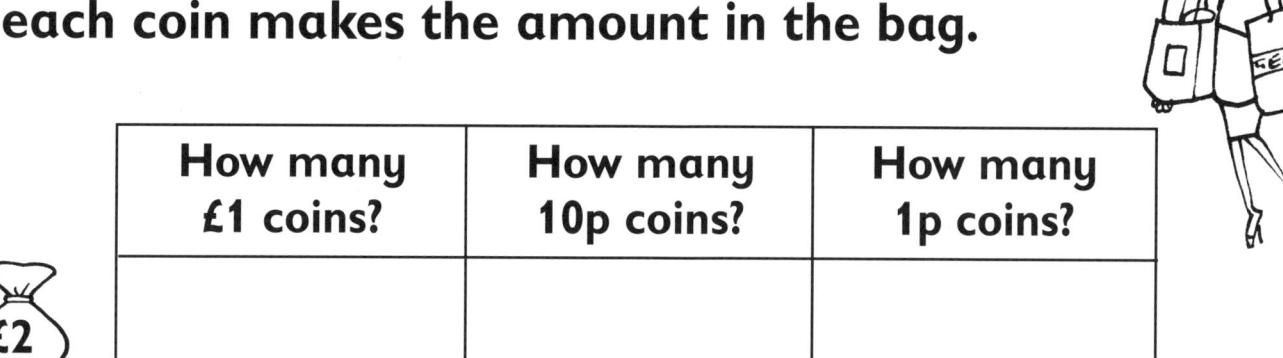

	How many £1 coins?	How many 10p coins?	How many 1p coins?
£2			
£4			
£5			
£8			
£9			
£11			

- **Explain what you notice about the number of £1, 10p and 1p coins.** _____

_____

_____

NOW TRY THIS!

- **Draw another table to show how many £2, 20p and 2p coins make £4, £6, £10 and £12.**

Teachers' note This activity encourages the children to see patterns in numbers that can be used to help them solve problems more quickly. Having completed the sheet, ask the children oral questions about the number of 10p, 1p or £1 coins that make different amounts. Encourage them to use the patterns they notice to explain how they answered them quickly.

A Lesson for Every Day
Maths
7-8 Years
© A&C Black

Toy sale

Each child has exactly $£1$ to spend. If they buy the toy shown, how much change do they each get?

1.  8p
92p

2.  95p
P

3.  80p
P

4.  21p
P

5.  15p
P

6.  40p
P

7.  45p
P

8.  77p
P

9.  55p
P

10.  82p
P

11.  63p
P

12.  74p
P

13.  16p
P

14.  32p
P

15.  47p
P

16.  66p
P

17.  27p
P

18.  19p
P

NOW TRY THIS!

• **Tick the pairs that have a total of** 100 .

| 84 | 26 | | 37 | 63 | | 52 | 48 | | 71 | 39 | | 17 | 84 |

Teachers' note This activity can help children to derive and recall number pairs with a total of 100.
Ensure the children realise that £1 is equal to 100p.

A Lesson for Every Day
Maths
7-8 Years
© A&C Black

Make one hundred: 1

- **Cut out the cards on both sheets.**
- **Play the game in a group.**

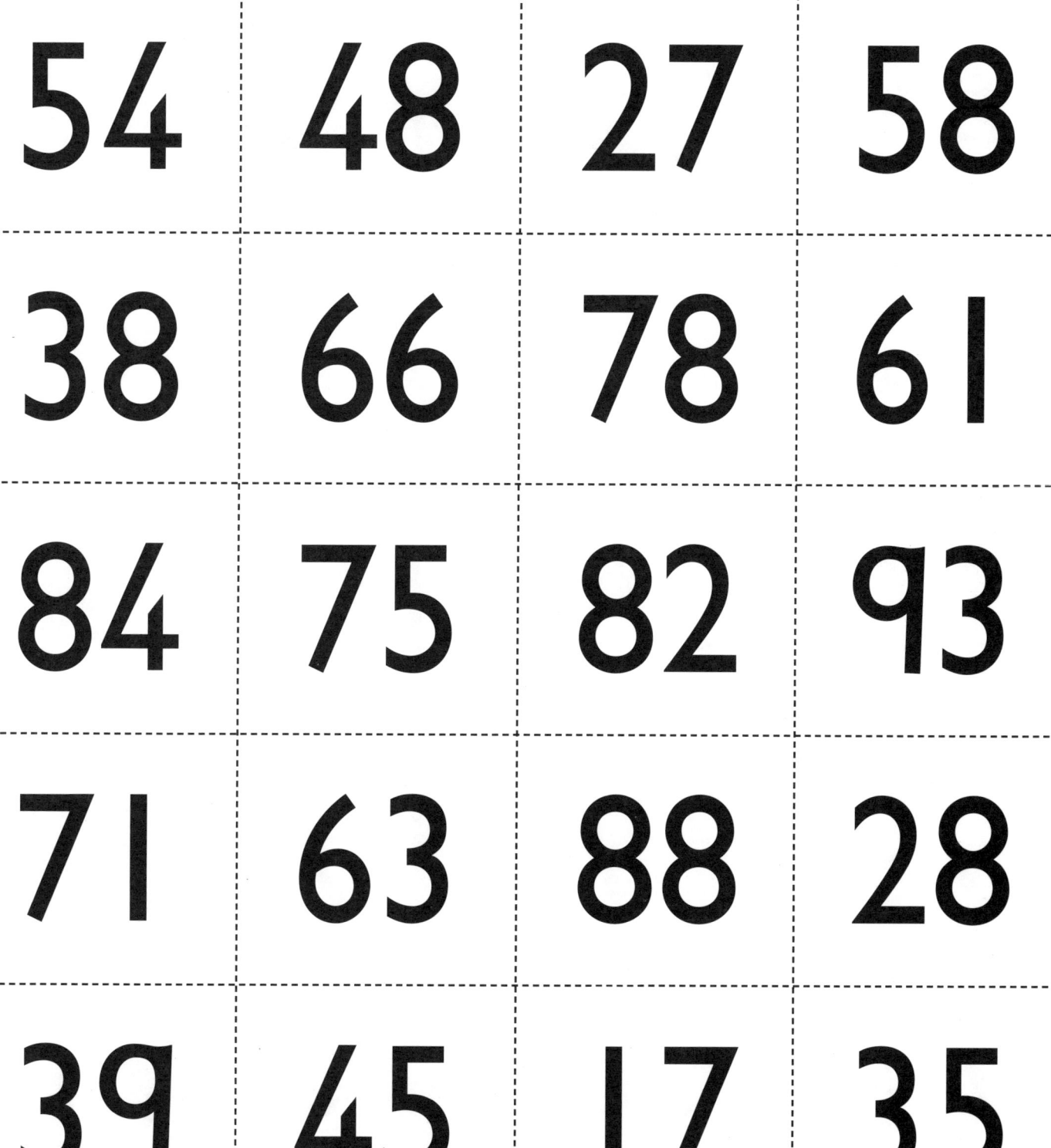

54	48	27	58
38	66	78	61
84	75	82	93
71	63	88	28
39	45	17	35

Teachers' note Use this sheet in conjuction with 'Make one hundred: 2'

A Lesson for Every Day
Maths
7–8 Years
© A&C Black

Make one hundred: 2

- **Cut out the cards on both sheets.**
- **Play the game in a group.**

46	52	73	42
62	34	22	39
16	25	18	7
29	37	12	72
61	55	83	65

Teachers' note Children play in even-numbered groups. Each group needs the cards from 'Make one hundred: 1 and 2'. Explain the following game: Deal out the cards. Player 1 places a card face up on the table. The player (could be Player 1) with the card that makes 100 places it down. They are then next to lay down a new card. The winner is the first player to lay down all their cards.

A Lesson for Every Day
Maths
7–8 Years
© A&C Black

Victorian classroom

In this Victorian classroom there are $\boxed{\text{six}}$ desks in every row.

• How many desks are there in

1.  5 rows?

2.  3 rows?

3.  10 rows?

4. 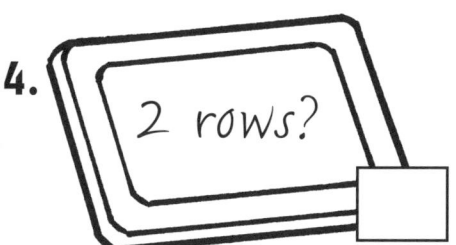 2 rows?

5.  7 rows?

6. 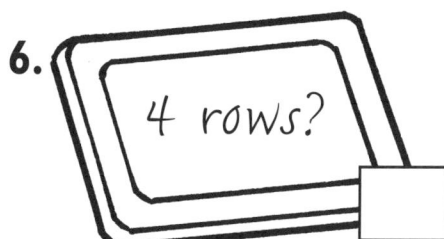 4 rows?

7. 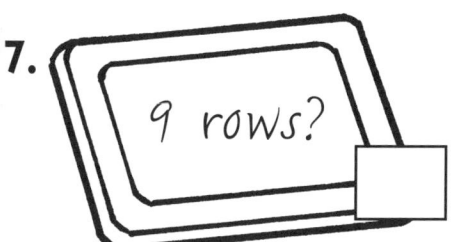 9 rows?

8. 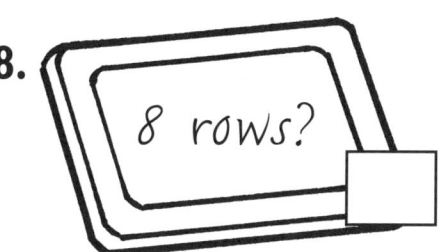 8 rows?

9.  6 rows?

NOW TRY THIS!

• Fill in these answers.

$1 \times 3 = \square$	$1 \times 6 = \square$	$2 \times 3 = \square$	$2 \times 6 = \square$
$3 \times 3 = \square$	$3 \times 6 = \square$	$4 \times 3 = \square$	$4 \times 6 = \square$
$5 \times 3 = \square$	$5 \times 6 = \square$	$6 \times 3 = \square$	$6 \times 6 = \square$
$7 \times 3 = \square$	$7 \times 6 = \square$	$8 \times 3 = \square$	$8 \times 6 = \square$
$9 \times 3 = \square$	$9 \times 6 = \square$	$10 \times 3 = \square$	$10 \times 6 = \square$

Teachers' note Children could use practical equipment to help them with these questions, for example collecting cubes in sticks of six and counting them or using squared paper and drawing rectangles with six squares in each row. When children have completed the extension activity, ask them what they notice about the answers to the 3 and the 6 times-tables.

A Lesson for Every Day
Maths
7–8 Years
© A&C Black

Draw and name game

- **Play this game with a partner.**
- **Draw and name...**

> **You need** a counter, a ruler, a pencil and some paper each, and a dice to share.

Start	a shape with four sides	a shape with three straight sides	a symmetrical shape	a shape with four right angles

a shape that has one curved side	a shape with ten straight sides	a shape that has five sides and one right angle	a shape that is half a circle

a shape with four lines of symmetry	**Finish**	a shape that has seven straight sides	a shape that has three sides and one right angle

a shape with four equal sides	a shape with three equal sides	a shape with three lines of symmetry	a shape with one line of symmetry

a shape with one right angle	a shape with three right angles	a symmetrical shape with six sides	a shape that has four sides and two right angles

a shape with six straight sides	a shape with more than four sides	a shape that has six sides and one right angle	a shape with five straight sides

a shape that is **not** symmetrical	a shape with eight straight sides	a shape with two lines of symmetry	a shape with no right angles

84

Teachers' note The children take turns to throw the dice and move their counter. As each child lands on a section of the trail he/she should draw a shape that matches the description. If the shape is drawn correctly he/she gets one point. A second point can be gained if the child can also name the shape. The winner is the player with the most points at the finish line.

A Lesson for Every Day
Maths
7–8 Years
© A&C Black

Shape all-sorts

Cut out the shapes cards.

- **Sort each shape onto the** Carroll diagram **and write its name in the correct place.**

	No circular faces	At least one circular face
At least one vertex	Cube	
No vertices		

NOW TRY THIS!

- **Draw a Carroll diagram with these labels:**
- **Sort the shapes again.**

No rectangular faces	At least one rectangular face
Not a prism	Prism

Teachers' note Ensure that the children know how to complete a Carroll diagram by demonstrating simple sorting with coloured 2-D shapes, for example red, not red, square, not square. For the extension activity, discuss that rectangles include squares and that prisms can include cubes, cuboids and cylinders as each has the same cross-section throughout its length.

A Lesson for Every Day
Maths
7-8 Years
© A&C Black

Symmetry Cemetery

- In Symmetry Cemetery, all the gravestones must be symmetrical .

- Tick ✔ the gravestones that are allowed in the cemetery and cross ✘ the ones that are not.

- Using a ruler, draw the lines of symmetry.

One has been done for you.

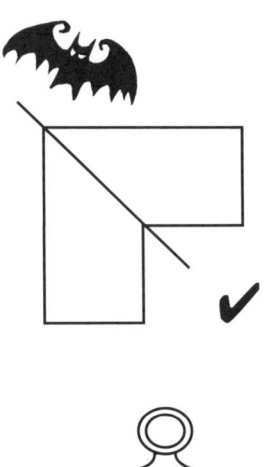   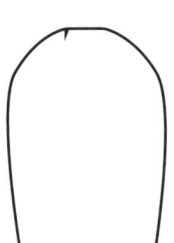 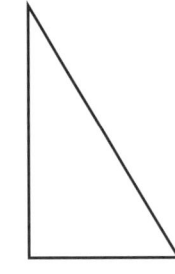

    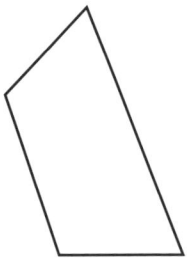

 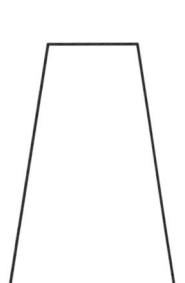 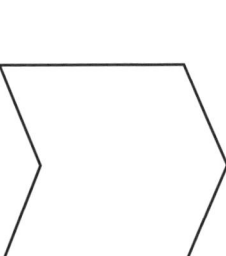 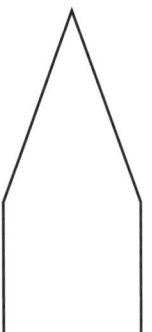 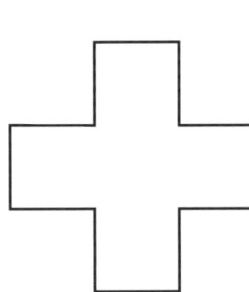

NOW TRY THIS!

- **Colour a gravestone with:**

  2 lines of symmetry **green**,

  4 lines of symmetry **blue**,

  1 **diagonal** line of symmetry **yellow**.

Teachers' note Ensure the children appreciate that the lines of symmetry do not need to be vertical in order for the gravestone to be allowed into the cemetery. As a further extension, the children could draw five more gravestones on the back of this sheet. They could then ask a partner to say whether these gravestones would be allowed in Symmetry Cemetery.

A Lesson for Every Day
Maths
7-8 Years
© A&C Black

Shape symmetry

- **Draw the** [reflection] **of each shape in the dotted mirror line.**

One has been done for you. Use a ruler.

1.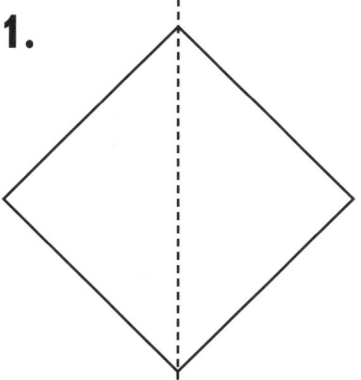

2.

3.

4.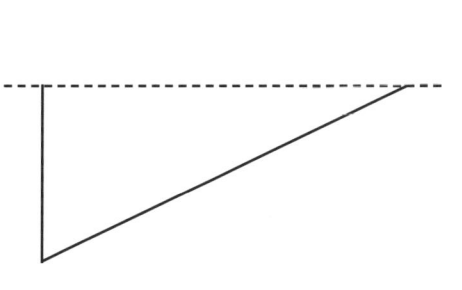

5.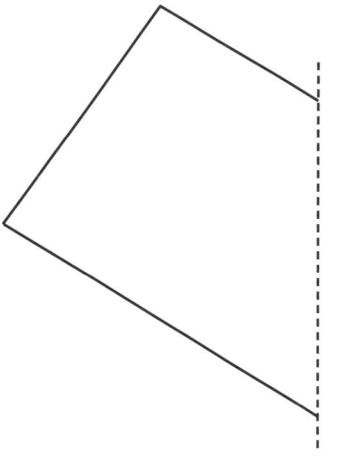

6.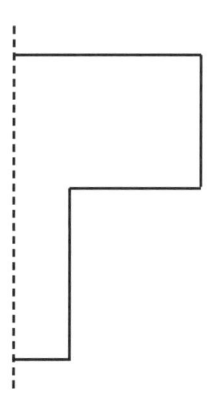

7.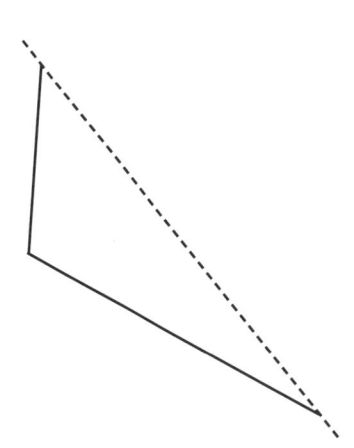

NOW TRY THIS!

- **Under each shape, write the name of the new shape you have made.**

Teachers' note Provide the children with mirrors and demonstrate how they should be used to help draw and check reflections. In this activity, the children place their mirrors along the dotted line (which is one side of the shape). If preferred, the children could use tracing paper to check reflections or help them to draw the shapes more accurately.

A Lesson for Every Day
Maths
7–8 Years
© A&C Black

Mosaic patterns

Each pattern is made from small tiles.
- ## Shade <u>two tiles</u> to make each pattern `symmetrical` .

One pattern has been done for you.

1.

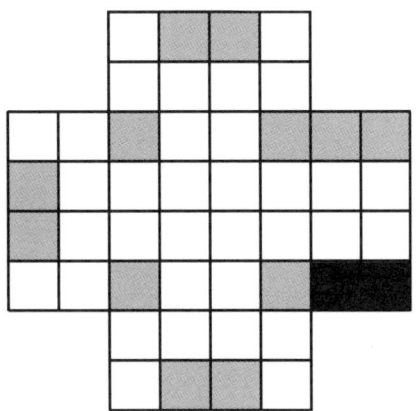

2.

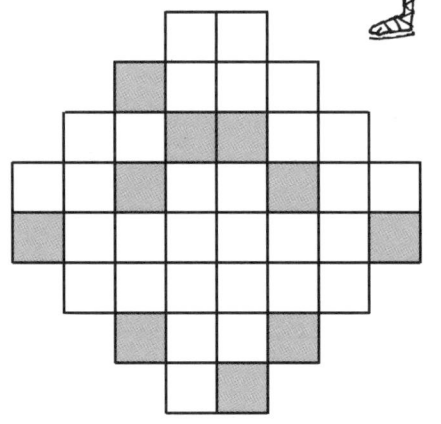

3.

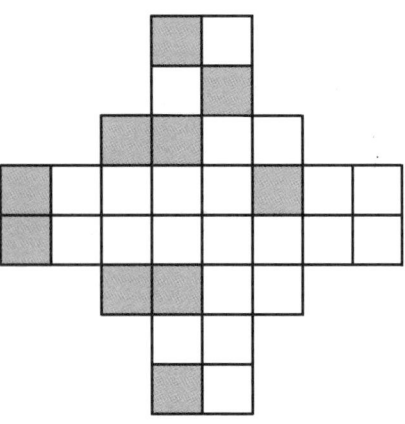

4.

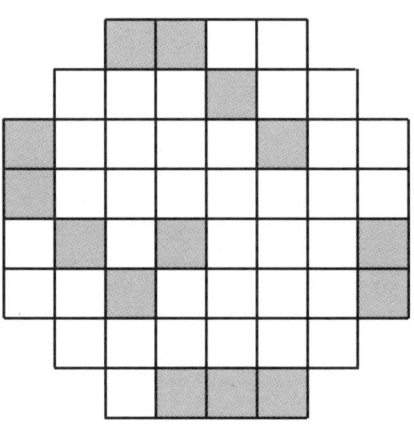

5.

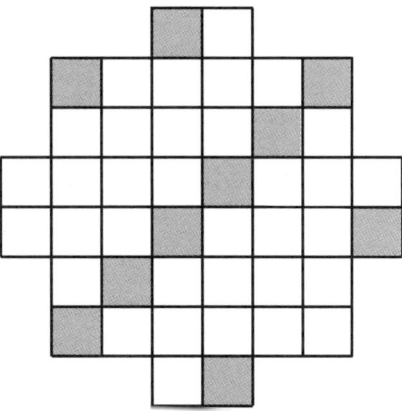

6.

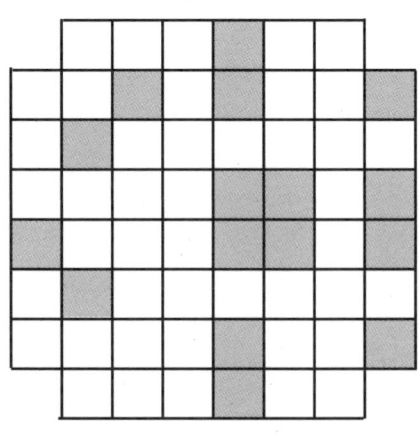

NOW TRY THIS!

- ## Now colour some of the patterns.

Make sure you keep them symmetrical.

Express pizza

- ## Use the menu to help you.

	small	medium	large
Pan	£4.99	£8.99	£10.49
Italian	£5.99	£10.99	£12.99
Soft crust	£6.49	£11.49	£13.99

* All include 4 toppings of your choice

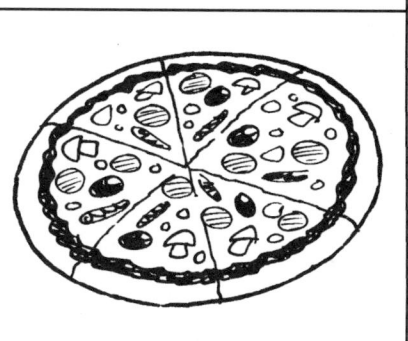

1 How much for:

a) 2 small Pan pizzas?

£ ____

b) 3 medium Italian pizzas?

£ ____

c) 2 large Soft crust pizzas?

£ ____

d) 1 large and 1 small Pan?

£ ____

e) 3 large Italian pizzas and 1 small Soft crust?

£ ____

f) 2 medium Soft crust pizzas and 2 small Italian pizzas?

£ ____

2 How much change from £20 for:

a) 3 small Italian pizzas?

£ ____

b) 1 large Pan pizza?

£ ____

c) 2 medium Pan pizzas?

£ ____

d) 4 small Pan pizzas?

£ ____

NOW TRY THIS!

- ## If you have £20, have you enough money to buy 3 small Soft crust pizzas? ____

Teachers' note Encourage children to round the prices and to work with whole or half pounds and then adjust for the pence when finding totals and giving change. Ask them to record their methods and the calculations they use on the back of the sheet.

A Lesson for Every Day
Maths
7-8 Years
© A&C Black

Loop the loop

* **Cut out the cards.**
* **Answer the 'start' card. Find the answer on one of the other cards. Then answer that question and so on.**
* **Put the cards in a loop on the table.**

Start **6 kg** Fi has 360 g of flour. She shares it equally into four bowls. How much in each bowl? **T**	**75 kg** 3 tins of beans each weigh 400 g and a tin of ravioli weighs 800 g. How much do the tins weigh altogether? **D**
68 kg A bowl and a potato together weigh 500 g. The bowl weighs 100 g more than the potato. How heavy is the bowl? **N**	**10 kg** A bucket weighs 500 g. A 2 kg brick is placed in the bucket. How heavy is it now? **T**
$2\frac{1}{2}$ kg Sally weighs 36 kg. She weighs 39 kg less than her mum. How heavy is her mum? **O**	**90 g** A baby weighed 3 kg. Its mass increased by 500 g a week for two weeks. How much does it weigh now? **R**
3 kg A dog weighs 24 kg. The dog is six times heavier than a cat. How heavy is the cat? **E**	**300 g** A dog weighs 6 kg more than a cat. The animals weigh 12 kg altogether. How heavy is the cat? **C**
4 kg A brick weighs $2\frac{1}{2}$ kg. What do four bricks weigh? **Y**	**2 kg** Sam is 12 kg lighter than Pete. Sam weighs 56 kg. How heavy is Pete? **A**

Teachers' note As a quick way of checking the children's answers, use the letters at the bottom right of each card. If correctly in order they should spell a phrase. Remind the children that 'g' stands for 'grams' and 'kg' stands for 'kilograms'.

A Lesson for Every Day
Maths
7-8 Years
© A&C Black

Sheep solutions

- **Work with a partner. In each barn are ewes and lambs.**
- **Use the clues to help you work out the | total | number of sheep in the barns.**

| In Barn A there are 3 more lambs than ewes. |

| Barn C has 4 lambs and some ewes. |

| Barn B has the same number of ewes as Barn C. |

| In Barn C there are 7 sheep altogether. |

| In Barn B there are 2 lambs. |

| In Barn A there is 1 ewe. |

- **How many sheep are in the barns | altogether | ?**
- **How many are: lambs? [ ]   ewes? [ ]**

NOW TRY THIS!

- **Draw 3 barns of your own and decide how many ewes and lambs are in each. Make up clues for a partner.**

Teachers' note For the extension activity encourage children to check whether they have given a clue for each barn, without saying how many lambs or ewes are in most of the barns. Write up sentences like 'more than', 'fewer than', 'the most', 'the fewest' and 'the same number' on the board to help them make up their own clues.

A Lesson for Every Day
Maths
7–8 Years
© A&C Black

Sensible statements

- Tick ✔ the most sensible number sentence for each problem.

1 There were 40 avocados in a shop. Sam sold some of them and then had 15 left. How many did he sell?

$\Diamond - 15 = 40$ $15 - \Diamond = 40$ $\Diamond - 40 = 15$ $40 - \Diamond = 15$

2 There are 42 cakes arranged on some plates. Each plate has 14 cakes on it. How many plates?

$\Diamond \div 14 = 42$ $42 \times \Diamond = 14$ $\Diamond \div 14 = 42$ $42 \div 14 = \Diamond$

3 Each packet holds 24 biscuits. Clive buys 3 packets of biscuits. How many biscuits?

$\Diamond \times 3 = 24$ $24 \div \Diamond = 3$ $24 \times 3 = \Diamond$ $\Diamond \times 3 = 24$

4 There were some peaches in a shop. Sam sold 14 of them and had 11 left. How many were there at the start?

$14 - \Diamond = 11$ $\Diamond - 14 = 11$ $11 - 14 = \Diamond$ $14 - 11 = \Diamond$

NOW TRY THIS!

- **Write** number sentences **to match these problems.**

  3 melons cost 90p. How much do 5 melons cost?

  5 apples cost 35p. How much do 12 apples cost?

Teachers' note Remind children that the focus is not on solving the problem, but rather on deciding which number sentence represents the situation. Encourage the children to describe their reasoning and to make up problems like these of their own.

A Lesson for Every Day
Maths
7–8 Years
© A&C Black

Coin quiz

- **Move along the track. Work out the total amount of money and find it below. Write the matching letter.**

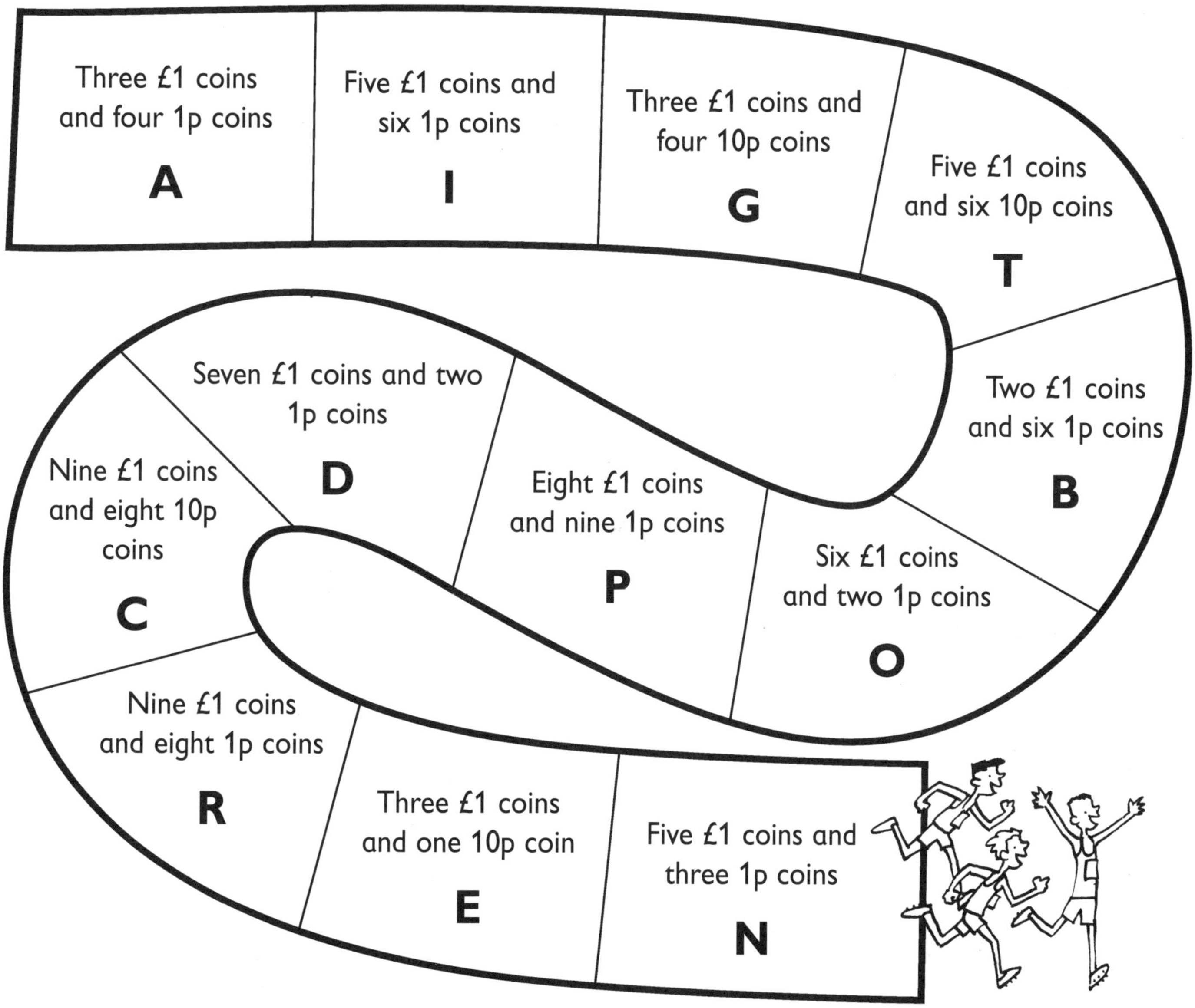

Three £1 coins and four 1p coins

A

Five £1 coins and six 1p coins

I

Three £1 coins and four 10p coins

G

Five £1 coins and six 10p coins

T

Seven £1 coins and two 1p coins

D

Nine £1 coins and eight 10p coins

C

Eight £1 coins and nine 1p coins

P

Two £1 coins and six 1p coins

B

Six £1 coins and two 1p coins

O

Nine £1 coins and eight 1p coins

R

Three £1 coins and one 10p coin

E

Five £1 coins and three 1p coins

N

£9.80		£3.04	A	£8.09	
£2.06		£5.06		£5.03	
£3.40		£3.10		£5.60	
£9.08		£6.02		£7.02	

- **What words are spelt in each line?** _____

Teachers' note Draw children's attention to the fact that some contain 10p coins and others 1p coins. Discuss the pounds/pence notation and encourage the children to say the total amounts in words.

A Lesson for Every Day
Maths
7–8 Years
© A&C Black

Right-angle wrangle

Tim has 8 identical right-angled triangles.
The other 2 angles in each
triangle are half right angles.

Tim fits them together, adding an extra triangle each time.

• Write what shapes are made and say how many right
angles each <u>whole</u> shape has.

1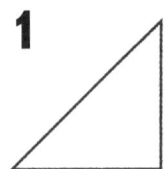

triangle
1 right angle

5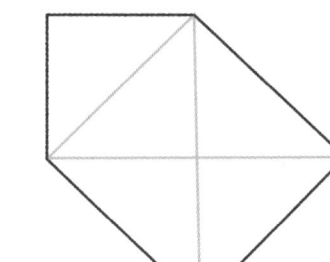

2

6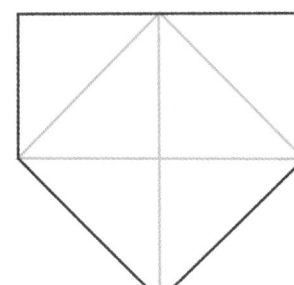

3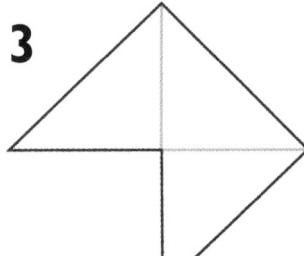

7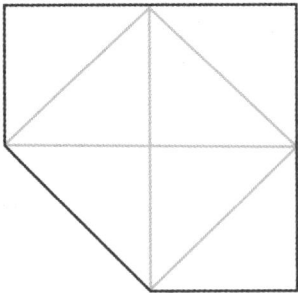

4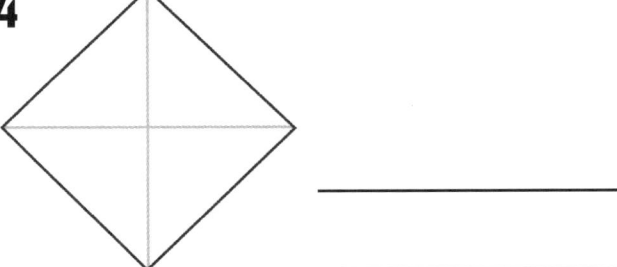

8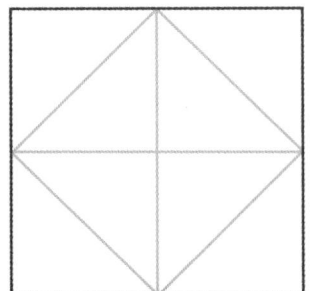

Teachers' note Children could investigate their own shapes formed using identical tiles of a different shape. Remind them that they should only count the right-angles that are formed INSIDE each shape and not those that are outside the shape. They could also use 'Right-angle tangle' as an extension. Ask the children to mark each right angle on the shapes.

A Lesson for Every Day
Maths
7-8 Years
© A&C Black

Right-angle tangle

Tim has 8 identical pentagons.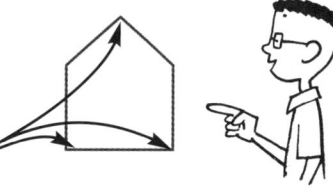
Three angles are right angles.
Tim fits them together, adding an extra pentagon each time.

• Write how many sides and how many right angles each <u>whole</u> shape has.

1

5 sides

3 right angles

5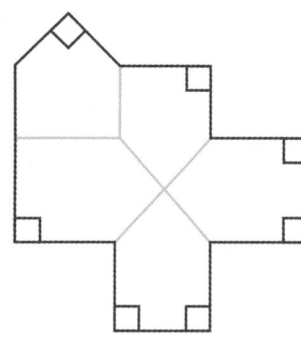

12 sides

7 right angles

2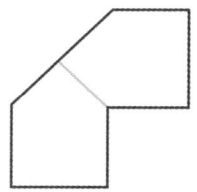

_____

_____

6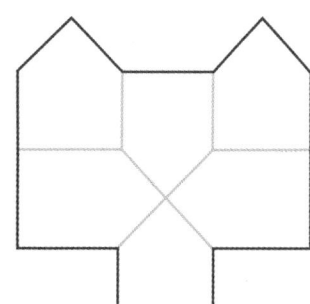

_____

_____

3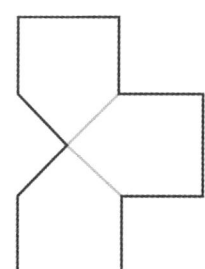

_____

_____

7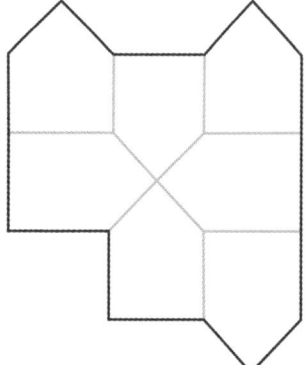

_____

_____

4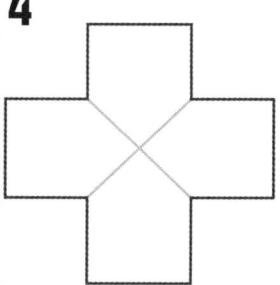

_____

_____

8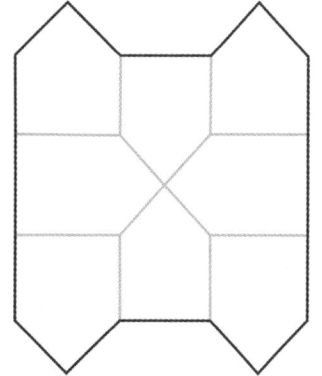

_____

_____

Teachers' note Ask the children to mark each right angle on the shapes. Remind them that they should only count the right-angles that are formed INSIDE each shape and not those that are outside the shape. Children could investigate their own shapes formed using identical tiles of a different shape.

A Lesson for Every Day
Maths
7–8 Years
© A&C Black

• **Through how many right angles does the minute hand turn between the times on the clocks in each pair?**

1

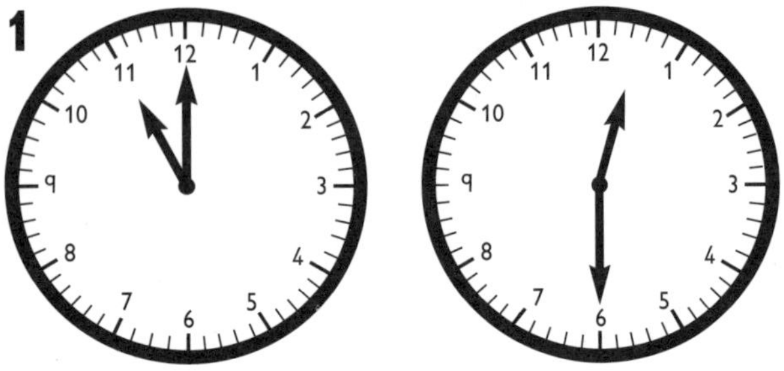

2

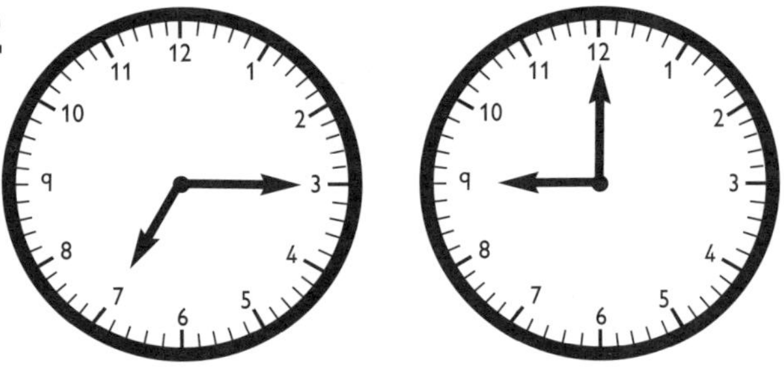

3

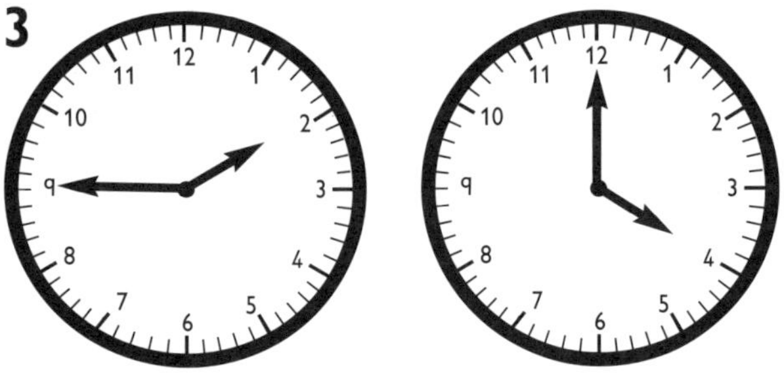

4

5

6

7

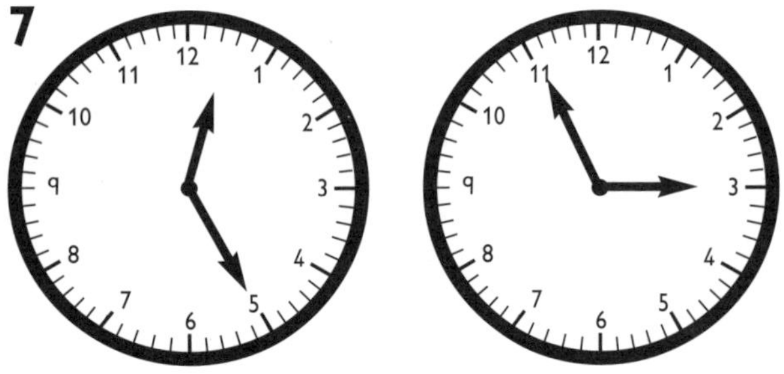

8

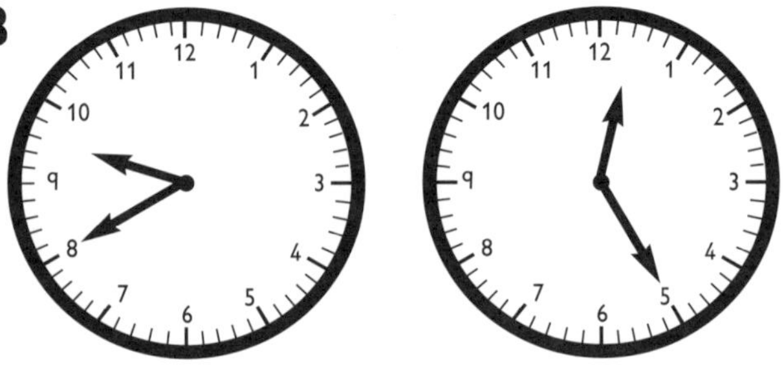

NOW TRY THIS!

• **Write different pairs of times in the afternoon where the minute hand goes through 11 right angles.**

Teachers' note Remind children that the minute hand is the longer hand and that it turns through 4 right angles in each hour. Also that it passes through a right angle when it moves between say the 2 and the 5. The hands on the clocks can be changed to create a variety of different question banks. For the extension activity, encourage the children to work systematically to write pairs of times.

A Lesson for Every Day
Maths
7–8 Years
© A&C Black

Magic carpets

- **Cut out the cards.**
- **Match the fractions with the rug patterns to show what fraction is shaded.**

$\dfrac{1}{6}$	$\dfrac{5}{10}$	$\dfrac{3}{4}$	$\dfrac{13}{15}$	$\dfrac{1}{9}$	$\dfrac{10}{12}$
$\dfrac{4}{7}$	$\dfrac{2}{5}$	$\dfrac{7}{12}$	$\dfrac{5}{9}$	$\dfrac{5}{12}$	$\dfrac{3}{6}$

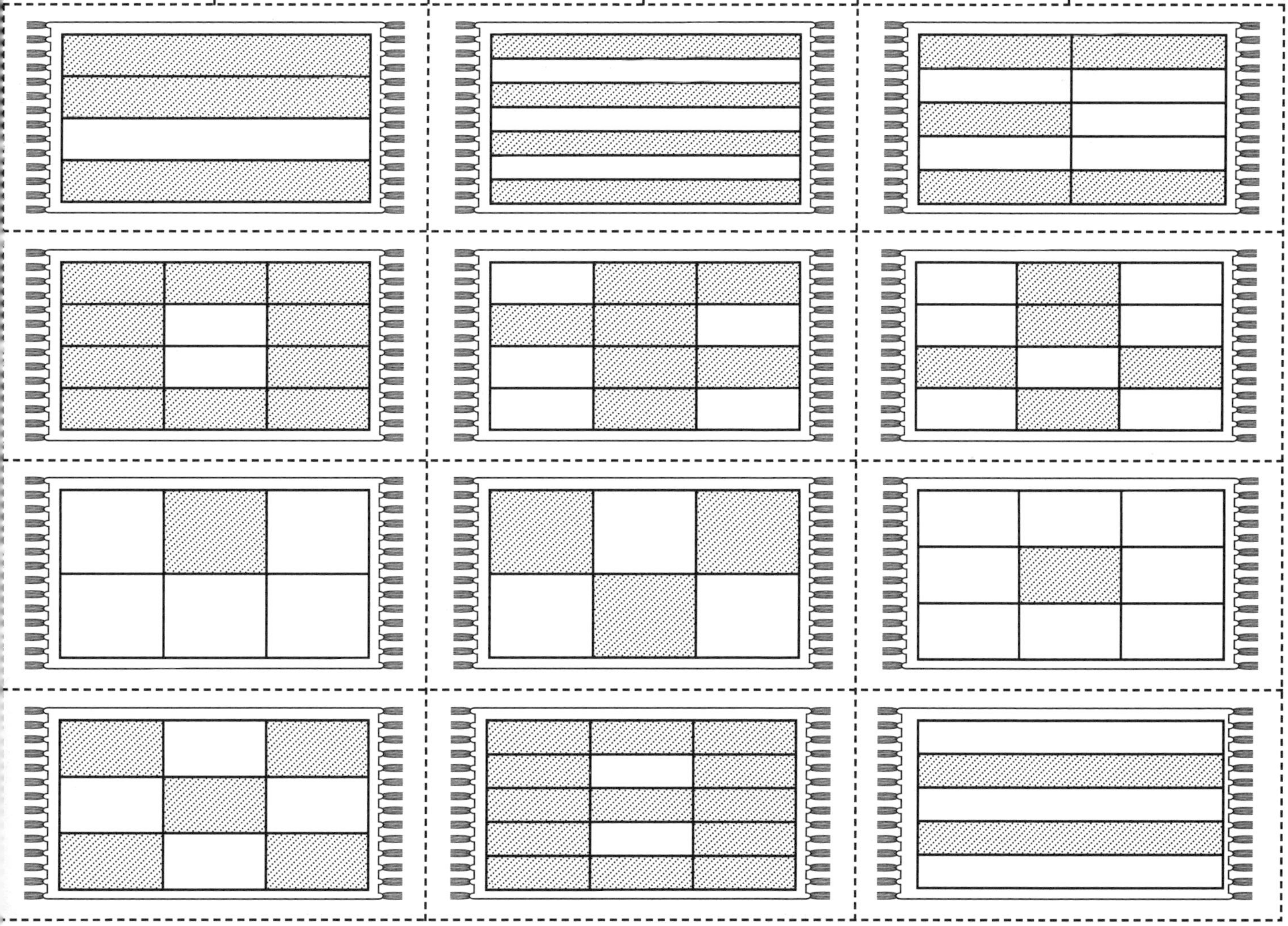

Teachers' note Watch out for the common error of writing the number of unshaded tiles as the denominator rather than the total number of tiles altogether, for example where 3 out of 7 tiles are shaded the children incorrectly write ¾ instead of ³⁄₇. See notes on the activity on page 12 for an alternative game.

A Lesson for Every Day
Maths
7–8 Years
© A&C Black

97

Gee-up horse!

- **Estimate** what fraction of the racecourse each horse has run.

| Start | | Finish | $\dfrac{1}{2}$ |

1

| Start | | Finish | $\underline{\quad}$ |

2

| Start | | Finish | $\underline{\quad}$ |

3

| Start | | Finish | $\underline{\quad}$ |

4

| Start | | Finish | $\underline{\quad}$ |

5

| Start | | Finish | $\underline{\quad}$ |

6

| Start | | Finish | $\underline{\quad}$ |

7

| Start | | Finish | $\underline{\quad}$ |

8

| Start | | Finish | $\underline{\quad}$ |

9

| Start | | Finish | $\underline{\quad}$ |

10

| Start | | Finish | $\underline{\quad}$ |

NOW TRY THIS!

- **Shade this line so that about three-eighths is shaded.**

Teachers' note At the start of the lesson, hold up some strips of paper. Fold them into equal parts and ask the children to say what fraction of the whole strip each part is worth. Then hold up a strip that has a quarter shaded but has no fold marks. Encourage the children to estimate the fraction shaded and demonstrate by drawing lines to show where the fold marks would go.

A Lesson for Every Day
Maths
7-8 Years
© A&C Black

Musical mental maths

• **Write a digit into each musical note to make the statements true. Do this as quickly as you can.**

1. 8 + 7 = ①⑤

2. 16 – 9 = ◯

3. 15 – 7 = ◯

4. 7 + 6 = ◯◯

5. 20 – ◯ = 11

6. 16 – ◯◯ = 4

7. 70 – 20 = ◯◯

8. 90 – 30 = ◯◯

9. 30 + 80 = ◯◯◯

10. 110 – 70 = ◯◯

11. 45 + ◯◯ = 100

12. 100 – ◯◯ = 16

NOW TRY THIS!

• **Fill in digits to make each of these statements true. There is more than one answer for each question.**

◯◯ + ◯◯ = 100

◯◯ – 9 = ◯

◯◯ + ◯◯ = 130

15 – ◯ = ◯

Teachers' note This sheet could be used as an assessment activity. It combines all the question types expected to be known by heart by the age of 8. Children could also time the activity to encourage speedy recall.

A Lesson for Every Day
Maths
7–8 Years
© A&C Black

Snap

- Write answers on each card in the pair.
- Write 'Snap' or 'Not snap' to show whether or not the answers are the same.

Snap!

$12 ÷ 6$ $24 ÷ 3$

2   8

Not snap

$24 ÷ 6$ $16 ÷ 4$

_____

$18 ÷ 6$ $6 ÷ 3$

_____

$42 ÷ 6$ $35 ÷ 5$

_____

$6 ÷ 6$ $30 ÷ 3$

_____

$36 ÷ 6$ $24 ÷ 4$

_____

$48 ÷ 6$ $45 ÷ 5$

_____

$60 ÷ 6$ $40 ÷ 4$

_____

$0 ÷ 6$ $3 ÷ 3$

_____

$30 ÷ 6$ $25 ÷ 5$

_____

$54 ÷ 6$ $32 ÷ 4$

_____

 **NOW TRY THIS!**

- Write three pairs of divisions that each 'Snap'.

Teachers' note For the extension activity answers could be written in, for example 4, 4, 7, 7 and 9, 9 to encourage the children to think carefully about the questions they choose.

A Lesson for Every Day
Maths
7-8 Years
© A&C Black

The dabble birds

Flynn is doing some calculating.

$$13 \times 8 =$$

The dabble birds want to undo what Flynn has done.

• **Write what the birds will do to undo Flynn's work.**
  Then write the answer to each question now.

1.
13×8 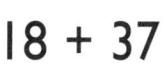 ÷ 8 = 13

2.
$18 + 37$

3.
$54 \div 9$

4.
$75 - 16$

5.
16×6

6.
$34 \div 5$

7.
$54 - 39$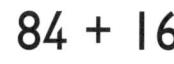

8.
$84 + 16$

9.
23×4

10.
$60 \div 4$

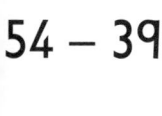 **NOW TRY THIS!**

• **Can you work out the answer to this question?**
  $100 + 7 - 7 \times 25 \div 25 - 4 + 4 =$ _____

Teachers' note This activity encourages the children to appreciate the inverse nature of addition, subtraction, multiplication and division. Children could also be given a calculator to check their answers.

A Lesson for Every Day
Maths
7-8 Years
© A&C Black

Taboo or not taboo

☆ Take turns to secretly pick a shape from the grid.

☆ Describe the shape to the others in your group.

☆ You must **not** say the name of the shape or name the shapes of the faces.

Work in a group of three or four.

 **Words you CANNOT use**	**Some words you CAN use**
~~sphere, cube, cuboid, cone, cylinder, prism, pyramid, hemisphere~~ ~~square, circle, triangle, rectangle, hexagon, pentagon~~	solid, faces, vertex, vertices, edges, surface curved, straight, flat, equal 

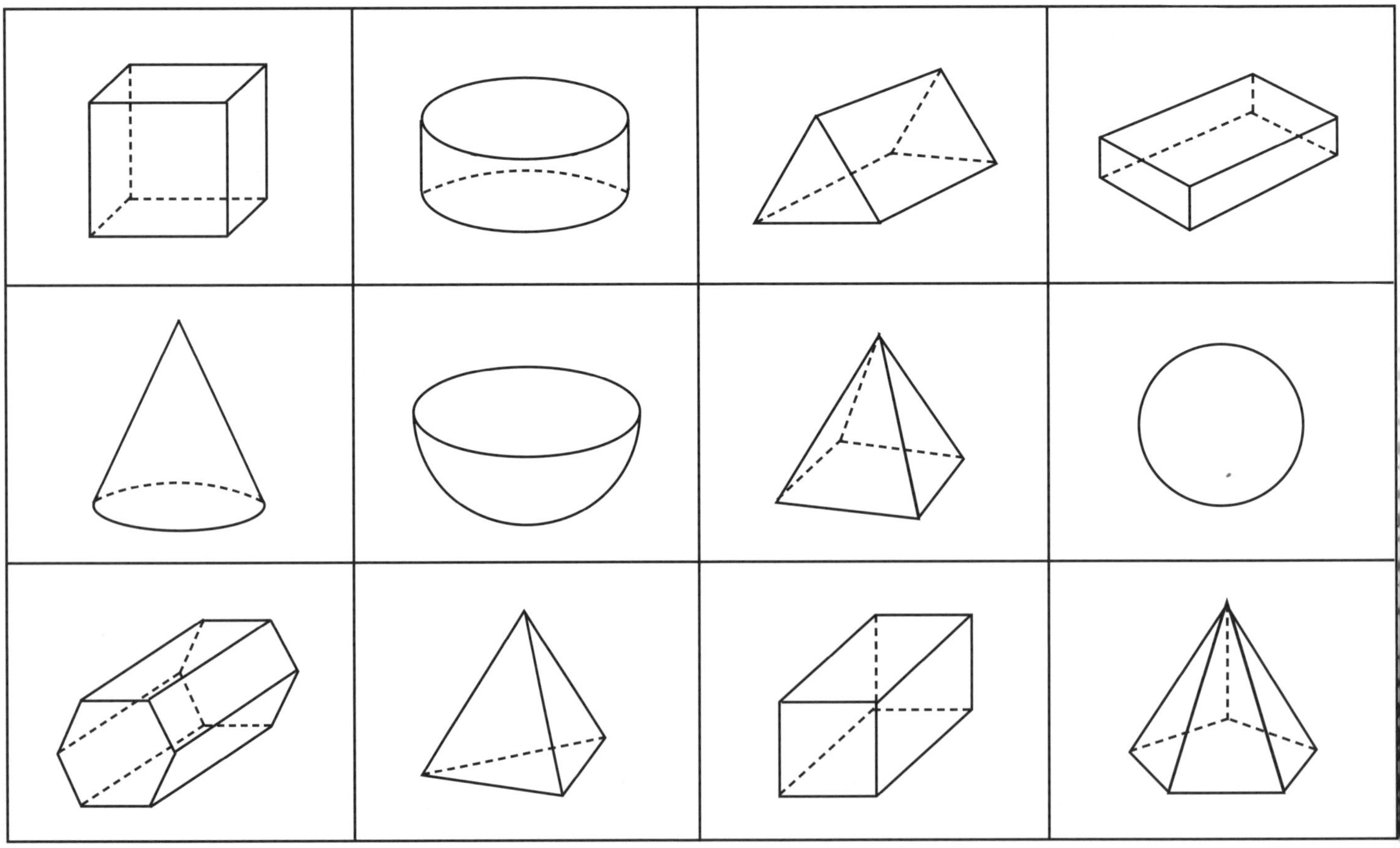

NOW TRY THIS!

• **Now each write a description of one shape, giving as much detail as you can.**

Teachers' note The 'listeners' must monitor whether any taboo words have been spoken, whilst trying to work out from the description which shape is being described. For the extension activity, remind children that they can't use the names of the shapes.

A Lesson for Every Day
Maths
7-8 Years
© A&C Black

Learning about turning

Jo faces the first letter of each word and turns to face the next letter. For each word, her turn is:

| less than a right angle | **or** | a right angle | **or** | more than a right angle |

- **Write each word under the correct heading below to show what kind of turn Jo has made.**

AM   AN

GO   ME

IS   BE

BY   AT

AS   OH

HE   ON

MY   TO

IN   HI

IT   SO

less than a right angle	a right angle	more than a right angle

Teachers' note For this activity, the children can decide whether to turn clockwise or anticlockwise for each turn. Encourage them to discuss their answers with a partner and to justify any disagreements. At the end of the lesson, discuss how a turn clockwise and a different turn anticlockwise can produce the same result.

A Lesson for Every Day
Maths
7–8 Years
© A&C Black

Angle art

Some angles are marked with an boxed:arc .

• **Colour:**

    – angles smaller than a right angle **yellow**,

    – right angles **red**,

    – angles larger than a right angle **blue**.

You need
yellow, red
and blue
coloured
pencils.

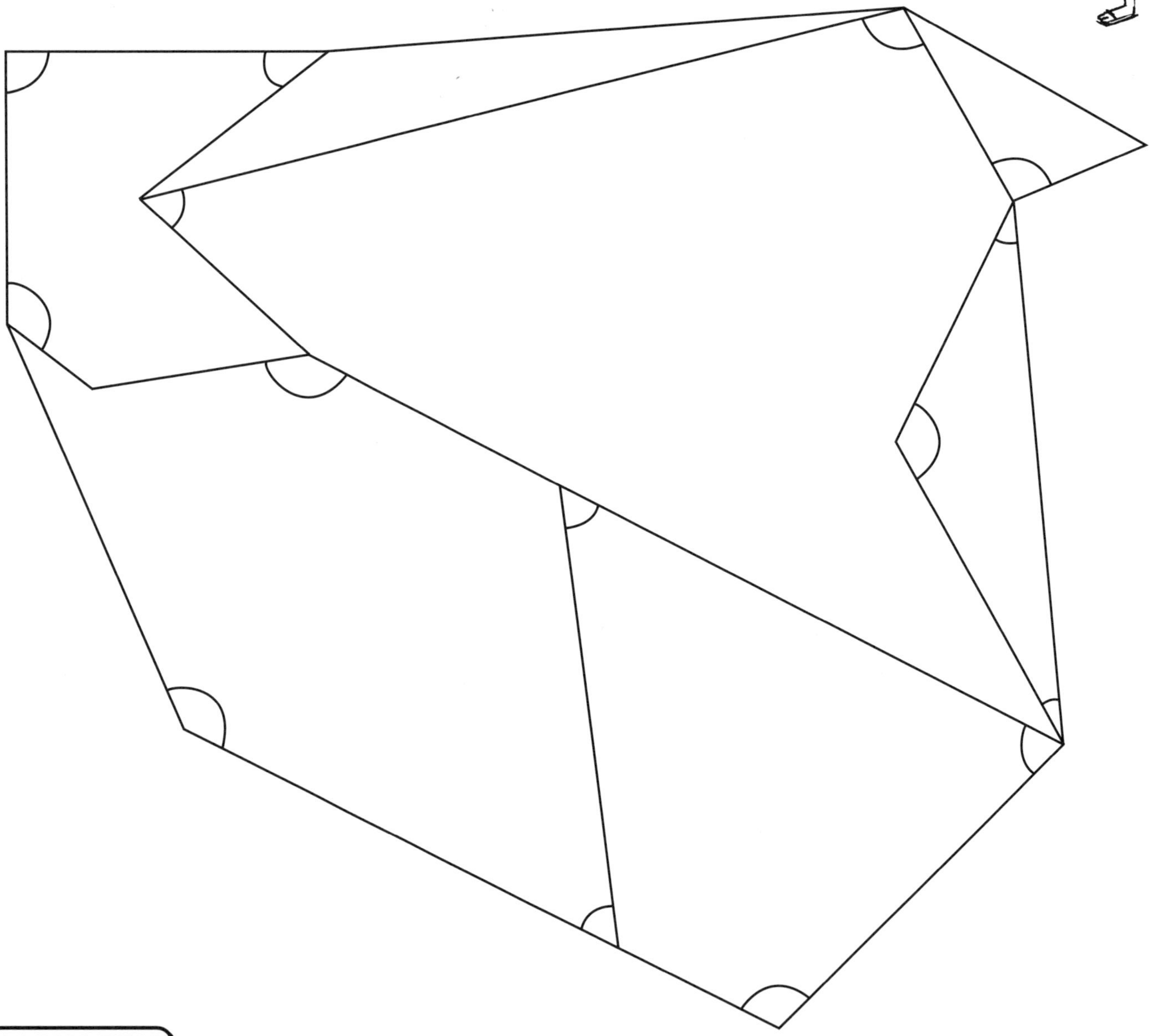

NOW TRY THIS!

• **Now use the same colours to colour the angles that are <u>not</u> marked with arcs.**

Teachers' note The children could be given a set-square or a right angle tester (such as the right angle gobbler from 'Bird's beaks') to help them complete this activity, or to help them check their answers. Discuss with the children who tackle the extension activity what they notice about the size of most of the angles outside the shape.

A Lesson for Every Day
Maths
7–8 Years
© A&C Black

Sorting coins

- **Use a full set of coins.**
- **Write where each coin would go in each** Venn **diagram.**

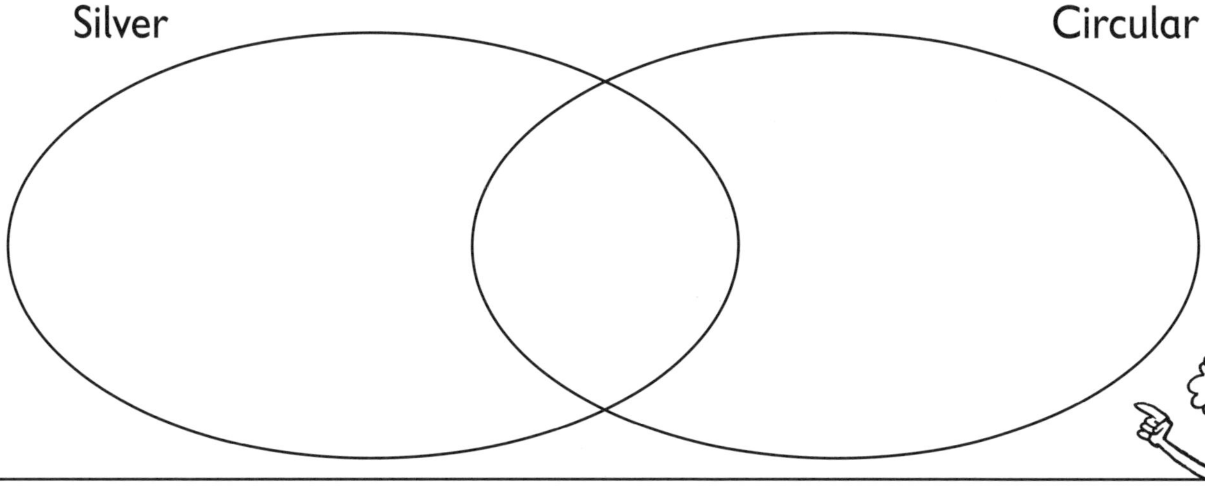

Silver   Circular

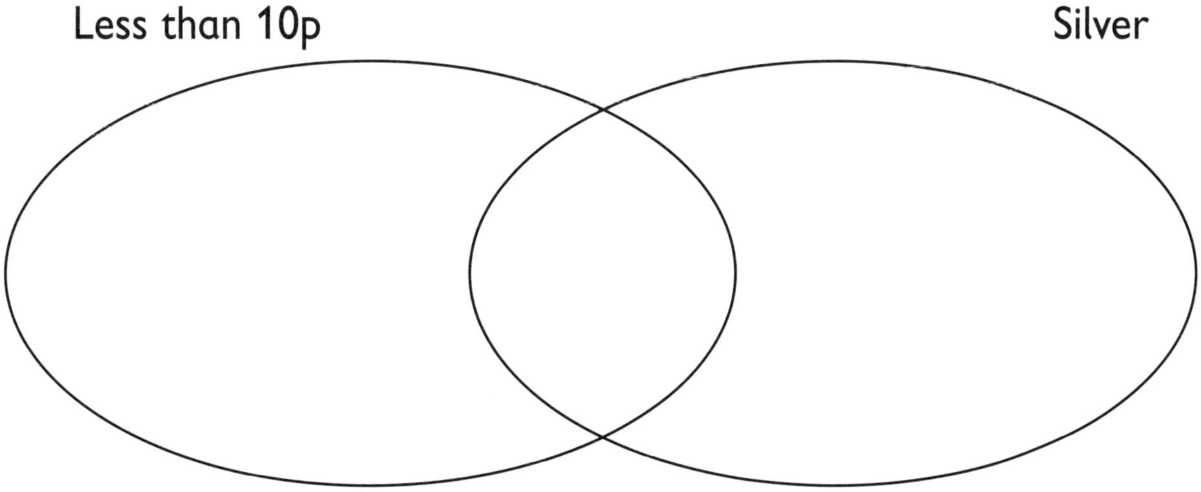

Less than 10p   Silver

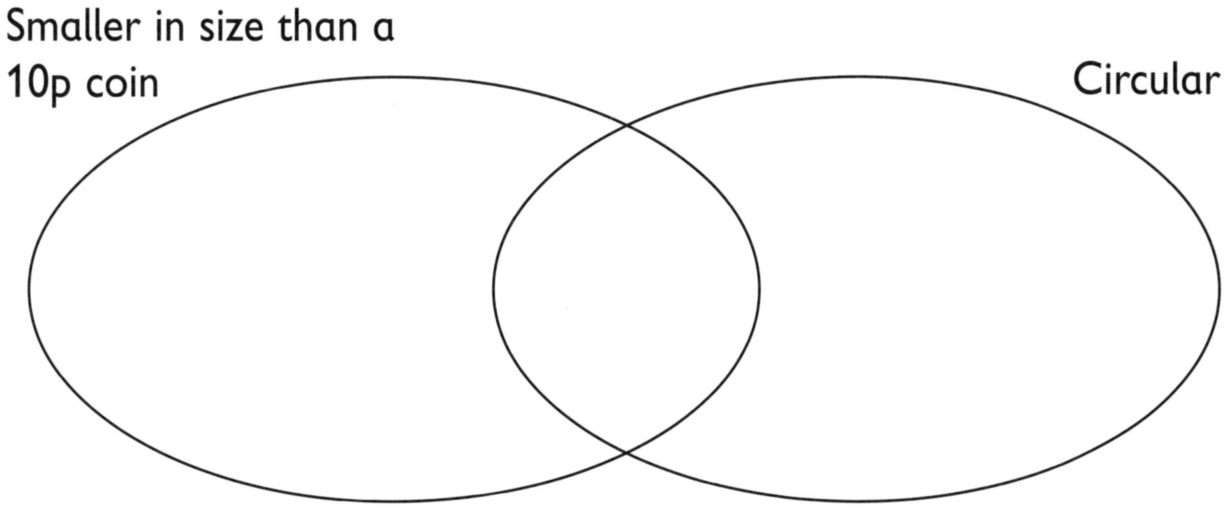

Smaller in size than a
10p coin   Circular

Teachers' note Provide the children with a £2, £1, 50p, 20p, 10p, 5p, 2p and 1p coin. Encourage them to compare the diagrams and to explain their decisions made when sorting the coins. As an extension activity, the children could draw their own Venn diagram and choose new labels or a different combination of labels than those here.

A Lesson for Every Day
Maths
7–8 Years
© A&C Black

Stream scheme

Scientists are measuring the depth of water in a stream at different times in the year.

- The measurements are written in metres. Change them to centimetres.

1. 4 m = $\boxed{400}$ cm

2. 7 m = $\boxed{}$ cm

3. 2 m = $\boxed{}$ cm

4. 3 m = $\boxed{}$ cm

5. 1 m = $\boxed{}$ cm

6. $\frac{1}{2}$ m = $\boxed{}$ cm

7. $\frac{1}{10}$ m = $\boxed{}$ cm

8. $6\frac{1}{2}$ m = $\boxed{}$ cm

9. 25 m = $\boxed{}$ cm

10. 10 m = $\boxed{}$ cm

11. $\frac{1}{4}$ m = $\boxed{}$ cm

12. $\frac{3}{4}$ m = $\boxed{}$ cm

NOW TRY THIS!

- Change these measurements to metres and centimetres.

(a) 518 cm = $\boxed{5}$ m $\boxed{18}$ cm

(b) 900 cm = $\boxed{}$ m $\boxed{}$ cm

(c) 150 cm = $\boxed{}$ m $\boxed{}$ cm

(d) 350 cm = $\boxed{}$ m $\boxed{}$ cm

(e) 125 cm = $\boxed{}$ m $\boxed{}$ cm

(f) 375 cm = $\boxed{}$ m $\boxed{}$ cm

(g) 120 cm = $\boxed{}$ m $\boxed{}$ cm

(h) 70 cm = $\boxed{}$ m $\boxed{}$ cm

Teachers' note Ensure that the children understand the abbreviations 'cm' and 'm', and that 100 cm is equal to 1 m. The numbers on this worksheet could be altered for differentiation.

A Lesson for Every Day
Maths
7–8 Years
© A&C Black

Question time

- **Cut out the cards.**
- **With a partner, decide which unit of measurement would be the best to use in each answer.**

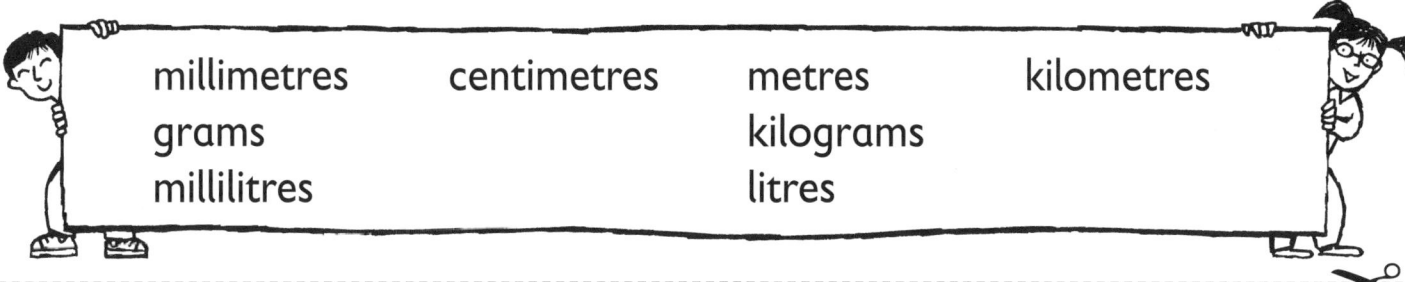

millimetres   centimetres   metres   kilometres

grams   kilograms

millilitres   litres

How far is it to fly from London to Paris?	How much milk comes from a cow each day?	How heavy is a conker?
How much cough medicine should I take?	How long is a worm? 	How far do people run in a marathon?
How tall is a giraffe? 	How much blood is inside a person?	How heavy is an elephant?
How long is an ant? 	How much petrol fills the tank in a car? 	How heavy is a blackbird?
What is the width of a football pitch? 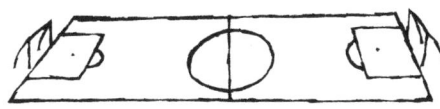	How heavy is a tennis ball? 	How tall is the Eiffel Tower? 

Teachers' note Ensure the children realise that they are not required to answer the questions. The children could write the unit on the back of each card. Discuss other units, such as Imperial units, if they arise, and at the end of the activity, compare and discuss the children's answers. As an extension, the children could write some questions of their own for another pair to discuss.

A Lesson for Every Day
Maths
7–8 Years
© A&C Black

107

Rulers rule

- **Read the** scale **on the ruler to find the length of each lizard.**

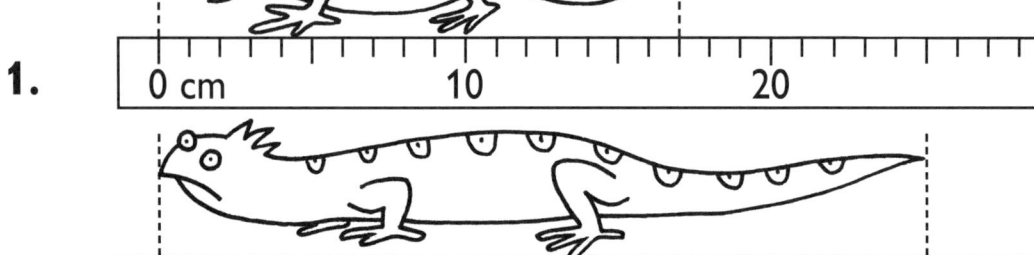

1.  | 17 | cm

2. | | cm

3. | | cm

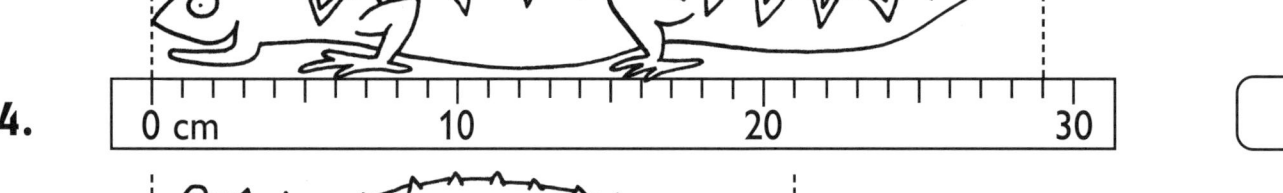

4.  | | cm

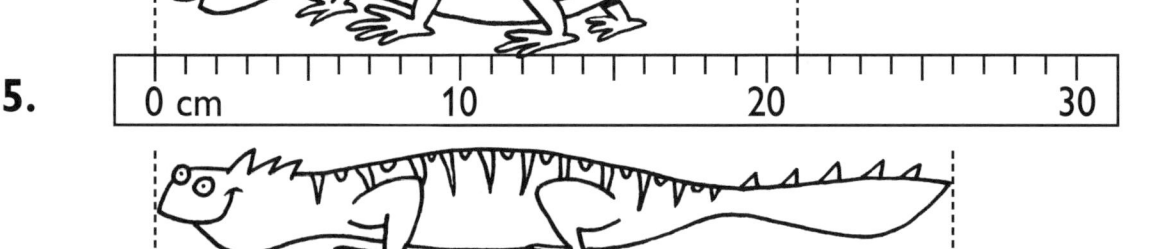

5.  | | cm

6. | | cm

NOW TRY THIS!

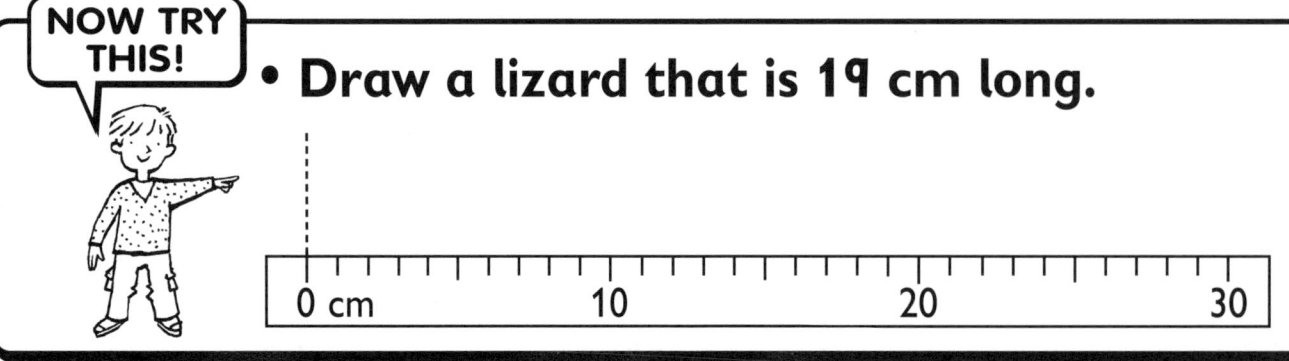

- **Draw a lizard that is 19 cm long.**

Teachers' note Some children who find this work difficult might benefit from having the sheet enlarged to A3 so that missing numbers can be written onto the scales.

A Lesson for Every Day
Maths
7–8 Years
© A&C Black

Vera's veggies

Vera has grown 3 types of vegetable. She is going to cook dinner for her grandchildren. She wants everyone to like at least one vegetable. These lists show the vegetables her grandchildren like.

I like beans
Suzie
Petra
Bobby
Sammy
Amanda
Pam

I like sweetcorn
Tim
Bobby
Ruth
Pam
Frankie
Sammy
Andy

I like peas
Suzie
Petra
Bobby
Ron
Amanda

1 How many grandchildren does Vera have? _____

2 Who likes all the vegetables? _____

3 Who only likes beans and sweetcorn? _____

4 Who only likes peas? _____

5 Which two vegetables should Vera cook? Why?

_____

NOW TRY THIS!

- **Which vegetables do you and four friends like? Add your names to the lists.**

- **Will this change what Vera should cook?**

_____

Teachers' note There is a certain amount of deduction required for solving this problem. Children may simply say that Vera should cook the most popular i.e. beans and sweetcorn. This is not correct as that will mean Ron will be left with nothing. Encourage them to find the two vegetables that everyone will eat at least one of.

A Lesson for Every Day
Maths
7–8 Years
© A&C Black

Newspaper sales

Mrs Print has made a ⟨ frequency table ⟩ to show last week's sales of the newspapers she sells.
She has been asked to answer a questionnaire.

• Help her to fill it in.

Daily Planet	1350
The Star	2000
The Comet	2500
The Meteor	1550
The Galaxy	750
Daily Moon	2300

Newspaper questionnaire

1 Which is the best-selling newspaper?

_____

2 Which sells fewest per week? _____

3 How many copies of each did you sell last week in order from

most to fewest? _____

_____

_____

4 If you could only stock 4 papers, which would they be and why?

_____

_____

Teachers' note Ask the children to read out the numbers for each newspaper sale. Discuss what a questionnaire is and why it is helpful. As an extension activity, ask the children to make up their own frequency table for six newspapers, and generate the sales numbers by creating four-digit numbers from throwing a dice four times. Then ask them to answer the questionnaire.

A Lesson for Every Day
Maths
7-8 Years
© A&C Black

Berries

Tom asked his friends if they liked blackberries or strawberries.

He recorded what they said.

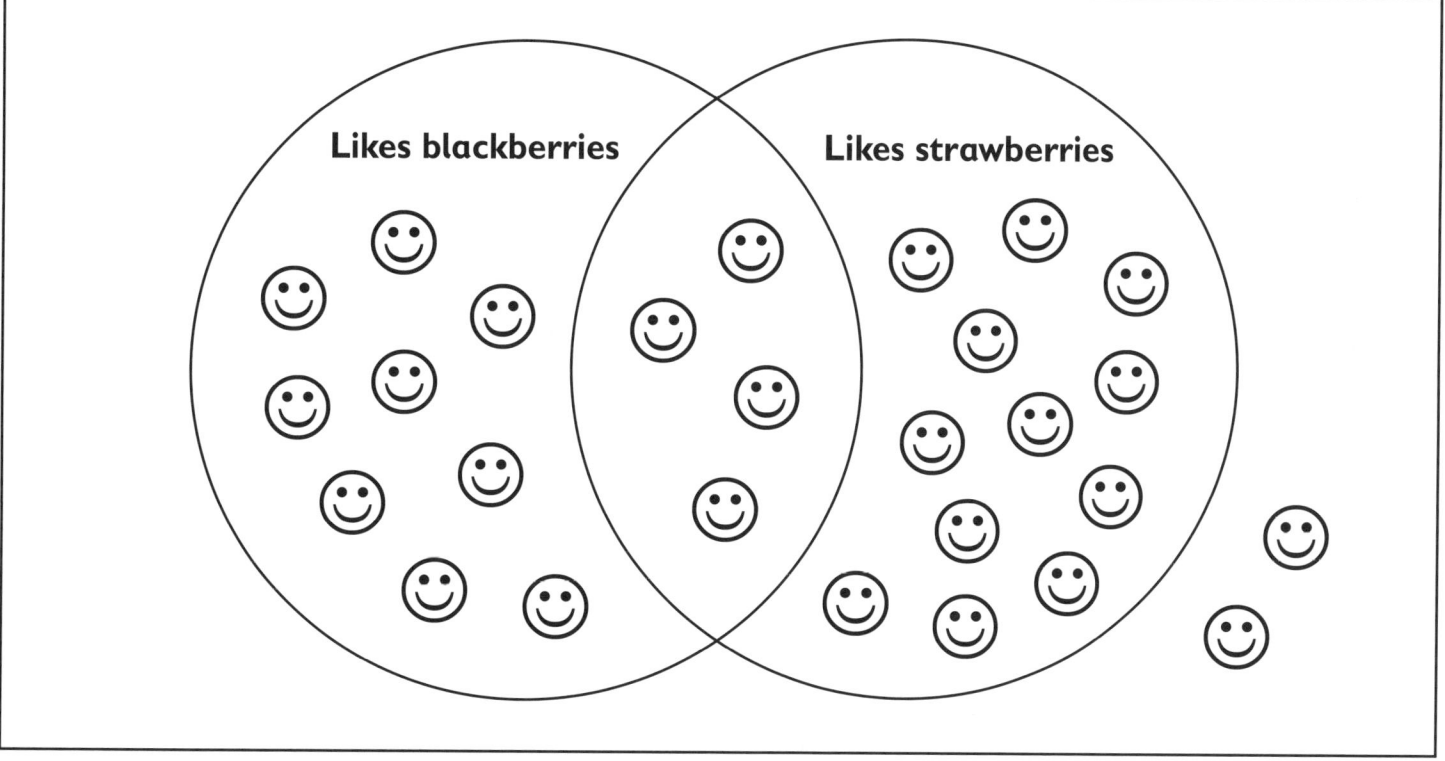

Likes blackberries   Likes strawberries

1 How many of Tom's friends like:

a Blackberries? _____   **b** Strawberries? _____   **c** Both? _____

d Only blackberries? _____   **e** Only strawberries? _____

f Neither? _____

2 How many of his friends did Tom ask? _____

NOW TRY THIS!

• **Make up three more questions about the Venn diagram for a partner to answer.**

Teachers' note Before you begin, you could demonstrate this activity using two fruits chosen by the children, for example apples and bananas. Draw two circles within a rectangle, label them and then ask the children where the smiley face should go to represent what they like. This will reinforce how to sort using Venn diagrams.

A Lesson for Every Day
Maths
7–8 Years
© A&C Black

Multiples

Shannon and Liam have been sorting some numbers.
This is how they did it, but they
have missed out two things.

1 Make the Venn diagram correct.

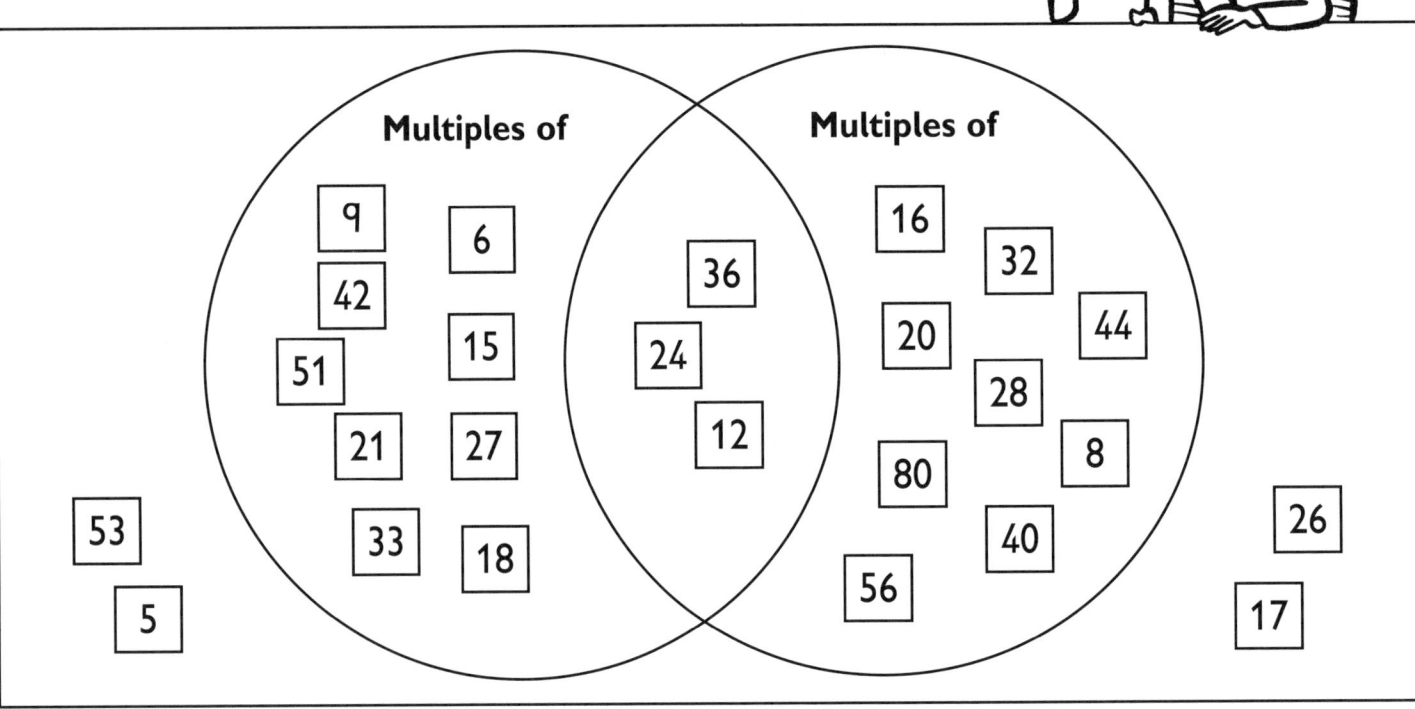

Multiples of ___

Multiples of ___

9 6
42
51 15
21 27
33 18

36
24
12

16
32
20 44
28
80 8
40
56

53
5

26
17

2 Use the Venn diagram to fill in the missing numbers:

a 15, 33, ___, ___, ___, ___, 42 and 6 are multiples of ___.

b 28, 40, ___, ___, ___, ___, ___, and ___ are not multiples of ___.

c ___, ___, ___ and ___ are not multiples of either number.

d ___, ___ and ___ are multiples of both.

NOW TRY THIS!

• **Write a label for the numbers that are not in either circle.** _____

Teachers' note To simplify, edit this page so that the multiples are below 40. To extend, edit to make higher multiples, some of which could be three-digit numbers.

A Lesson for Every Day
Maths
7–8 Years
© A&C Black

Party food: 1

James wants to sort the cost of the party foods into this Venn diagram.

- **Use the foods from 'Party food: 2' to help him.**

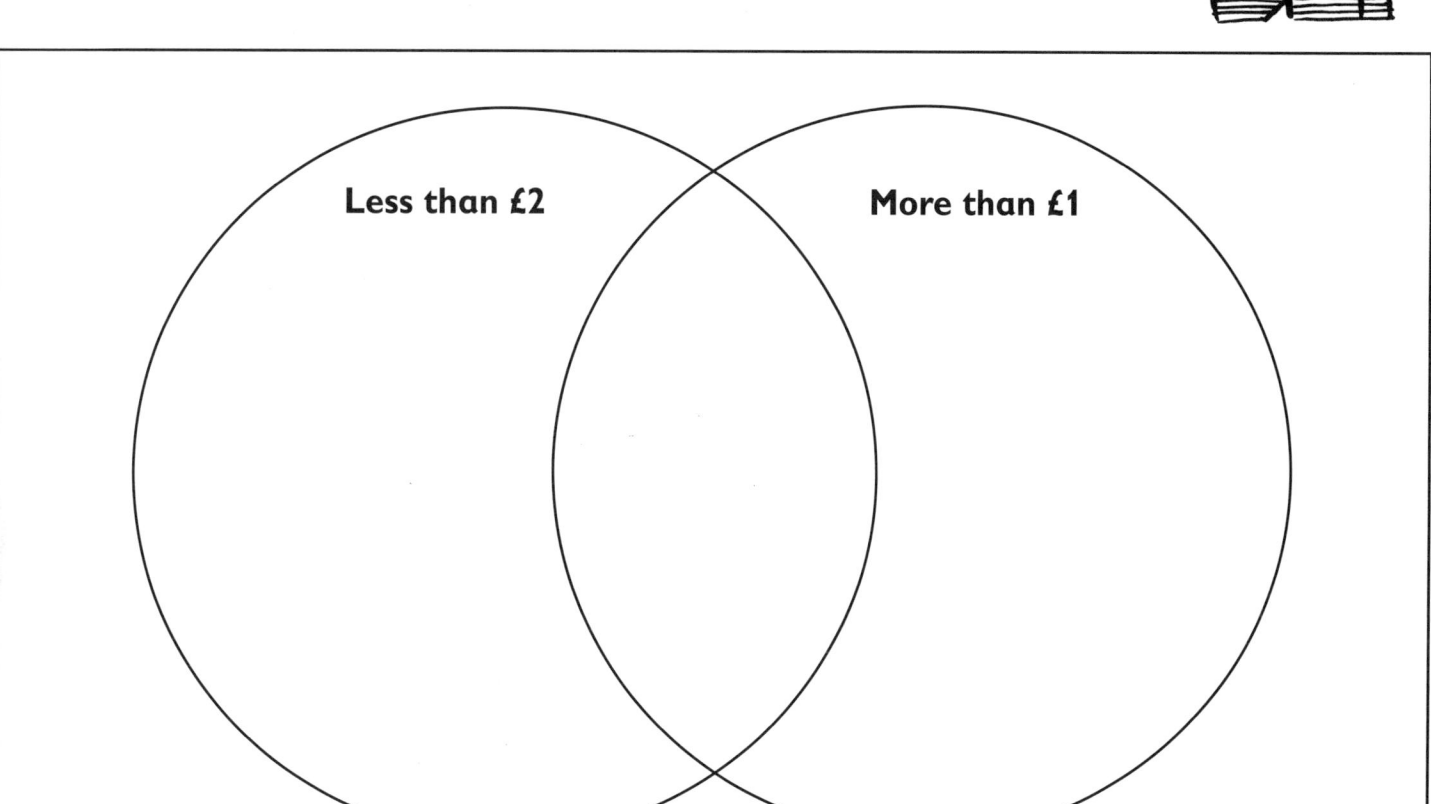

Less than £2   More than £1

1 Which party foods cost less than £2?

2 Which party foods cost more than £2?

3 Which party foods cost between £1 and £2?

4 Choose party foods that James could buy for **exactly** £2.

NOW TRY THIS!

- **Sort the foods into another Venn diagram.**
- **Use the labels 'More than £1' and 'More than £2'. What do you notice?**

Teachers' note Give the children a copy of 'Party food: 2'. Ask them to cut out the pictures and then place them in piles in the correct section of the Venn diagram. For the extension activity, provide scrap paper for children to sketch the Venn diagram while they work out what it will look like.

A Lesson for Every Day
Maths
7–8 Years
© A&C Black

Party food: 2

Cut out the cards.

Pizza £1.75 	**Pies** 35p each 	**Baguette** £1.20 	**Nuts** 75p per bag 
Mini quiches £1.00 for 3 	**Couscous** £2.00 	**Potato salad** £2.00 	**Green salad** £1.00 
Gateau £5.00 	**Mini burgers** £3.00 for 10 	**Juice £1.50** 	**Crisps** 50p per bag 
Carrot sticks £1.75 	**Dips** £1.25 per tub 	**Samosas** 75p each 	**Satay sticks** 50p each 

Teachers' note Use in conjunction with 'Party food: 1'.

A Lesson for Every Day
Maths
7–8 Years
© A&C Black

Someone said: 1

- **Work with a partner.**
- **Read through the questions and choose one of them to work with.**
- **You will need a copy of 'Someone said: 2'.**

Someone said that more than half the children in our class bring an apple to school.

Is this true?

Someone said that fewer than half the children in our class have one brother.

Is this true?

Someone said that about half the children in our class have the letter 'e' in their name.

Is this true?

Someone said that more than half the children in our class have a shoe size larger than 12.

Is this true?

Someone said that fewer than half the children in our class walk to school.

Is this true?

Someone said that more than half the children in our class go to bed by 9 o'clock.

Is this true?

- **Cut out your chosen question and stick it onto the 'Someone said: 2' activity sheet.**

Teachers' note This activity should be done in pairs. The children should choose a question from this sheet and stick it on to 'Someone said: 2'. They should then plan how they would go about answering the question. The focus should be on planning the investigation and time should be spent discussing all the children's work.

A Lesson for Every Day
Maths
7–8 Years
© A&C Black

Someone said: 2

- **Write your names.**

  _____

  _____

- **Show how you could find out whether your statement is** $\boxed{\text{true}}$ **.**

	Stick your chosen question here.

What information we need:

How we would collect it:

What we think we will find and why:

How we would show the information:

Teachers' note Use in conjunction with 'Someone said: 1'.

A Lesson for Every Day
Maths
7–8 Years
© A&C Black

How far?

This map shows how far from school some children live.

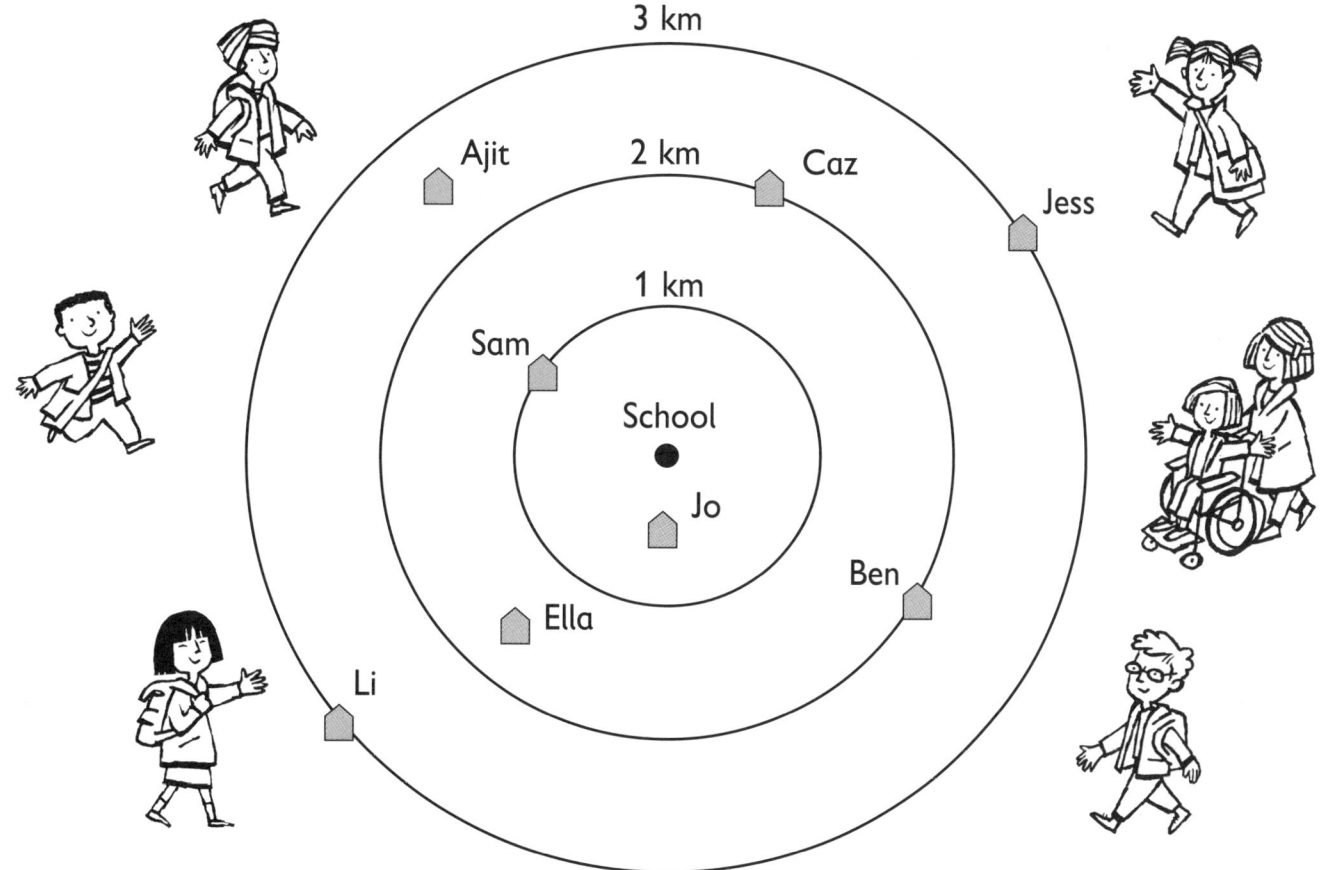

- 3 km
- 2 km
- 1 km
- Ajit
- Caz
- Jess
- Sam
- School
- Jo
- Ben
- Ella
- Li

• **Tick** ✔ **to show whether each statement is** true **or** false .

	true	false
1. Sam lives about 1000 m from school.	☐	☐
2. Jess lives about 300 m from school.	☐	☐
3. Ben lives about 2000 m from school.	☐	☐
4. Li lives about 3000 m from school.	☐	☐
5. Jo lives about 500 m from school.	☐	☐
6. Ajit lives about 2500 m from school.	☐	☐

 **NOW TRY THIS!**

• **Write** true **statements to say how far from school Caz and Ella live.** (Use metres.)

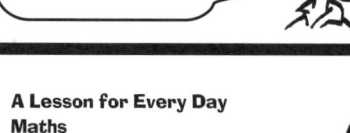

Teachers' note At the start of the lesson ensure that the children understand the abbreviations 'm' and 'km', and that 1000 m is equal to 1 km. Discuss how far this distance is in relation to the school. Explain how the diagram works by showing, with a piece of string, how all the points that are the same distance from the school form a circle.

A Lesson for Every Day
Maths
7-8 Years
© A&C Black

Woolly jumpers

- **Using a piece of string and a ruler, measure the length of each loose thread.**

Work with a partner.

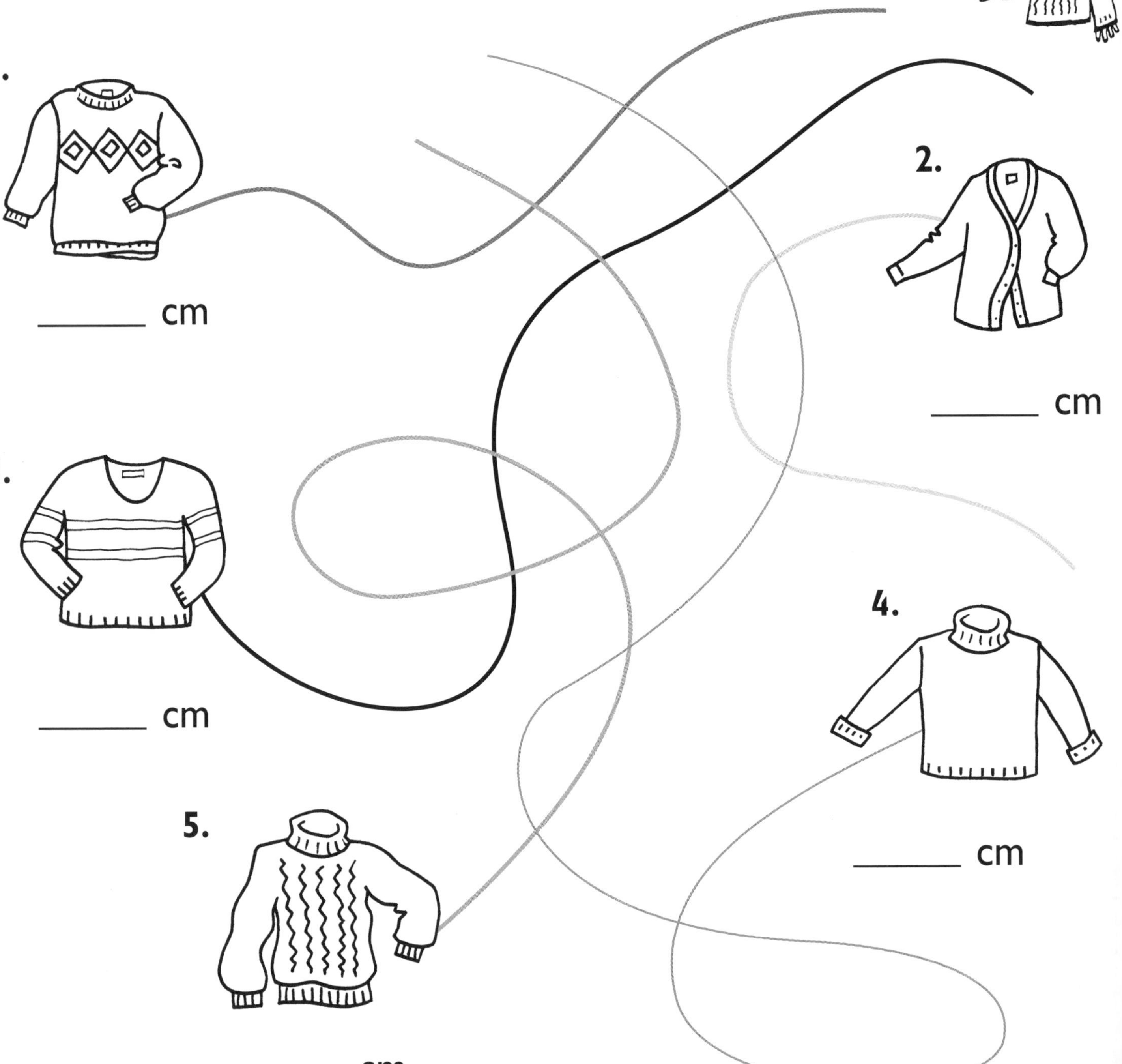

1.

_____ cm

2.

_____ cm

3.

_____ cm

4.

_____ cm

5.

_____ cm

NOW TRY THIS!

- **On the back of this sheet, draw a jumper with a loose thread that is <u>exactly</u> 24 cm long.**

Teachers' note Demonstrate how to lay string along a curved or wiggly line, mark it and straighten it along a ruler or metre stick to find its length. The children should measure the loose threads to the nearest centimetre. More confident children could be encouraged to measure the threads to the nearest half-centimetre, for example 5½ cm or 2.5 cm.

A Lesson for Every Day
Maths
7–8 Years
© A&C Black

Kitchen scales

• **Draw an arrow on the scale to show the weight given.**

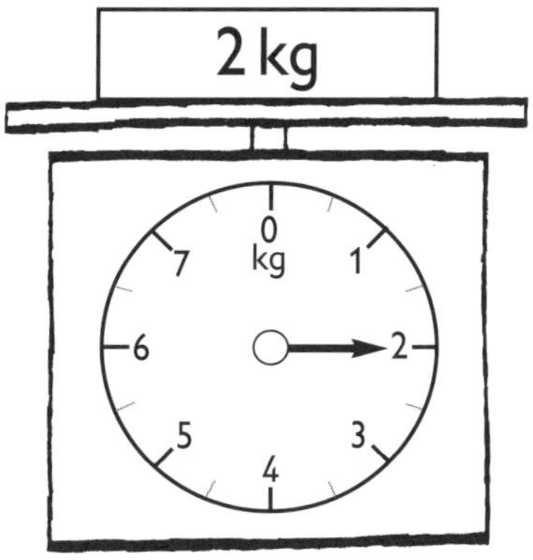

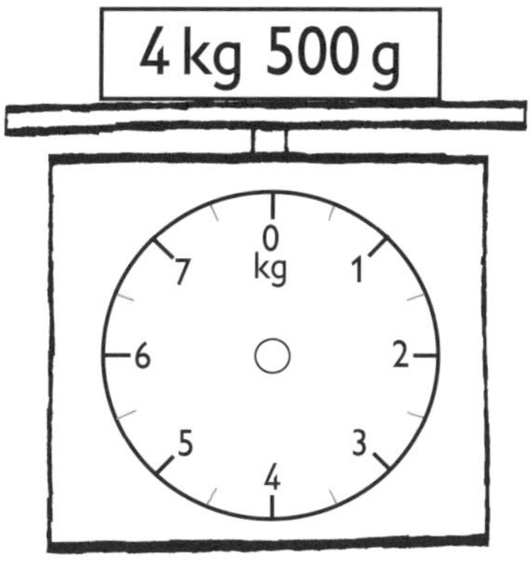

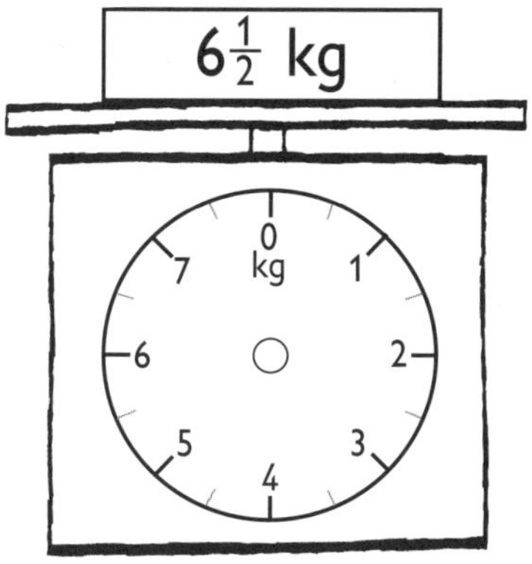

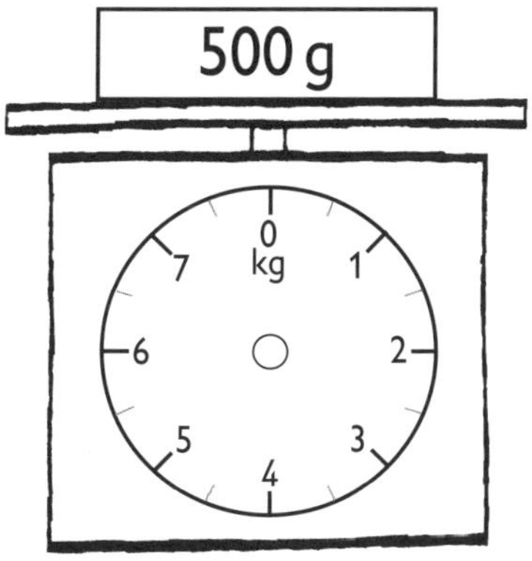

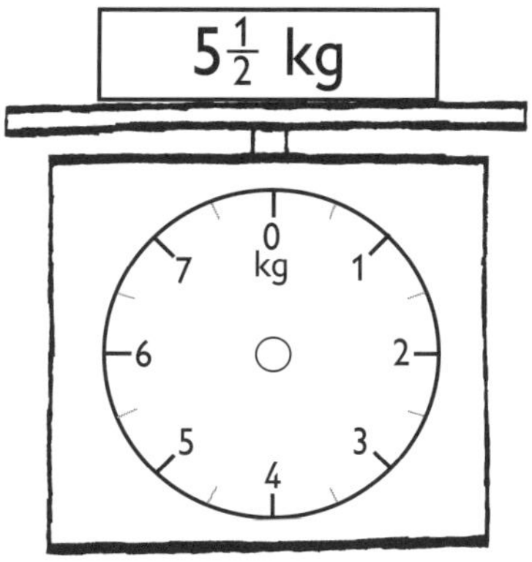

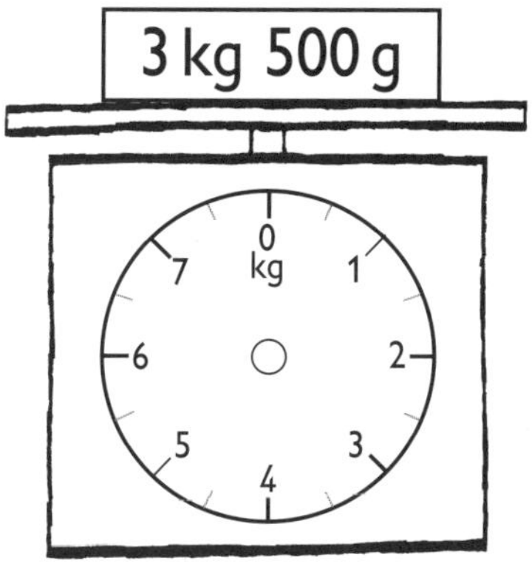

2 kg	4 kg 500 g	6 ½ kg

500 g	5 ½ kg	3 kg 500 g

NOW TRY THIS!

• **Now try these.**

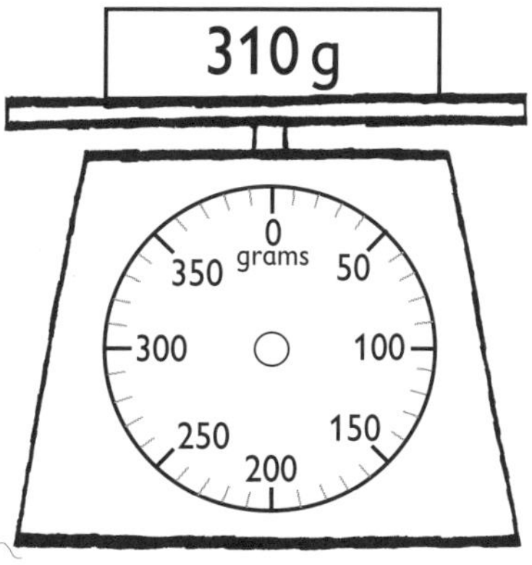

310 g	120 g

290 g	330 g	¼ kg

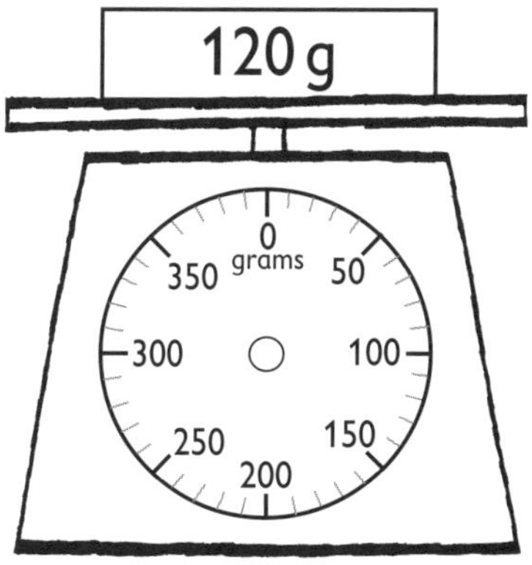

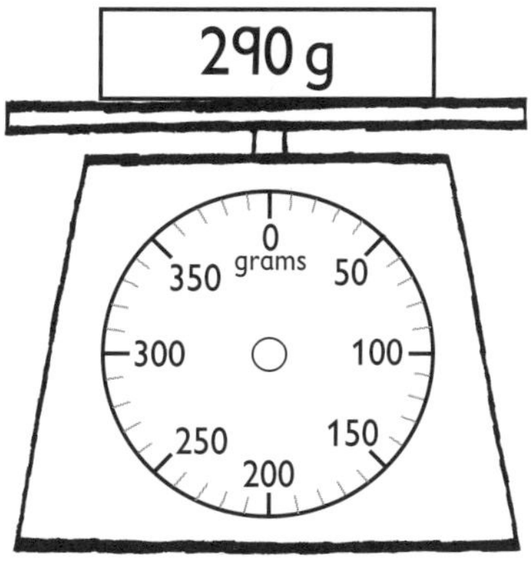

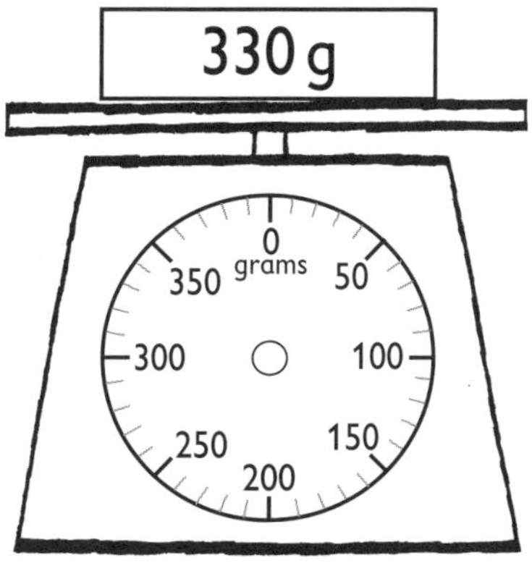

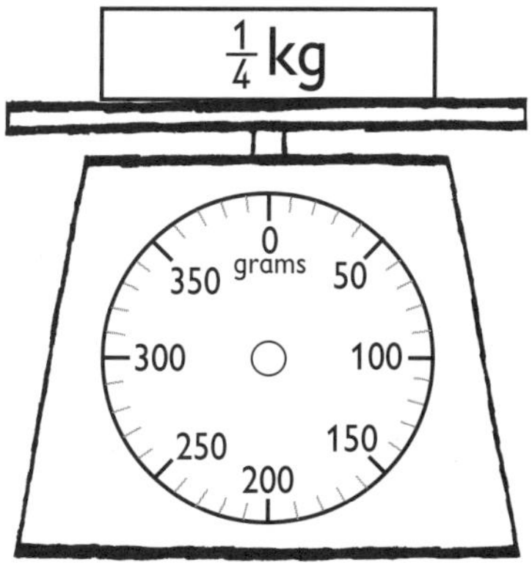

Teachers' note Some children might benefit from the sheet being enlarged to A3 size so that missing numbers can be written onto the scales.

A Lesson for Every Day
Maths
7–8 Years
© A&C Black

What time
would it be
2 hours later?

What time
would it be
10 minutes later?

What time
would it be
$\frac{1}{2}$ an hour earlier?

What time
would it be
5 hours later?

What time
would it be $\frac{3}{4}$ of
an hour earlier?

What time
would it be
10 minutes later?

What time
would it be
2 hours earlier?

What time
would it be
50 minutes later?

What time would
it be 40 minutes
earlier?

What time
would it be
6 hours later?

What time would
it be $\frac{1}{4}$ of an
hour earlier?

What time
would it be
5 minutes later?

What time would
it be 45 minutes
earlier?

What time
would it be
4 hours later?

What time
would it be
40 minutes later?

What time
would it be
2 hours earlier?

Teachers' note Give a loop card to each child in a large group (two sets could be used to make 32 cards). Choose a child to say the time and read the question. The first child to stand up with the correct card reads out the time and the new question. Alternatively, the cards can be used as an individual or pair activity where the children place them correctly in a loop.

A Lesson for Every Day
Maths
7–8 Years
© A&C Black

At the laundry

Mrs Bubble made a pictogram to keep track of her washing.

- **Has she got it right? Check to see.**
- **Add more bubbles if they are needed. Cross out any that are not needed.**

◯ = 1 piece of clothing

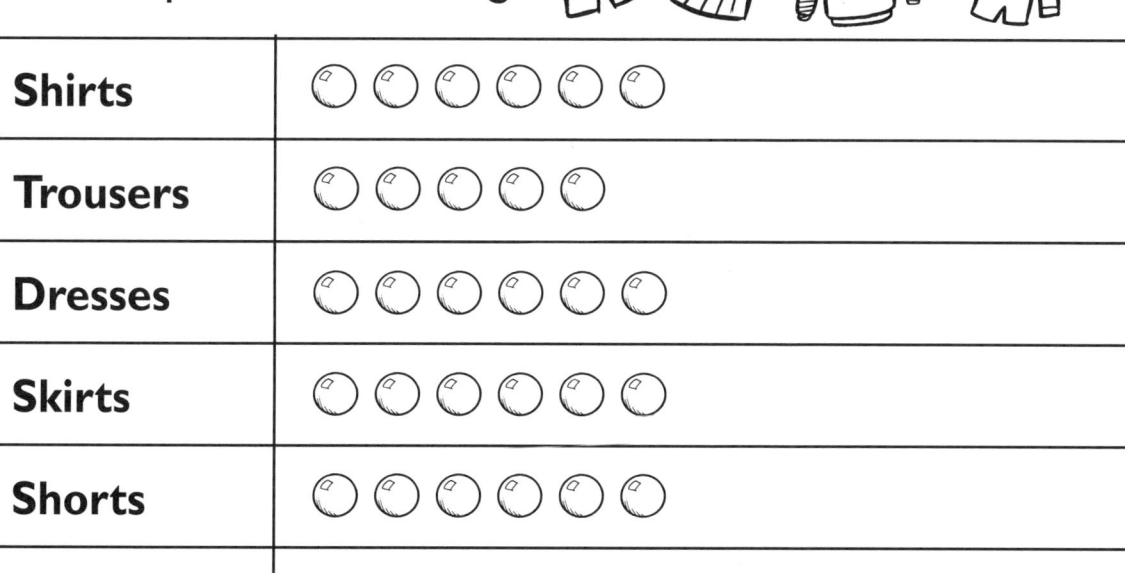

Shirts	◯ ◯ ◯ ◯ ◯ ◯
Trousers	◯ ◯ ◯ ◯ ◯
Dresses	◯ ◯ ◯ ◯ ◯ ◯
Skirts	◯ ◯ ◯ ◯ ◯ ◯
Shorts	◯ ◯ ◯ ◯ ◯ ◯
Jumpers	◯ ◯ ◯

Number of clothes

- **How many of each item of clothing does Mrs Bubble have?**

Skirts _____   Jumpers _____   Dresses _____

Shirts _____   Shorts _____   Trousers _____

NOW TRY THIS!

- **How many items of clothing are there in total?** _____

Teachers' note The children need to identify the clothes, count how many there are and then check Mrs Bubble's pictogram adding or crossing off bubbles as appropriate. As a further extension, ask them to make up five questions about the information to ask the class during the plenary.

A Lesson for Every Day
Maths
7–8 Years
© A&C Black

Birthday presents

The **Gift Store** wanted to know what the most popular presents were this year. They asked 100 children. This pictogram shows what the children said.

= 2 toys

Number of toys

Table football	Remote control car	Skateboard	Magic set	Keyboard	Painting set	Puzzles

1 How many of each present did the children vote for?

Table football _____   Remote control car _____   Skateboard _____

Magic set _____   Keyboard _____   Painting set _____   Puzzles _____

2 Which were the three most popular presents?

_____

NOW TRY THIS!

• **Ask** ten **friends what present they would like. Make a pictogram to show this.**

Teachers' note Encourage the children to count the presents and double them for the actual number and to use one column to help them work out others, for example 7 whole presents for table football, car is one more making 8, so 16 votes. To simplify, provide counters and ask them to count out two for every present. Encourage them to make statements from the pictogram.

A Lesson for Every Day
Maths
7–8 Years
© A&C Black

Oranges and lemons

Mr Frute has a fruit stall. He sells oranges and lemons.
He wants to know how many of each to buy.
He asked his customers which they liked.

⊛ = 1 person

	Likes oranges	Doesn't like oranges
Likes lemons	⊛ ⊛ ⊛ ⊛ ⊛ ⊛ ⊛ ⊛ ⊛ ⊛ ⊛ ⊛ ⊛	⊛ ⊛ ⊛ ⊛
Doesn't like lemons	⊛ ⊛	⊛ ⊛ ⊛ ⊛ ⊛ ⊛

1 How many people like oranges and lemons? _____

2 How many people don't like either? _____

3 How many people like lemons? _____

4 How many people just like oranges? _____

5 He decides to buy 50 lemons. How many oranges should he buy? _____

NOW TRY THIS!

• **Make a** Venn diagram **to show this information.**

Teachers' note The children should identify how many people like each fruit and establish that twice as many like oranges than lemons and that Mr Frute should buy twice as many oranges as lemons. To simplify edit the last question so that it simply asks a data question, for example how many like lemons but not oranges.

A Lesson for Every Day
Maths
7-8 Years
© A&C Black

Monkey business

The monkeys in Gordon's zoo are very fussy eaters.
Every day he gives them apples and bananas.

- **Sort out the monkeys' likes and dislikes on this** | Carroll diagram | .

Sam

Dan

Flo

Ian

Jon

Ann

Eli

Sara

Paul

Bob

Ella

Rosa

	Apples	No apples
Bananas		
No bananas		

1 How many monkeys like bananas? _____

2 How many monkeys like apples? _____

3 How many monkeys like both apples and bananas? _____

4 Gordon gives raisins to the monkeys who don't like apples

  or bananas. How many monkeys have raisins? _____

You need the shapes on 'Symmetry: 2'.

• **Put them in the correct places on the** Carroll **diagram.**

	Symmetrical	Not symmetrical
4 sides		
Not 4 sides		

1 How many shapes have 4 sides? _____

2 How many shapes are not symmetrical? _____

3 How many shapes have 4 sides and are symmetrical? _____

4 How many shapes do not have 4 sides? _____

5 How could you use the Carroll diagram to describe a circle?

Teachers' note Use in conjunction with 'Symmetry: 2'. If you would like the children to stick their shapes into the Carroll diagram, enlarge the sheet before copying. As an extension activity, ask the children to make their own Carroll diagram and sort the second set of shapes from 'Symmetry: 2' in a different way.

A Lesson for Every Day
Maths
7-8 Years
© A&C Black

Symmetry: 2

• **Cut out the cards.**

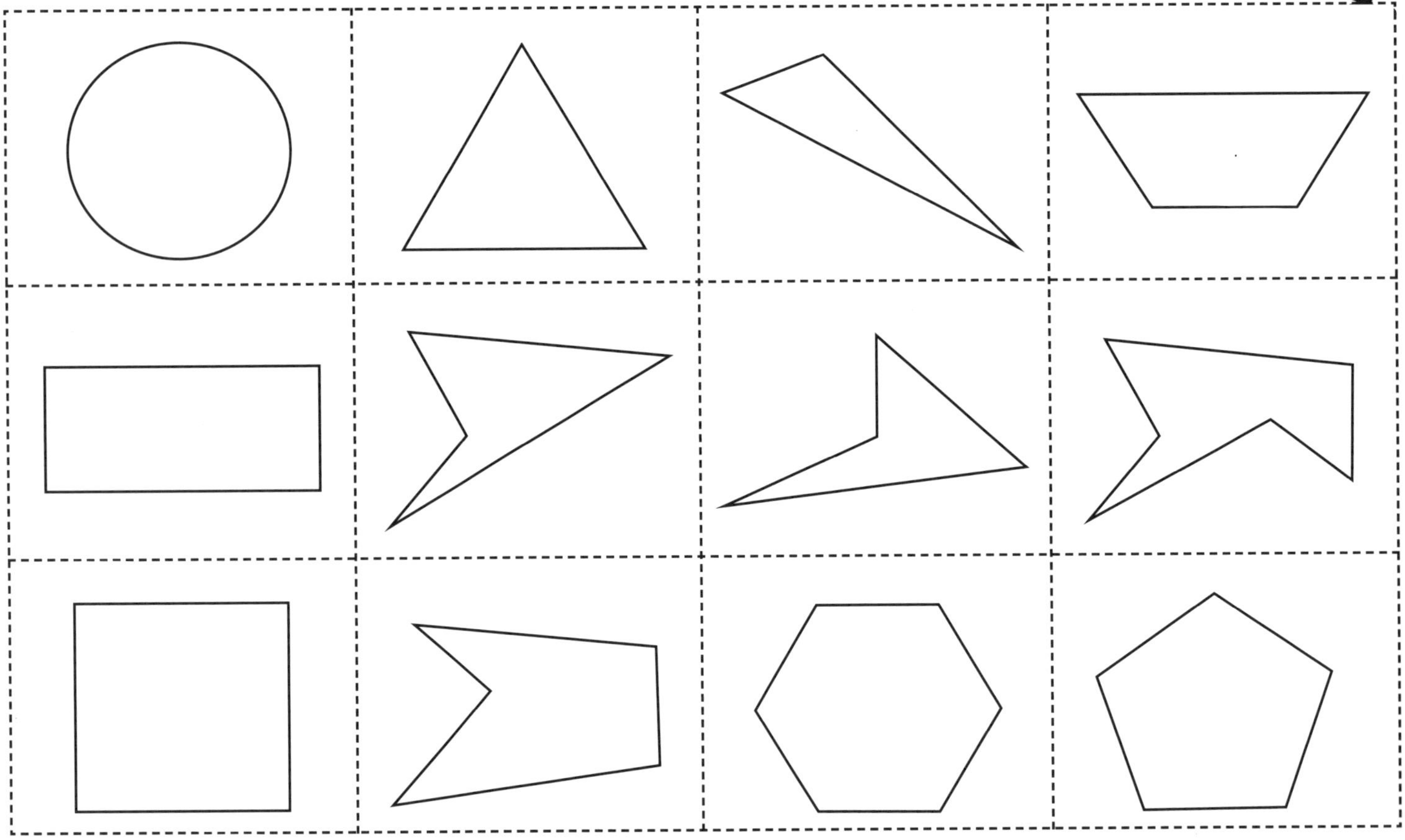

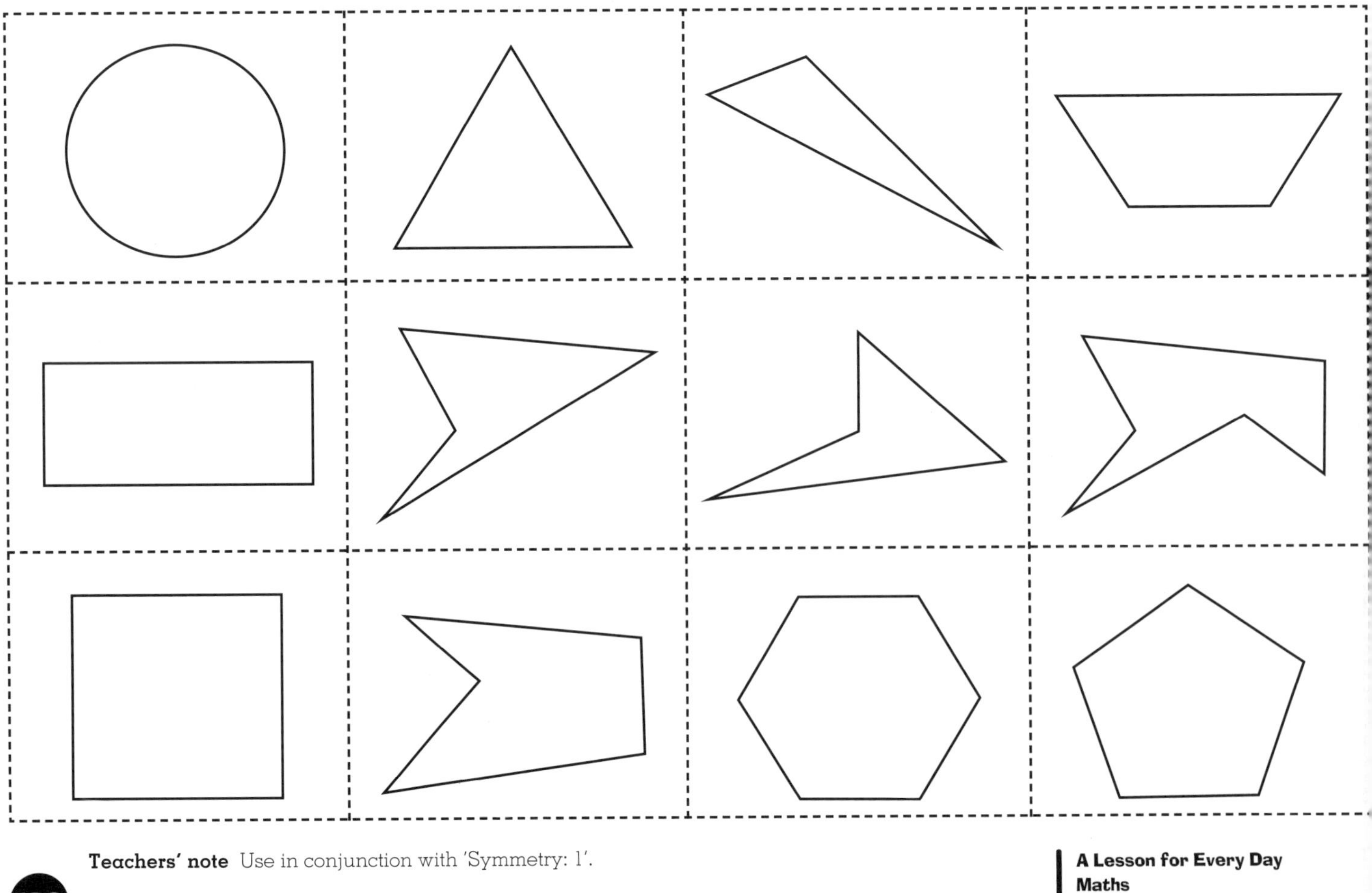

Teachers' note Use in conjunction with 'Symmetry: 1'.

A Lesson for Every Day
Maths
7–8 Years
© A&C Black

Lines of enquiry

- **Cut out the cards.**
- **Investigate the problem and find a solution.**
- **Explain to the rest of the class what you did and how you found the answer.**

What is the largest odd number that can be made by multiplying the numbers on two dice?

What is the largest remainder you can have when you divide a number by 4?

What is the total of the first five multiples of 3?

What is the smallest even number that is in the five- and the three-times tables?

What is the largest remainder you can have when you divide a number by 3?

When counting on in fours from zero, what is the first multiple of 10 you reach?

What is the total of the first five multiples of 4?

What is the smallest odd number that is in the five- and the seven-times tables?

What is the largest odd number that can be made by adding the numbers on three dice?

What is the largest number that divides into 24 that is not a multiple of 3?

Teachers' note These cards could be copied onto thin card and laminated for a more permanent classroom resource. The children could be given specific cards or be allowed to choose their own to investigate. They could write explanations of their investigation in the form of a leaflet or poster for others to understand.

A Lesson for Every Day
Maths
7–8 Years
© A&C Black

Share and share alike

Some children put their money together and share it equally .

- **Predict how much they will each get.**
- **Work out the answer.**

4p	9p	7p	8p

Prediction [ ] p

Answer [ ] p

3p	7p	6p	8p

Prediction [ ] p

Answer [ ] p

10p	6p	7p	5p

Prediction [ ] p

Answer [ ] p

9p	10p	8p	9p

Prediction [ ] p

Answer [ ] p

7p	9p	11p	5p

Prediction [ ] p

Answer [ ] p

11p	3p	6p	8p

Prediction [ ] p

Answer [ ] p

NOW TRY THIS!

- **Talk to a partner about how you answered these.**
- **Can you think of a different way to do it?**
- **How could you record what you did so that someone else could read and understand it?**

Teachers' note Discuss different strategies that could be used and the means of recording the method so that others could understand and follow it. For example, only taking money from those children with more money and giving it to those with less, or beginning with the lowest amount and making sure each child has that much, only sharing out the extra coins above this amount.

A Lesson for Every Day
Maths
7–8 Years
© A&C Black

Broken keys

• **Write how you would answer each question on the calculator without using the keys marked with a** | cross |.

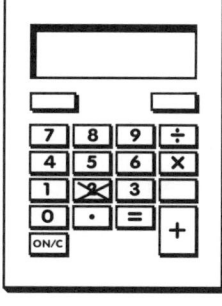

| 21 x 20 | _____ |

_____

_____

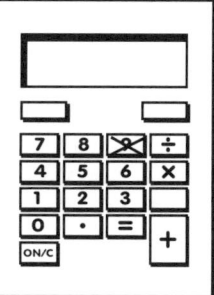

| 99 x 12 | _____ |

_____

_____

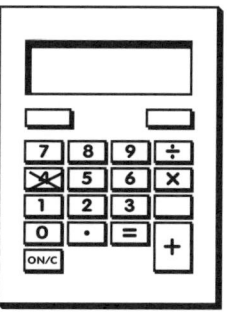

| 444 + 333 | _____ |

_____

_____

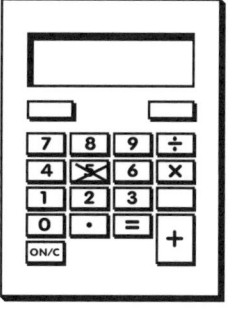

| 500 − 235 | _____ |

_____

_____

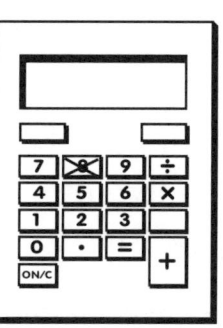

| 104 ÷ 8 | _____ |

_____

_____

Teachers' note These calculations require considerable thought as the children must find a way of answering the calculation without using the key marked with a cross. Encourage them to discuss their different approaches together and say which they think are most easily understood. The calculations can be altered before copying to provide differentiation and variety.

A Lesson for Every Day
Maths
7-8 Years
© A&C Black

Milkshake mistakes

These children are making milkshakes.

- Tick ✔ to show who is right each time.

1. 
This is the same as 10 litres. ☐
1000 ml
No, it's the same as 1 litre. ✔

2. 
This is the same as $\frac{1}{2}$ litre. ☐
500 ml
No, it's the same as 5 litres. ☐

3. 
This is the same as 2 litres. ☐
2000 ml
No, it's the same as $\frac{1}{2}$ litre. ☐

4. 
This is the same as $1\frac{1}{2}$ litres. ☐
1500 ml
No, it's the same as 15 litres. ☐

5. 
This is the same as 25 litres. ☐
2500 ml
No, it's the same as 2·5 litres. ☐

6. 
This is the same as 30 litres. ☐
3000 ml
No, it's the same as 3 litres. ☐

NOW TRY THIS!

- Try these in the same way.

(a) 
This is the same as 50 ml. ☐
0·5 l
No, it's the same as 500 ml. ☐

(b) 
This is the same as 3500 ml. ☐
$3\frac{1}{2}$ l
No, it's the same as 350 ml. ☐

Teachers' note Ensure that the children understand the abbreviations 'ml' and 'l', and that 1000 ml is equal to 1 l. The children may require assistance with interpreting numbers written as decimals or fractions in this activity. The numbers on this worksheet could be altered for differentiation.

A Lesson for Every Day
Maths
7–8 Years
© A&C Black

Pyramid picture

☆ **Estimate** the length of each numbered line.

☆ Write your estimates in the table below.

☆ Then use a ruler to measure the lines and record their lengths.

To the NOT-SO-GREAT PYRAMIDS

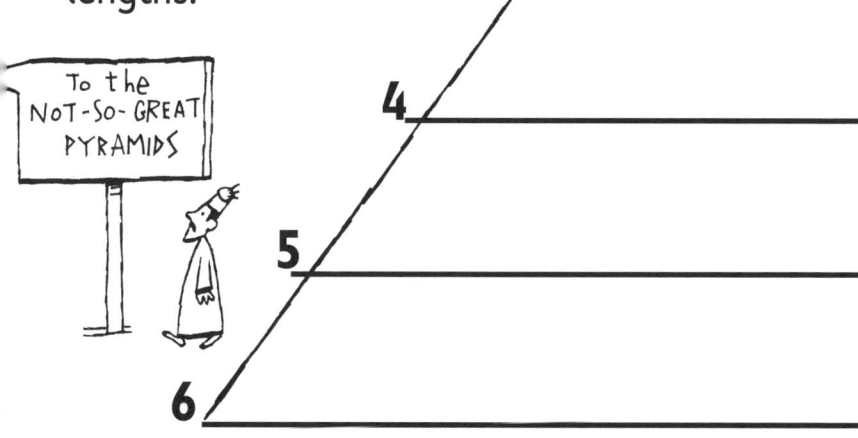

Line	Estimate	Measure
1		
2		
3		
4		
5		
6		

NOW TRY THIS!

• **Add the lengths. Do they total more than 1 m?** _____

• **On the back of this sheet, draw your own pyramid where the lengths come to more than 1 m.**

Teachers' note Encourage the children to accurately measure the lengths of the horizontal lines to the nearest half-centimetre, or if appropriate, to the nearest tenth of a centimetre. For the extension activity, more confident children could try to make the total length of the lines as close to 1 m as they can.

A Lesson for Every Day
Maths
7-8 Years
© A&C Black

Game show

• **Colour the best estimate to win the game show!**

1. The weight of a mobile phone

100 g
1 kg
1 g

2. The length of a swimming pool

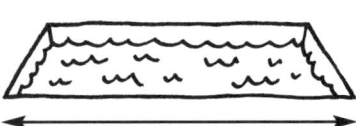

30 m
3 cm
3 m

3. The capacity of a wheely bin

300 ml
300 l
3 l

4. The height of a kettle

25 m
25 cm
250 m

5. The weight of a tin of baked bins

50 kg
5 g
500 g

6. The capacity of a jam jar

40 l
4 l
400 ml

7. The depth of a bath

400 cm
4 m
40 cm

8. The width of a door

70 m
70 cm
700 cm

NOW TRY THIS!

• **Write three more estimate questions for a partner to solve.**

Teachers' note Have available metre sticks, kilogram and hundred gram weights and measuring containers to help the children to visualise the lengths, masses or capacities more clearly. Encourage the children to compare their answers with a partner and to discuss their reasons.

A Lesson for Every Day
Maths
7-8 Years
© A&C Black

Measuring jugs

• **Use a blue pencil to show the water level on each jug.**

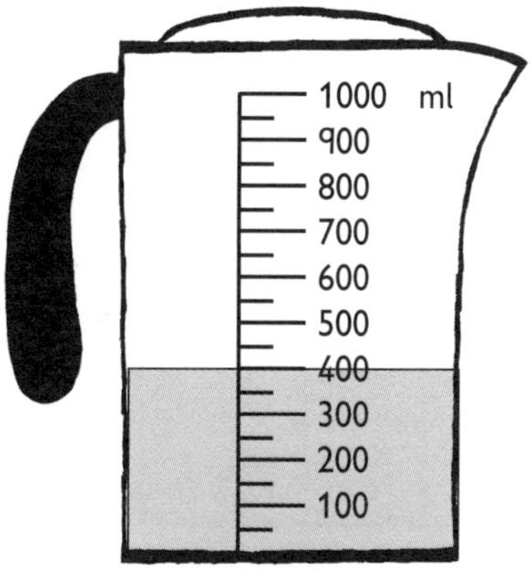

1000 ml / 900 / 800 / 700 / 600 / 500 / 400 / 300 / 200 / 100	1000 ml / 900 / 800 / 700 / 600 / 500 / 400 / 300 / 200 / 100	1000 ml / 900 / 800 / 700 / 600 / 500 / 400 / 300 / 200 / 100
400 ml	**50 ml**	**250 ml**
1000 ml / 900 / 800 / 700 / 600 / 500 / 400 / 300 / 200 / 100	1000 ml / 900 / 800 / 700 / 600 / 500 / 400 / 300 / 200 / 100	1000 ml / 900 / 800 / 700 / 600 / 500 / 400 / 300 / 200 / 100
550 ml	**650 ml**	**75 ml**
1000 ml / 900 / 800 / 700 / 600 / 500 / 400 / 300 / 200 / 100	1000 ml / 900 / 800 / 700 / 600 / 500 / 400 / 300 / 200 / 100	1000 ml / 900 / 800 / 700 / 600 / 500 / 400 / 300 / 200 / 100
25 ml	**175 ml**	**425 ml**

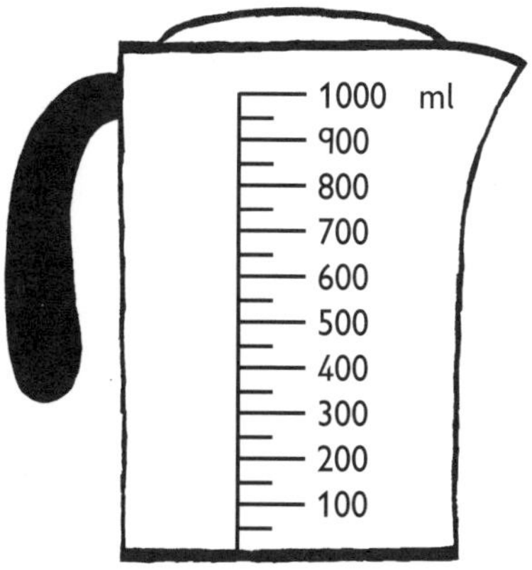

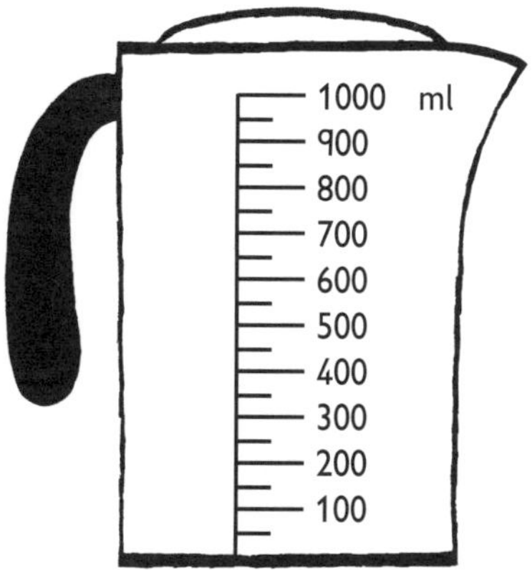

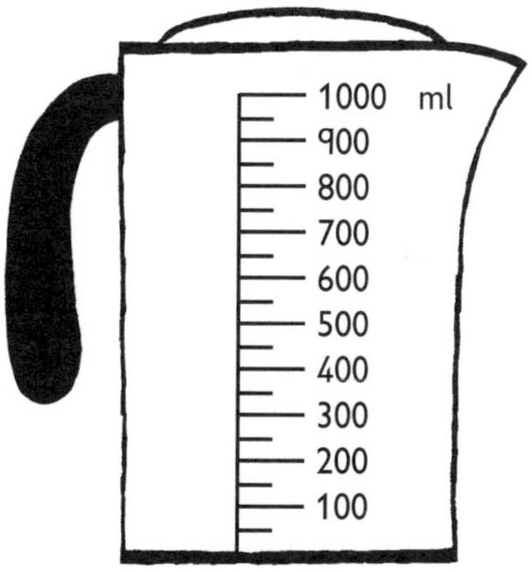

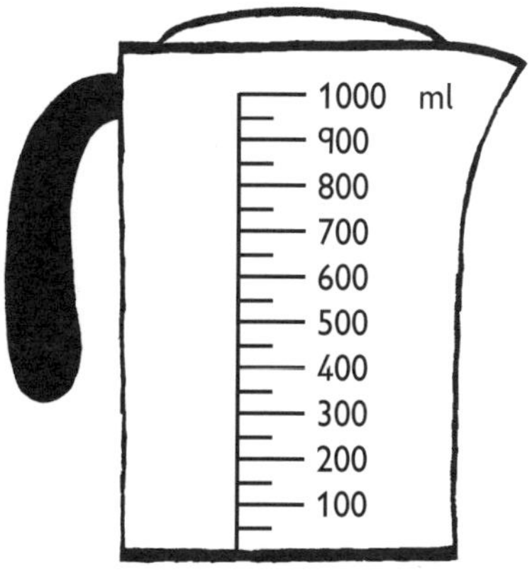

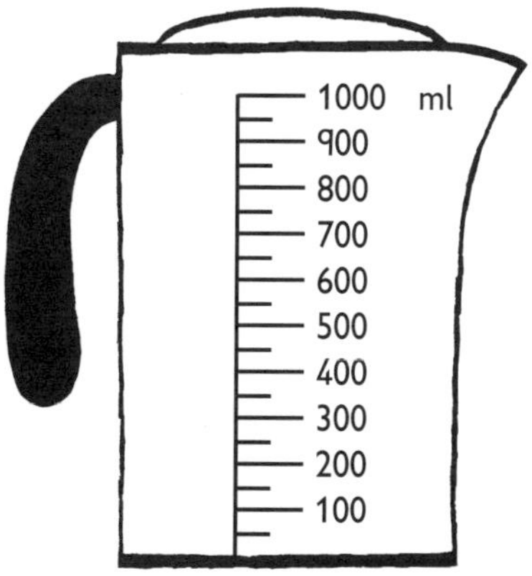

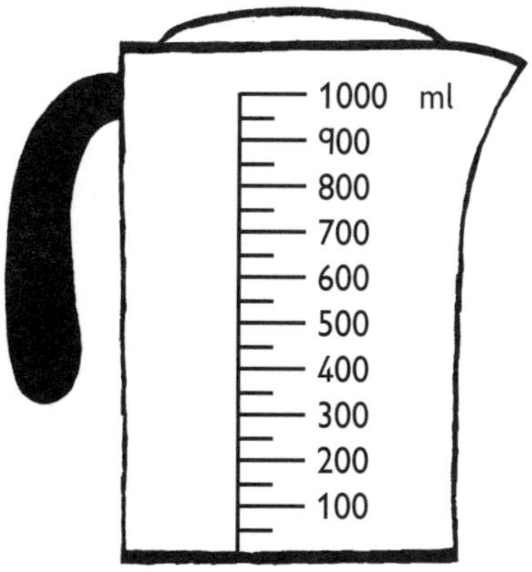

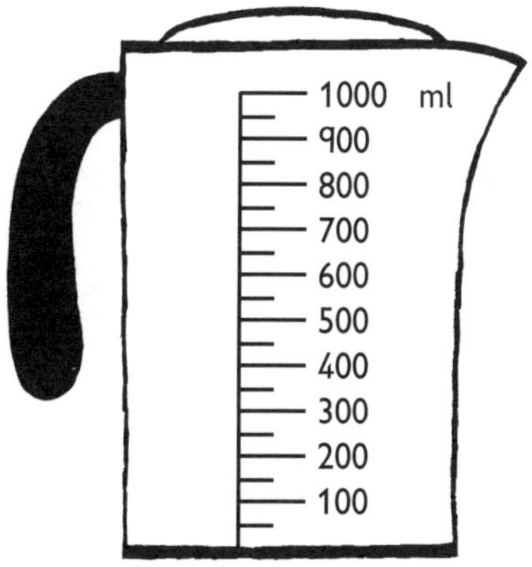

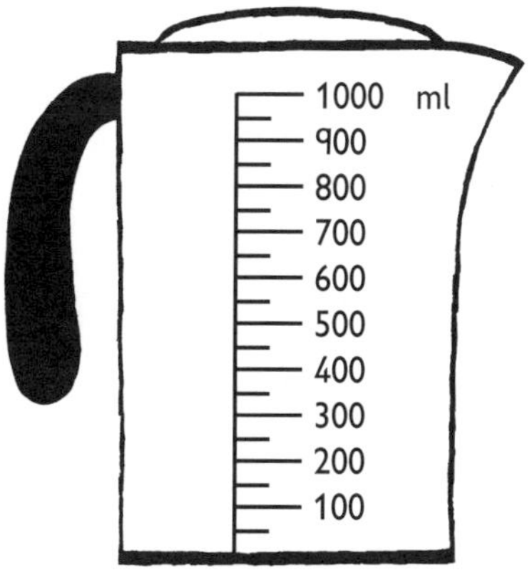

NOW TRY THIS!

• **On a sheet of paper, write how many more millilitres of water are needed in each jug to make 1 litre.**

Teachers' note The measurements can be altered to provide a wider range of variety and practice. For the extension activity, remind the children that 1000 ml is the same as 1 litre.

A Lesson for Every Day
Maths
7-8 Years
© A&C Black

Thirsty work

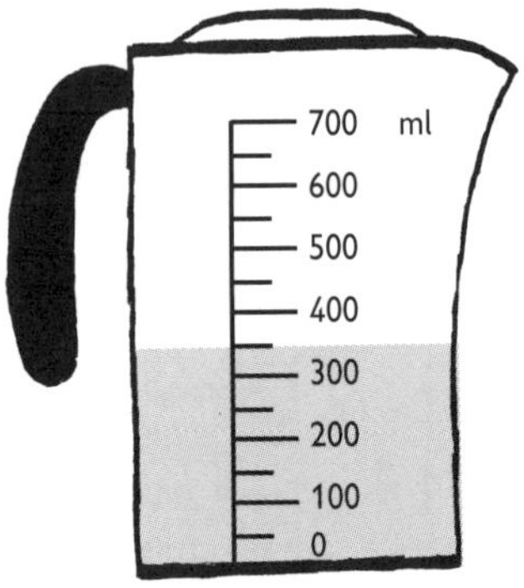

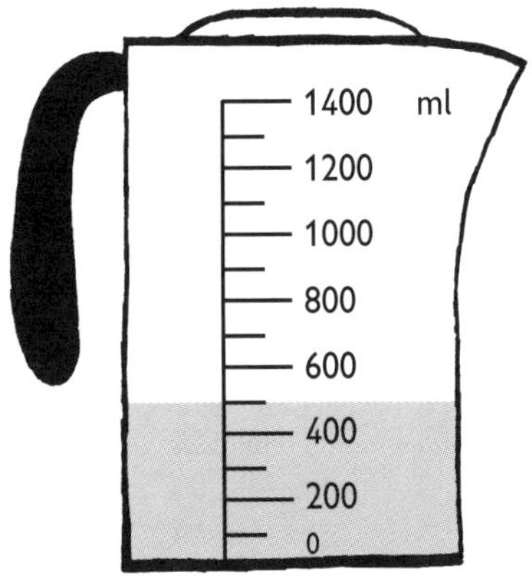

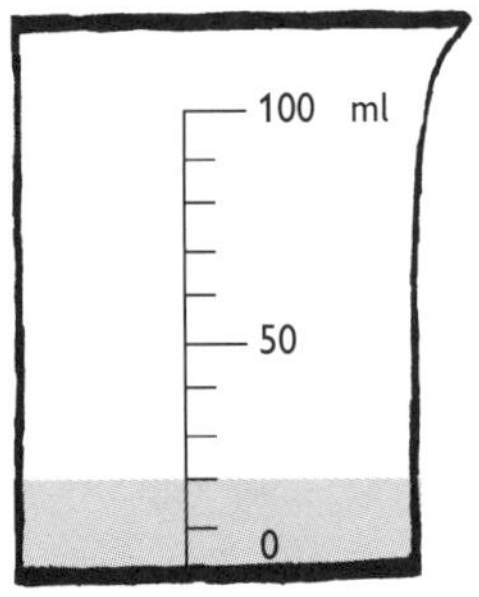

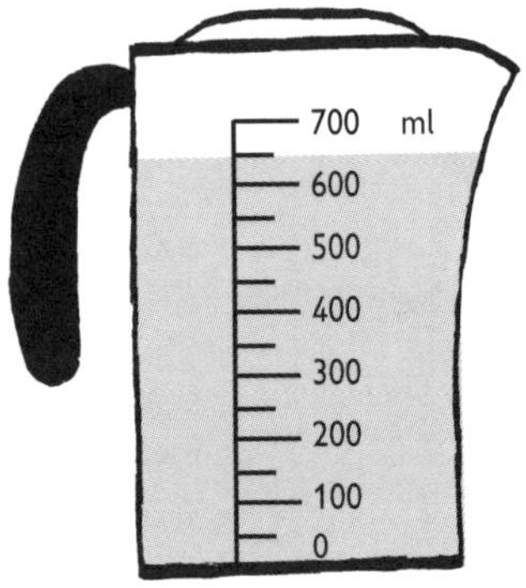

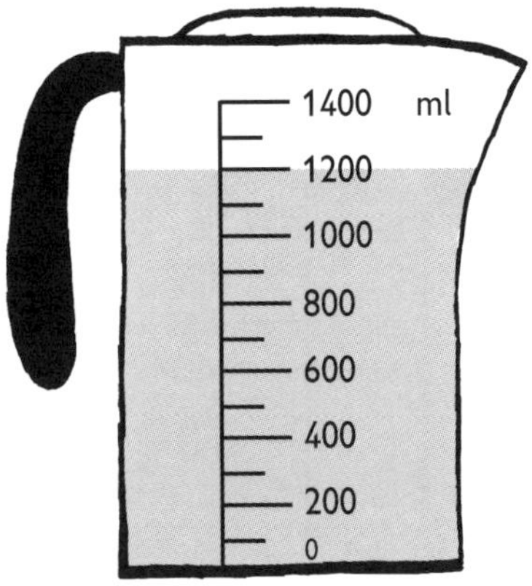

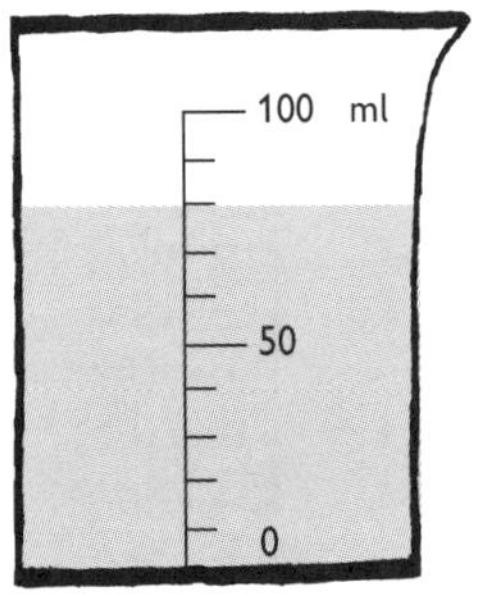

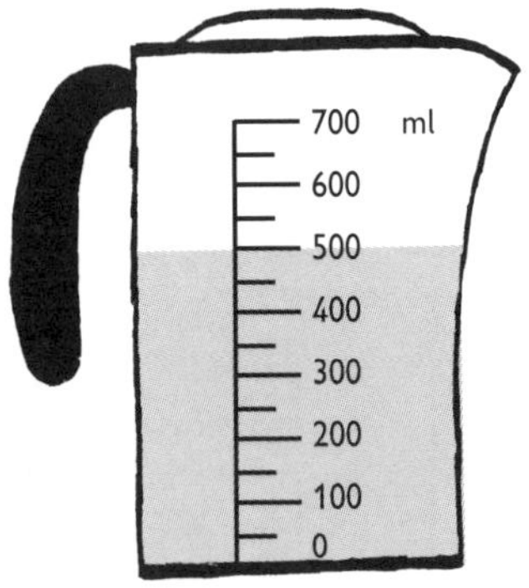

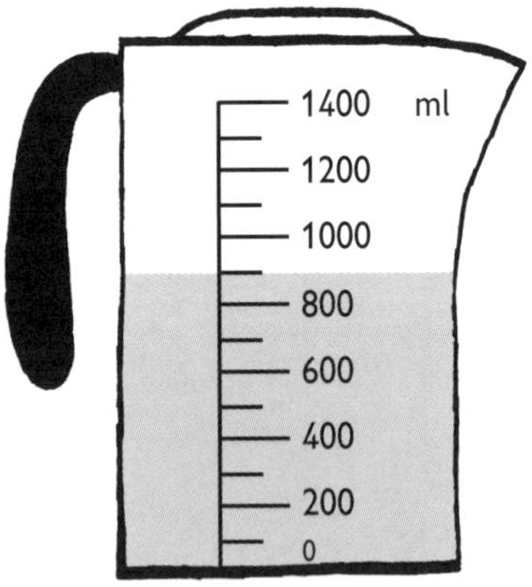

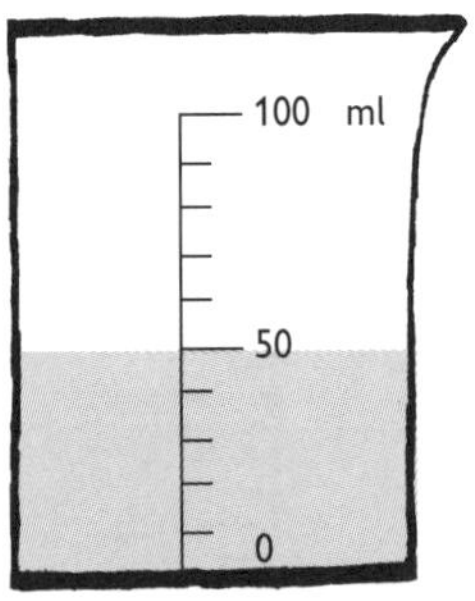

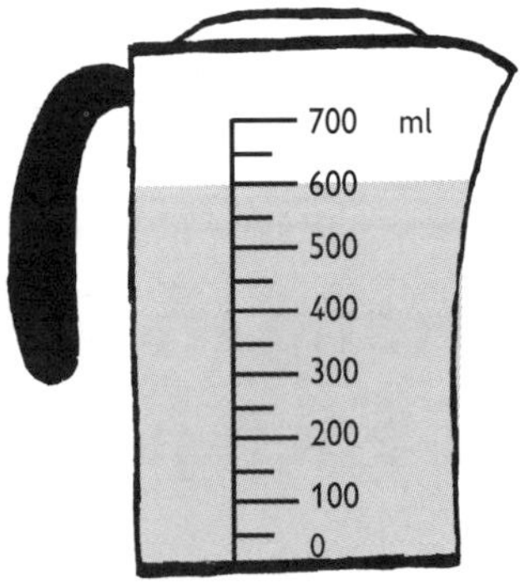

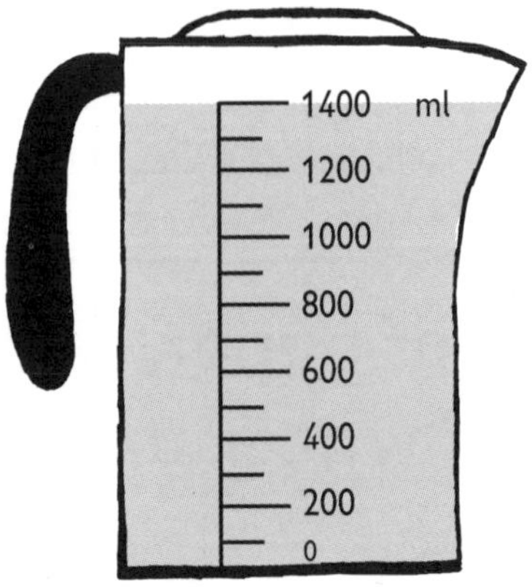

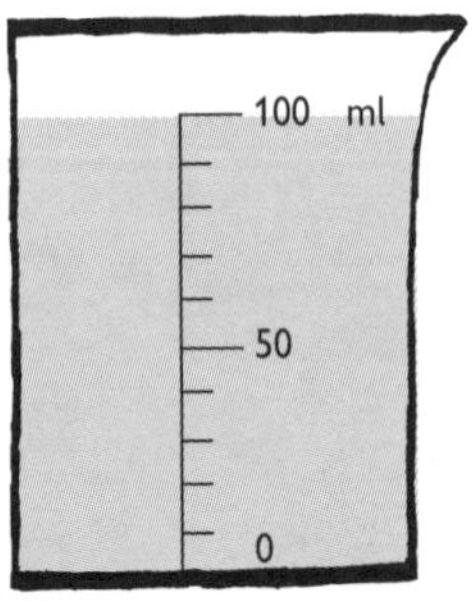

Teachers' note These cards can be used to play three different games. The rules can be found in the notes on the activity on page 15.

A Lesson for Every Day
Maths
7–8 Years
© **A&C Black**

Hobbies: 1

Class 3S voted for their favourite hobbies.
- **Look at the pictures on 'Hobbies: 2'.**
- **Make up a tally to show the information.**

Activity	Tally

1 How many children voted for each hobby?

reading ____ sport ____ making models ____ music ____

watching TV ____ playing computer games ____

2 List the hobbies in order from most popular to least popular.

_____

3 Make up three questions to ask about the information in the tally chart.

1 _____

2 _____

3 _____

NOW TRY THIS!

- **Ask 10 friends about their favourite hobbies. Now answer the questions again, including those you made up.**

Teachers' note To simplify, you could give the children half the number of pictures or ask them to look for three of the hobbies and make a tally of these. Some children might find it helpful to have the names of the activities written on the board for them to refer to for spellings: reading, computer games, music, sport, making models, watching TV.

A Lesson for Every Day
Maths
7–8 Years
© A&C Black

• **Use these pictures to make a tally of the children's favourite hobbies.**

Teachers' note Use this sheet in conjunction with 'Hobbies: 1'.

A Lesson for Every Day
Maths
7-8 Years
© A&C Black

The Basketeers

These children belong to a basketball team called The Basketeers. They made a tally to show their coach the number of baskets they each scored that season.

Player	Tally
	‖‖ ‖‖ ‖‖ ‖‖ I
Jack	
	‖‖ ‖‖ ‖‖ ‖‖ ‖‖ I
	‖‖ ‖‖ ‖‖ ‖‖ IIII
Jill	

Jack 26   Jim 24   Jon 19

Jan 21   Jade 26   Jill 15

Something has gone wrong with the tally chart.
• Correct it so that it shows all the information.

One of the players is hoping to win the **Basketeer Cup.**

• **Who do you think it might be?** _____

• **Why?** _____

• **Write down 5 things you know from the tally chart.**

    1 _____

    2 _____

    3 _____

    4 _____

    5 _____

Teachers' note The children look at the number of baskets the players scored and compare with the tally, identifying those whose scores are tallied, making the tally for those named and finding out who has been left off completely and adding them. As an extension activity, tell the children to write three questions to ask a partner about the tally chart.

A Lesson for Every Day
Maths
7–8 Years
© A&C Black

Email

Zak made a frequency table to show the number of messages in his email folders.

Email folder	Number of emails
Inbox	7
Saved	9
Sent	11
Deleted	3
Draft	9
Junk	2

• **Make a bar chart to show this information**

Bar chart to show the number of emails

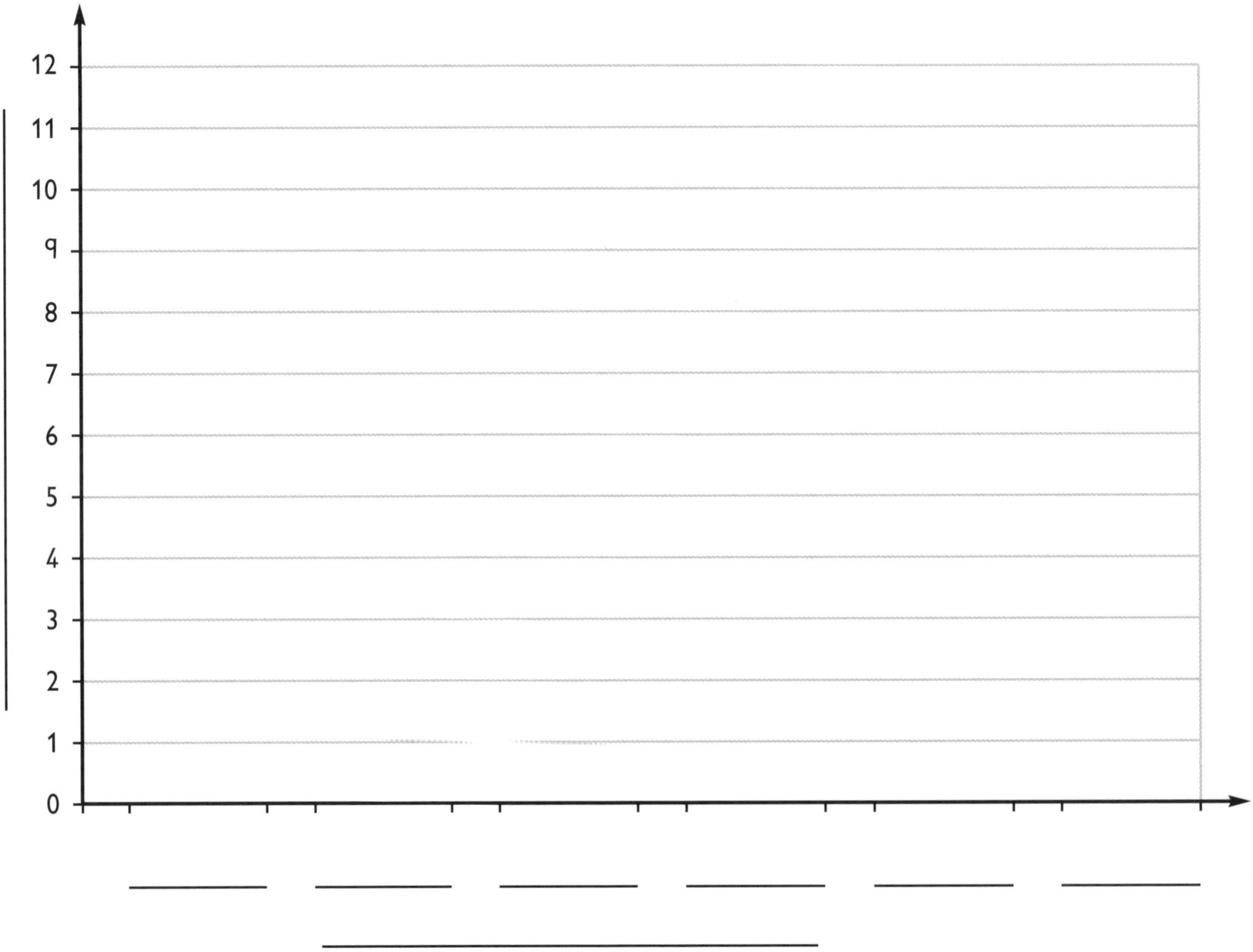

12
11
10
9
8
7
6
5
4
3
2
1
0

Teachers' note To simplify, add the axis labels before copying. To extend, delete the numbers on the vertical axis and ask the children to write those in as well. As an extension activity, ask the children to make up six questions to ask a partner about Zak's email account.

A Lesson for Every Day
Maths
7-8 Years
© A&C Black

Mr Woods is sorting out his library.
How many books are there for each subject?

1 Complete the frequency table. Then make the
bar chart on 'The great library sort out: 2'.

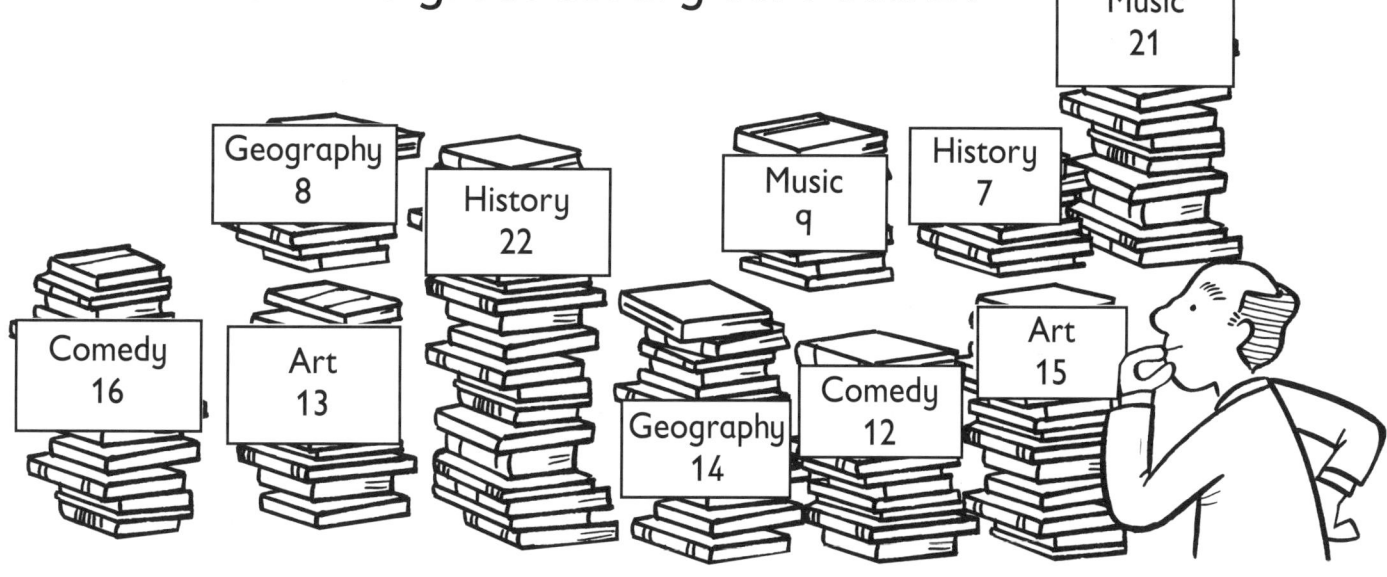

Music 21
Geography 8
History 22
Music 9
History 7
Comedy 16
Art 13
Geography 14
Comedy 12
Art 15

Subject	Number of books
Comedy	

2 How many books does Mr Woods

have altogether in his library? _____

NOW TRY THIS!

• **Make up five questions about
your bar chart to ask a partner.**

Teachers' note Give the children a copy of 'The great library sort out: 2' for this activity. Ask them to first find the total of each type of book by adding the numbers on the sticky notes and completing the frequency table. Then they construct a bar graph to show the information. Remind them about labels and numbering the axis (the scale should be in 2s).

A Lesson for Every Day
Maths
7-8 Years
© A&C Black

The great library sort out: 2

- **Use your frequency table from 'The great library sort out: 1' to help you complete the bar chart.**

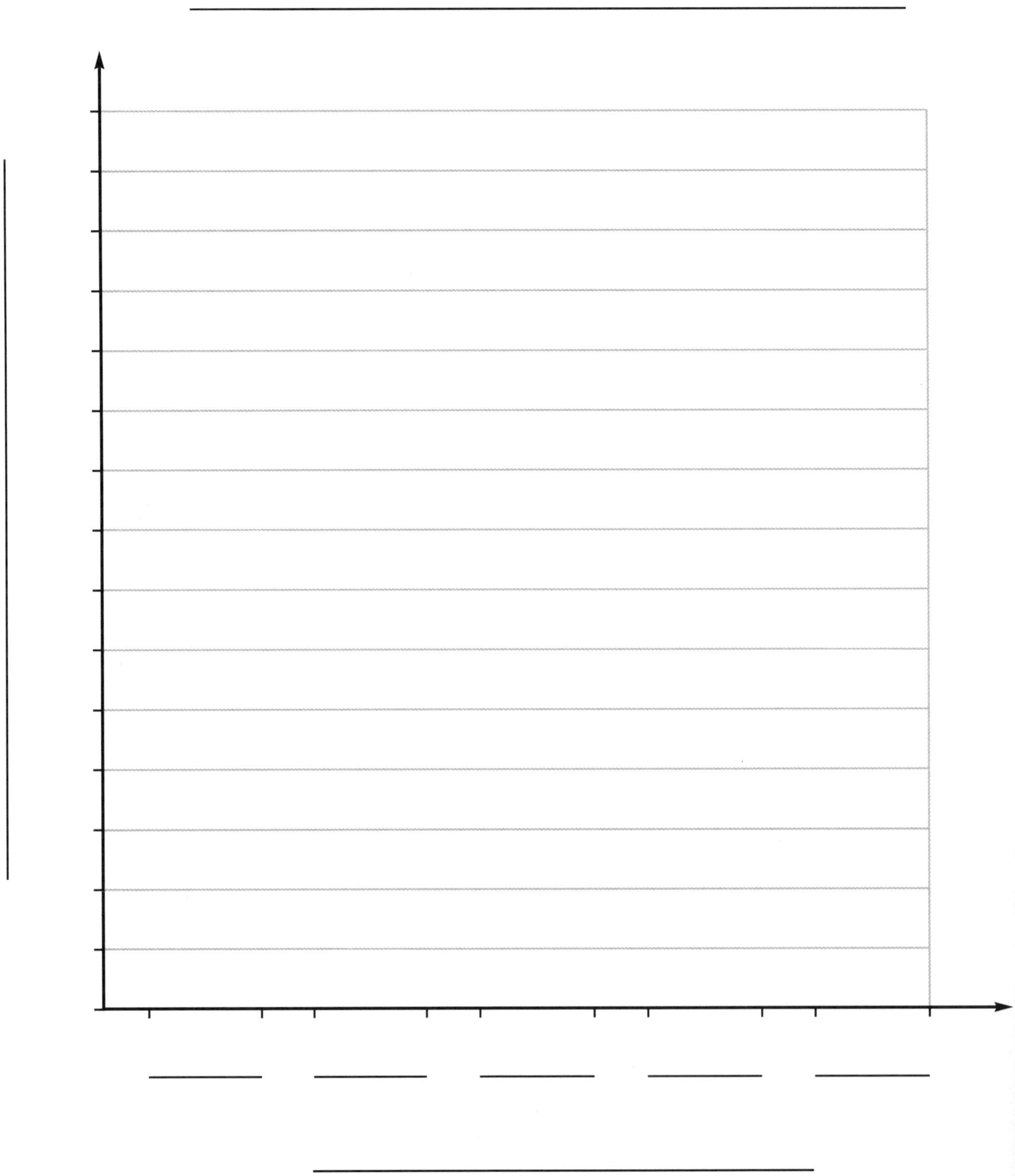

Teachers' note Use this sheet in conjuction with 'The great library sort out: 1'.

A Lesson for Every Day
Maths
7–8 Years
© A&C Black

Chocolate matters

There are 36 chocolates in a box.
17 are milk chocolate, 6 are white chocolate
and the rest are dark chocolate.

• **Write a calculation for each problem and solve it.**

1 How many in each box are dark chocolate?

2 From a box, how many people can have 5 chocolates each?

3 How many chocolates are there in 3 boxes?

4 James has a whole box. He eats a quarter of them.
How many are left in the box?

5 If you wanted 24 white chocolates, how many boxes
would you need?

6 The Jones family have a box. Tom eats 8, Isobel eats half as
many as Tom and Mum eats 3. How many are left?

NOW TRY THIS!

• **Write** 3 **word problems of your
own about the box of chocolates.**

Teachers' note The numbers can be altered before copying to provide differentiation. Encourage the children to write each question as a calculation and to describe their strategy for working out each answer, including showing this on a number line, using a written method or on a 100-square.

A Lesson for Every Day
Maths
7-8 Years
© A&C Black

Fruit corner

- **Answer each question.**
- **Show your working.**

---

1 6 apples are cut into quarters. How many children can have 3 pieces each?

2 Jo has 3 satsumas. Each satsuma has 12 segments. How many children can have 4 segments each?

3 9 pears are cut in half. How many children can have 3 pieces each?

4 5 peaches are cut into quarters. How many children can have 2 pieces each?

5 A bowl holds 30 grapes. 8 children are given 3 each. How many grapes in the bowl now?

6 3 apples are cut into eighths. How many children can have 3 pieces each?

7 A pineapple is cut into 8 slices. Each slice is cut into 5 chunks. How many chunks altogether?

8 Some bananas are cut into 15 slices each. There are 60 slices altogether. How many bananas?

 **NOW TRY THIS!**

- **Make up 2 fruit questions for a partner to solve.**

 142

Teachers' note The numbers can be altered before copying to provide differentiation. Encourage the children to use pictorial methods or to write each question as a calculation and describe their strategy for working out each answer.

A Lesson for Every Day
Maths
7–8 Years
© A&C Black

What's the difference?

Some shapes are made with numbered balls and rods.

• Write the │ difference │ between the numbers joined by each rod.

1.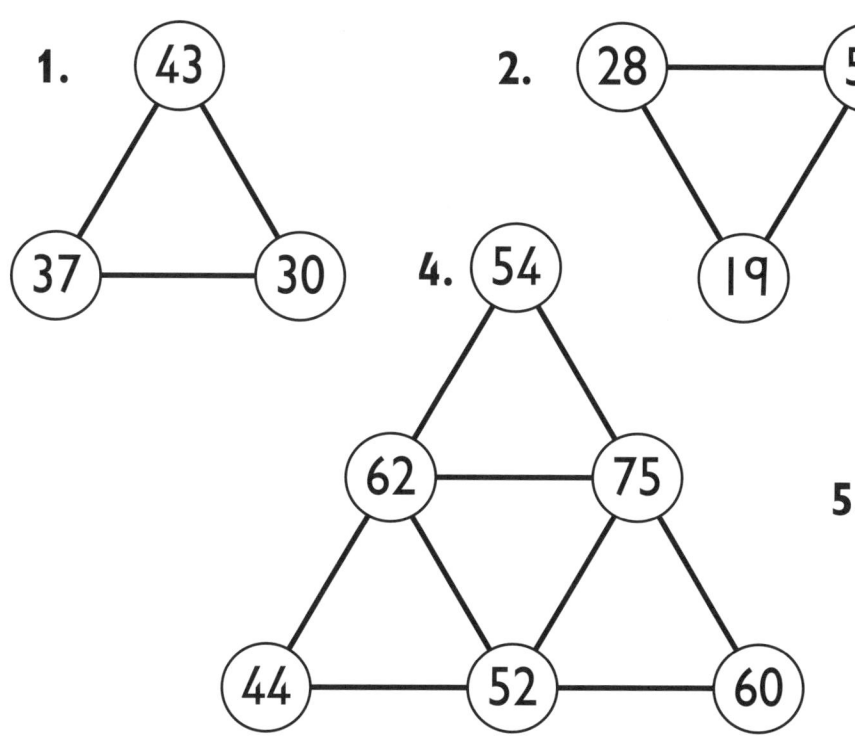

2.

3.

4.

5.

6.

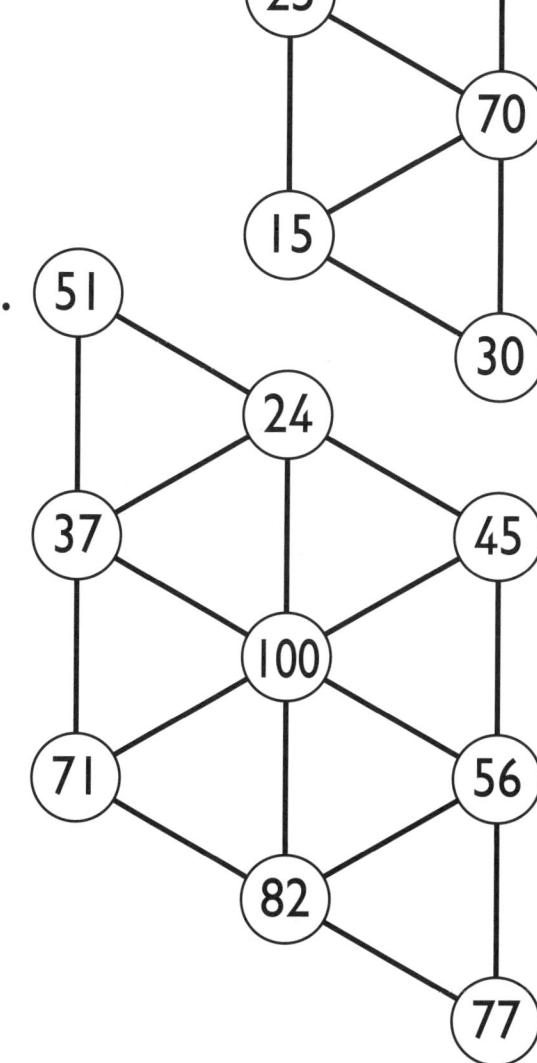

Teachers' note Encourage the children to use and draw their own number lines to help them find differences. Discuss how, for numbers close to each other, it is easier to count up from the smaller number to find the difference, whereas for numbers further apart it is often easier to do a subtraction by taking the smaller number away from the larger one.

A Lesson for Every Day
Maths
7–8 Years
© A&C Black

Counter tracker

A counter is placed on a square and then moved.

- **Write where the counter ends up each time.**

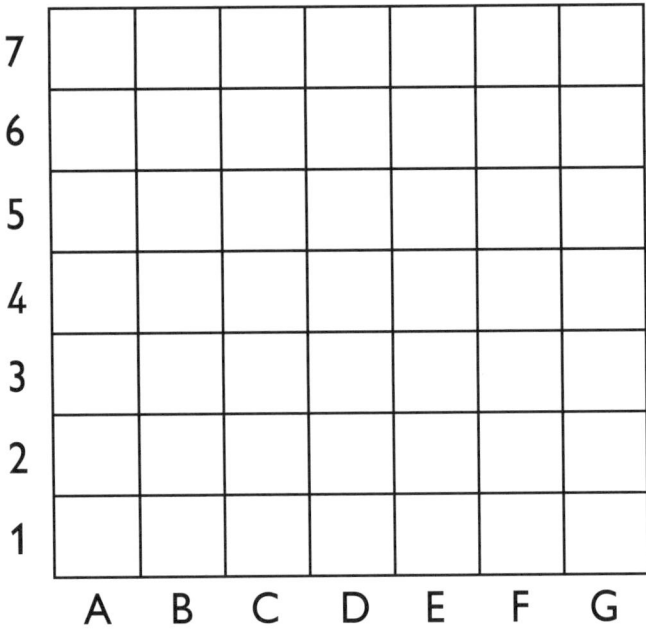

1. | The counter is put on D3. It is moved 2 squares East and 4 squares North. | It is now on ☐

2. | The counter is put on F6. It is moved 4 squares South and 2 squares West. | It is now on ☐

3. | The counter is put on A4. It is moved 3 squares North and 5 squares East. | It is now on ☐

4. | The counter is put on G5. It is moved 6 squares West and 2 squares South. | It is now on ☐

5. | The counter is put on E1. It is moved 4 squares North and 3 squares West. | It is now on ☐

NOW TRY THIS!

- **Make up three puzzles of your own for a partner to solve.**

Teachers' note Remind the children of the directions North, South, East and West at the start of the lesson.

A Lesson for Every Day
Maths
7–8 Years
© A&C Black

Ribbons

A shop sells lots of different ribbons.
These ribbons measure ⏐ 1 metre ⏐ .

- **Write how much ribbon is left if some is cut off.**

1.

50 cm is cut off

[50] cm is left

2.

70 cm is cut off

[   ] cm is left

3.

5 cm is cut off

[   ] cm is left

4.

17 cm is cut off

[   ] cm is left

5.

24 cm is cut off

[   ] cm is left

6.

67 cm is cut off

[   ] cm is left

7.

28 cm is cut off

[   ] cm is left

8.

35 cm is cut off

[   ] cm is left

9.

59 cm is cut off

[   ] cm is left

NOW TRY THIS!

- **Try these ⏐ 2 metre ⏐ ribbons.**

(a)

48 cm is cut off

[   ] cm is left

(b)

154 cm is cut off

[   ] cm is left

Teachers' note Begin the lesson by practising number pairs that total 100 (see the notes on the activity on page 16) as knowledge of these are required for the activity. The children could use the tape measure from 'DIY tape measure' to help them with this activity.

A Lesson for Every Day
Maths
7–8 Years
© A&C Black

Measure master

☆ Work with a partner. **You need** a dice and counters in two colours.

☆ Take turns to roll the dice and look at the measuring equipment for that dice number.

☆ Match it to a square on the grid and cover the square with a counter in your colour.

☆ The winner is the first to cover four squares in a line.

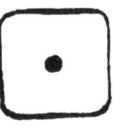					
ruler	metre stick or tape measure	trundle wheel	weighing scales	measuring jug	stopwatch or egg-timer

How long does it take to boil an egg?	How much coffee will fill a flask?	How large is your hand?	How heavy is a brick?	How long is this line?
			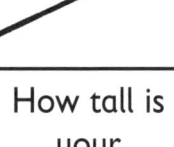	
How heavy is a coin?	How far is it from your hall to the playground?	How much water does a cup hold?	How much does your friend weigh?	How tall is your classroom door?

How long does it take to walk around your playground?	How much cola is in a bottle?	How long is a ladybird?	How wide is your table?	How much milk is in a carton?

How heavy is a marble?	What is the distance all the way round your head?	How deep is the sink?	How long does it take to count to 100?	How far is it from your classroom to the hall?
			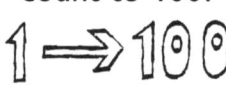	
How wide is your classroom?	How tall is your teacher?	How heavy is a jam jar?	How much water does a jug hold?	How long does it take to skip 10 times?
	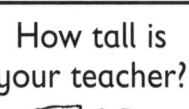		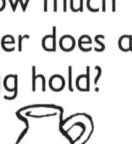	

Teachers' note Enlarge this sheet to A3 size for easier use. Ensure the children understand that the piece of measuring equipment must be the most suitable piece of equipment for the situation described on the square. If a player feels that the situation chosen is not most appropriate, they can challenge. The winning line can be horizontal, vertical or diagonal.

A Lesson for Every Day
Maths
7-8 Years
© A&C Black

Cookery class

- **Draw an arrow on each timer to show the correct number of minutes.**

1.

| 6 minutes |

2.

| 45 minutes |

3.
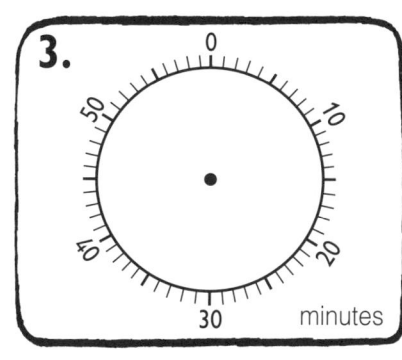

| 21 minutes |

4.
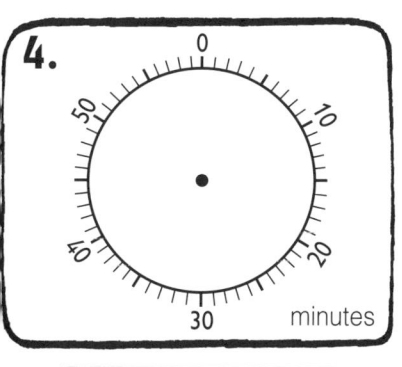

| 37 minutes |

5.
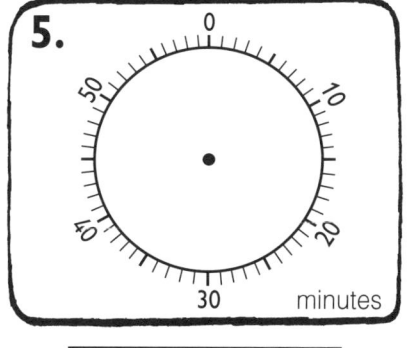

| 58 minutes |

6.
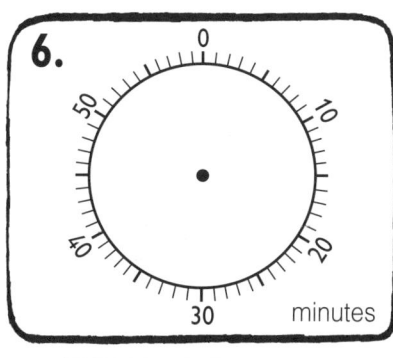

| 23 minutes |

7.
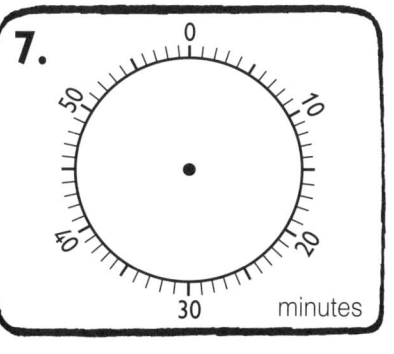

| 17 minutes |

8.
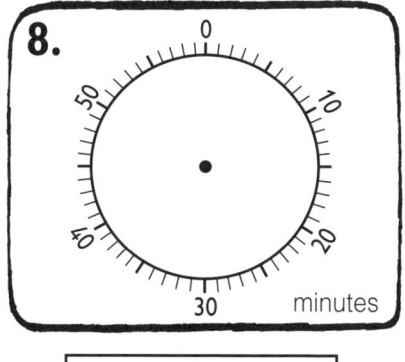

| 54 minutes |

9.
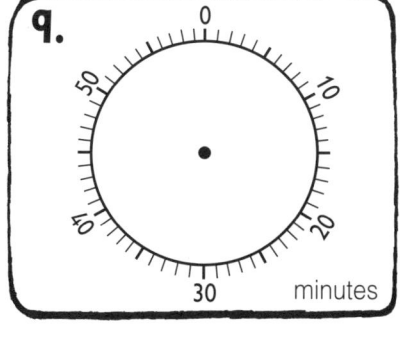

| 39 minutes |

NOW TRY THIS!

- **Under each timer, write how many minutes less than one hour it shows.**

Teachers' note Some children might benefit from the sheet being enlarged to A3 size so that missing numbers can be written onto the scales. Arrows could be drawn on each timer and the numbers removed to provide an alternative activity for practising the reading of scales.

A Lesson for Every Day
Maths
7-8 Years
© A&C Black

Time quiz

- **Your teacher has chosen one of these times and will give you some clues.**
- **Can you work out which time has been chosen?**

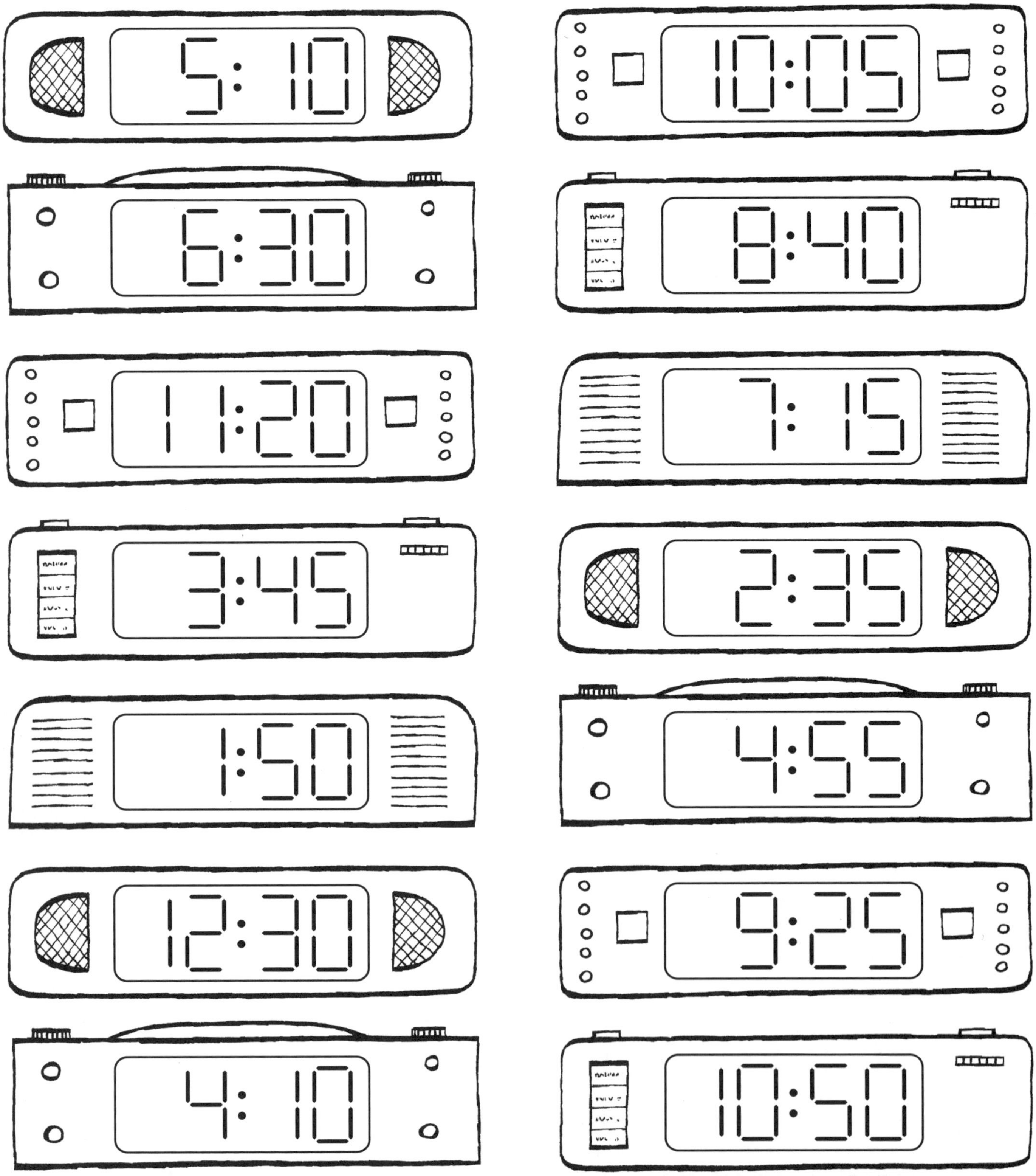

5:10

10:05

6:30

8:40

11:20

7:15

3:45

2:35

1:50

4:55

12:30

9:25

4:10

10:50

Digital puzzles

You need the Time quiz worksheet.

1. Which clock shows ten to two?

1 : 50

2. Which clock shows ten past five?

3. Which clock shows quarter to four?

4. Which clock shows twenty to nine?

5. Which time is one hour after quarter past six?

6. Which time is five minutes after half past two?

7. Which time is closest to 11 o'clock?

8. Which time is half an hour after 8:55?

NOW TRY THIS!

• Write a puzzle for this time:

11:20

Teachers' note Use this sheet in conjunction with 'Time quiz' as an assessment. It could be altered to provide more challenging questions. As an extension the children could be asked to find pairs of times that are a given period apart, for example 45 minutes (6:30 and 7:15, 1:50 and 2:35, etc).

A Lesson for Every Day
Maths
7-8 Years
© A&C Black

TV times: 1

- **Cut out these cards, and the cards from TV times: 2.**
- **Sort them into pairs.**

The time now is	Cartoons are at	The time now is	The Y Factor is at

The time now is	The News is at	The time now is	Football is at

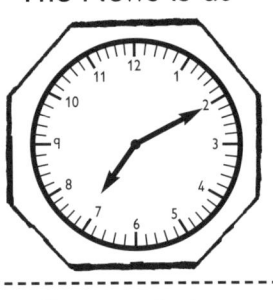

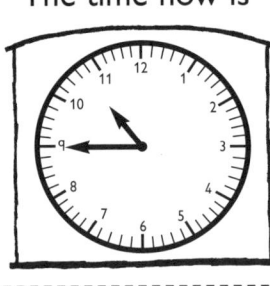

The time now is	Art-magic is at	The time now is	Em Street is at

The time now is	Now-a-story is at	The time now is	Dino World is at

The time now is	Dina Warrior is at	The time now is	Westenders is at

Teachers' note Use this sheet in conjunction with 'TV times: 2'. The children could also be given this sheet only and asked to write how long they would have to wait for each programme to start. Both sets of cards could also be used by children working in pairs, to play games such as Pairs, Snap or Pelmanism.

A Lesson for Every Day
Maths
7–8 Years
© A&C Black

- **Cut out these cards, and the cards from TV times: 1.**
- **Sort them into pairs.**

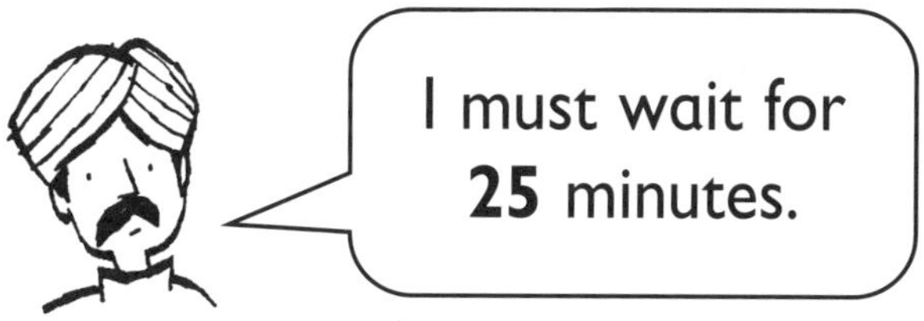

I must wait for **25** minutes.	I must wait for **50** minutes.
I must wait for **45** minutes.	I must wait for **40** minutes.
I must wait for **15** minutes.	I must wait for **35** minutes.
I must wait for **20** minutes.	I must wait for **55** minutes.
I must wait for **5** minutes.	I must wait for **30** minutes.

Teachers' note Use this sheet in conjunction with 'TV times: 1'. The children could also be given this sheet only and a set time, and asked to write at what time each programme would start. Both sets of cards could also be used by children working in pairs to play games such as Pairs, Snap or Pelmanism.

A Lesson for Every Day
Maths
7–8 Years
© A&C Black

Campsite capers

- **Work with a partner.**
- **Use the clues to help you work out the** | total | **number of children in the tents.**

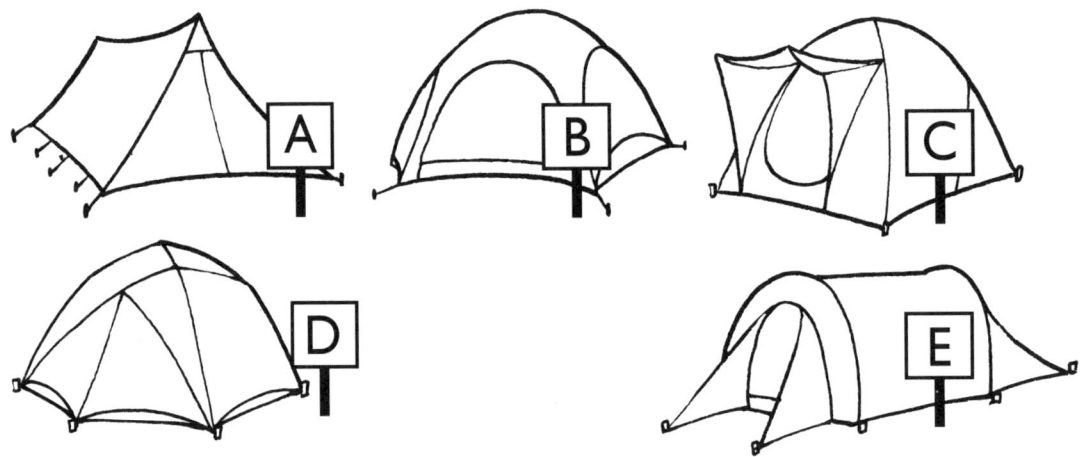

In Tent B there are 3 more children than in tent E.

Tent D has the most children in.
It has 1 more child than in any other tent.

In Tent C there are 2 fewer children than in tent A.

In Tents A and E there are the same number of children.

In Tent B there are 6 children.

- **How many children are at the camp** | altogether | **?**

NOW TRY THIS!

- **Draw** | 5 | **tents of your own and decide how many children are in each. Make up clues for a partner.**

Teachers' note For the extension activity encourage the children to check whether they have given a clue for each tent, without saying how many are in most of the tents. Write up sentences like 'more than', 'fewer than', 'the most', 'the fewest' and 'the same number' on the board to help them make up their own clues.

**A Lesson for Every Day
Maths
7–8 Years
© A&C Black**

Ship ahoy!

To mend his boat, **Captain Sprat** nails planks of wood together to make ⬚ 1 metre ⬚ lengths. If the length is over 1 metre, he cuts off the extra bit.

• **For each pair of planks, write how much Sprat needs to cut off.**

1. 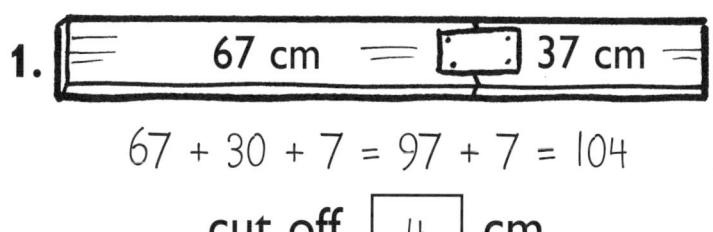 67 cm ═ 37 cm

$67 + 30 + 7 = 97 + 7 = 104$

cut off ⬚ 4 ⬚ cm

2. 74 cm ═ 28 cm

cut off ⬚ ⬚ cm

3.  56 cm — 77 cm

cut off ⬚ ⬚ cm

4. 71 cm ═ 39 cm

cut off ⬚ ⬚ cm

5. 85 cm ═ 38 cm

cut off ⬚ ⬚ cm

6. 66 cm — 45 cm

cut off ⬚ ⬚ cm

7. 45 cm — 86 cm

cut off ⬚ ⬚ cm

NOW TRY THIS!

A length of wood is ⬚ 134 cm ⬚.

• **Write how long it will be if Sprat cuts off:**

(a) 42 cm _____   **(b)** 67 cm _____   **(c)** 79 cm _____

Teachers' note This method of addition involves beginning with the larger number, partitioning the smaller number and first adding the multiple of 10, and then adding the ones. Demonstrate this method at the start of the lesson and encourage the children to come to the front of the class to practise it before beginning the sheet.

A Lesson for Every Day
Maths
7–8 Years
© A&C Black

Odd one out

- **Work with a partner.**
- **Colour the bead which is the odd one out in each row.**

1.

| $\frac{1}{2}$ of 40 | 40 ÷ 2 | one-half of forty | 40 × 2 | 20 |

2.

| $\frac{1}{3}$ of 30 | three-quarters of thirty | 10 | one-third of thirty | 30 ÷ 3 |

3.

| $\frac{1}{5}$ of 20 | one-fifth of twenty | 5 ÷ 20 | 4 | 20 ÷ 5 |

4.

| $\frac{1}{4}$ of 28 | 28 ÷ 4 | one-quarter of twenty-eight | 6 | 7 |

5.

| $\frac{1}{10}$ of 700 | 700 ÷ 10 | 7 | 70 | one-tenth of seven hundred |

6.

| $\frac{1}{6}$ of 24 | one-sixth of twenty-four | 24 × 6 | 4 | 24 ÷ 6 |

NOW TRY THIS!

- **Write three matching statements for each bead.**

| $\frac{1}{3}$ of 27 | | | |
| $\frac{1}{4}$ of 32 | | | |

Teachers' note This activity encourages the children to see the relationship between division and finding unit fractions of numbers. The children should work in pairs for this activity to encourage them to share ideas. Explain that for each odd one out, they must be able to explain to the class why it is different.

154

A Lesson for Every Day
Maths
7–8 Years
© A&C Black

Secret symmetry

• Play this game with a partner.

Keep your pattern secret.

☆ First make a **symmetrical** pattern by drawing 20 spots on this grid. Two have been done for you.

My pattern

☆ Take turns to say the position of a square on the grid (such as B4).

☆ The other player must say whether he/she has a spot in that square.

If the answer is 'yes', record the spot on the grid below and have another go.

If the answer is 'no', it's the other player's turn.

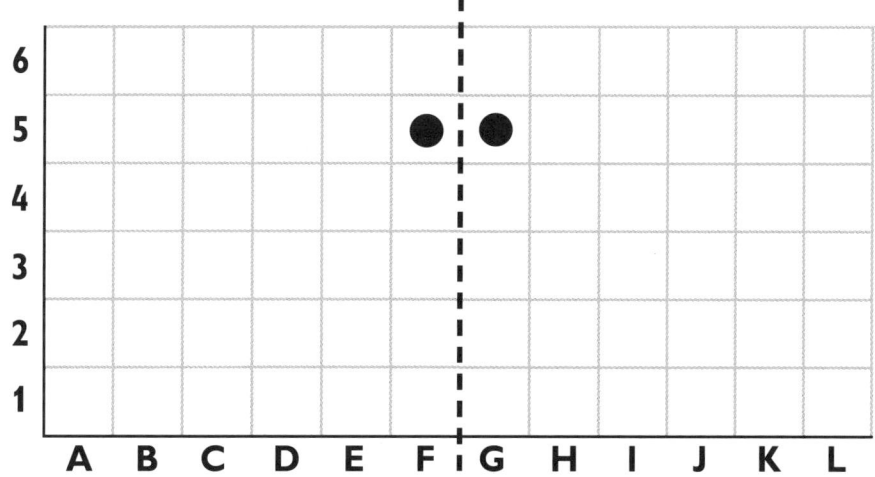

The other player's pattern

☆ The first person to work out the other player's pattern is the winner.

NOW TRY THIS!

• Colour some empty squares in the grid above.

Make sure the patterns are still symmetrical.

Teachers' note Give each child a copy of this sheet. The children will need a screen, for example a large book or a folder, to hide their patterns from their partners'. Encourage the children to mark with crosses those squares they have found that do not contain spots.

A Lesson for Every Day
Maths
7-8 Years
© A&C Black

Dotty symmetry

- **Draw the** `reflection` **of each shape in the mirror line.**

- **Use a mirror to check your reflections.**

Teachers' note Provide the children with mirrors and demonstrate how they should be used to help draw and check reflections. For the extension activity, encourage the children to turn the sheet round to make the mirror lines vertical or horizontal.

A Lesson for Every Day
Maths
7-8 Years
© A&C Black

Map work

- **Complete each sentence using numbers and the directions**

| North |, | South |, | East |, **or** | West |.

You need a ruler.

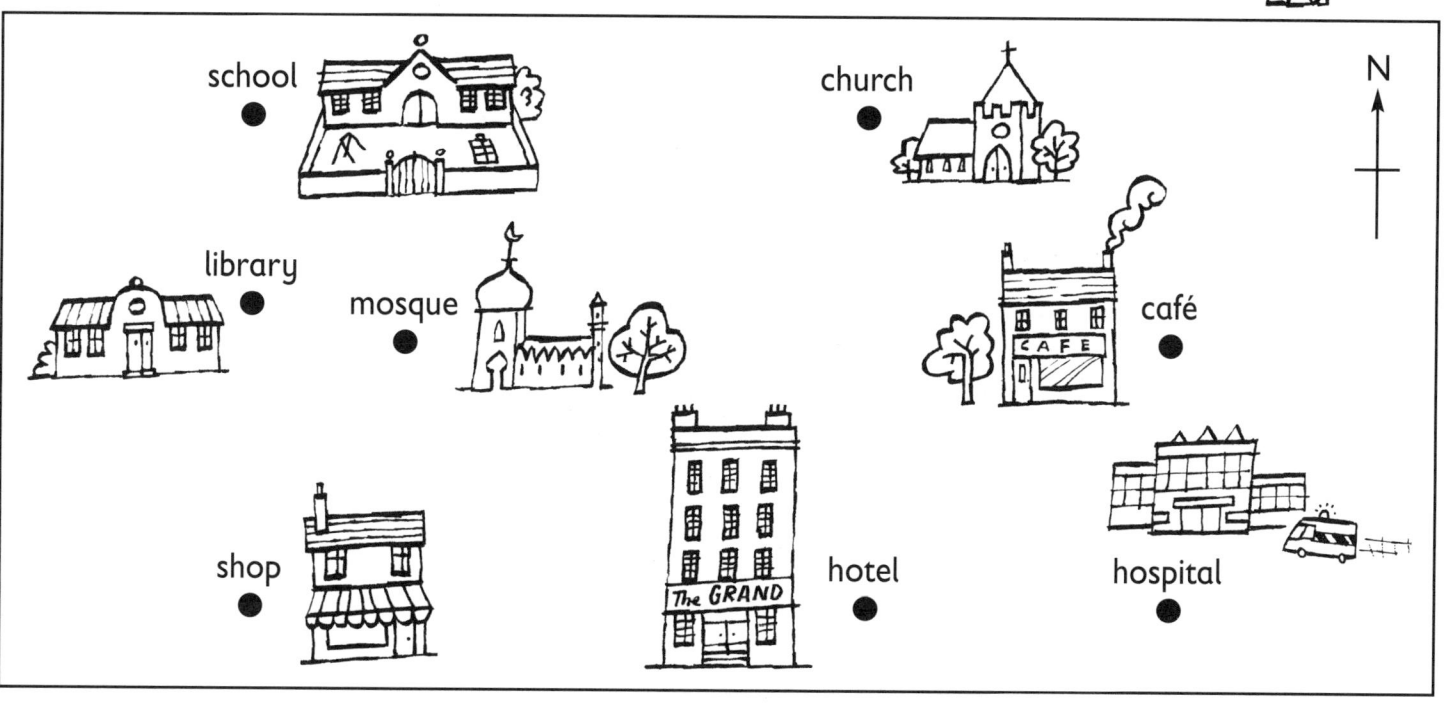

school

church

library

mosque

café

shop

hotel

The GRAND

hospital

N

- **On the map:**

1. the church is | 8 | cm | East | of the school

2. the shop is | | cm | | of the hospital

3. the library is | | cm | | of the school

4. the library is | | cm | | of the shop

5. the hospital is | | cm | | of the cafe

6. the café is | | cm | | of the mosque

NOW TRY THIS!

- **Write four more sentences of your own about the map.**

Teachers' note Encourage the children to measure from dot to dot rather than from word to word. For the extension activity, the children could find distances and directions between places on opposite sides of the map, eg. the shop and church. As a further extension, the children could draw their own maps on squared paper and write sentences about them.

A Lesson for Every Day
Maths
7–8 Years
© A&C Black

Learner driver

- **Mark all the** | right angles | **in this picture.**
- **Use the 'L' shape to help you check each angle.**

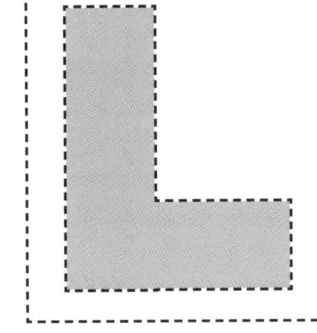

Mark the right angles with a coloured pencil.

Leeds 64m

Driving School

Teachers' note If necessary, explain to the children that people learning to drive have to stick an 'L' sign on their car when they are driving. As an extension, the children could draw their own picture with as many right angles in it as they can. Some children could use the right angle symbol ⌐ if they are ready to.

A Lesson for Every Day
Maths
7–8 Years
© A&C Black

Weight lifters

- **For each weight lifter, colour both weights if they are the same.**

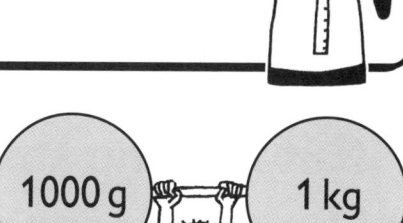

1.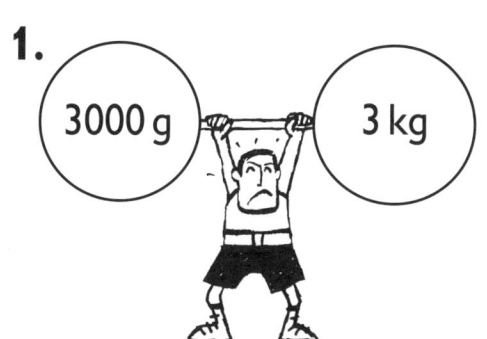
3000 g 3 kg

2.
200 g 2 kg

3.
500 g $\frac{1}{2}$ kg

4.
6000 g 6 kg

5.
4000 g 4 kg

6.
3 g 300 kg

7.
500 g 0·5 kg

8.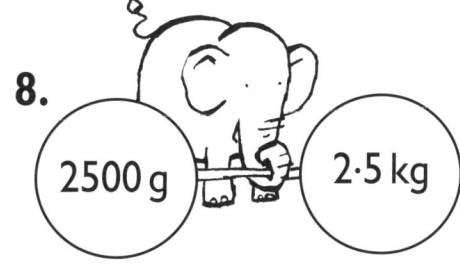
2500 g 2·5 kg

9.
3·5 g 3500 kg

10.
1500 g 1·5 kg

11.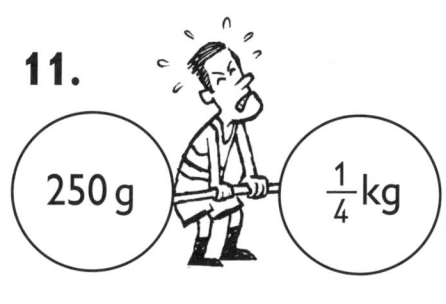
250 g $\frac{1}{4}$ kg

12.
1250 g $1\frac{1}{4}$ kg

NOW TRY THIS!

- **On the back of this sheet, draw three more weight lifters with weights that are equal amounts.**

Teachers' note Ensure that the children understand the abbreviations 'g' and 'kg', and that 1000 g is equal to 1 kg. Encourage them to look out for the correct units and to look closely at the numbers to see whether the measurements are equivalent. The numbers could be altered for further differentiation.

A Lesson for Every Day
Maths
7–8 Years
© A&C Black

DIY tape measure

- **Cut out the strips and tape them together.**
- **Use your tape measure to find the size of your:**

wrist	elbow	ankle	knee	thigh	waist
0					
1	21	41	61		81
2	22	42	62		82
3	23	43	63		83
4	24	44	64		84
5	25	45	65		85
6	26	46	66		86
7	27	47	67		87
8	28	48	68		88
9	29	49	69		89
10	30	50	70		90
11	31	51	71		91
12	32	52	72		92
13	33	53	73		93
14	34	54	74		94
15	35	55	75		95
16	36	56	76		96
17	37	57	77		97
18	38	58	78		98
19	39	59	79		99
20	40	60	80		1m

Teachers' note The children may need help sticking the strips together with transparent tape or glue. The children should keep their own tape measure (naming it on the reverse) and use it for a range of measuring activities in and around the school, measuring to the nearest centimetre.

A Lesson for Every Day
Maths
7–8 Years
© A&C Black

Time for TV

• **Use the TV times to help you answer the questions.**

Remember to watch:
News - 1:00 p.m.   Watchdog - 7:30 p.m.
Brainy Quiz - 2:15 p.m.   Film - 8:50 p.m.

1 The News runs for 25 minutes.

What time does it end? _____

2 How long after midday does

Brainy Quiz come on? _____

3 Brainy Quiz runs for 30 minutes.

What time does it end? _____

4 Watchdog ends at 7:55 p.m.

How long does the show last? _____

5 Mrs Smith looks at her watch at 8:10 p.m. How long does she

have to wait until the film starts? _____

6 The film runs for 1 hour and 45 minutes.

When does it end? _____

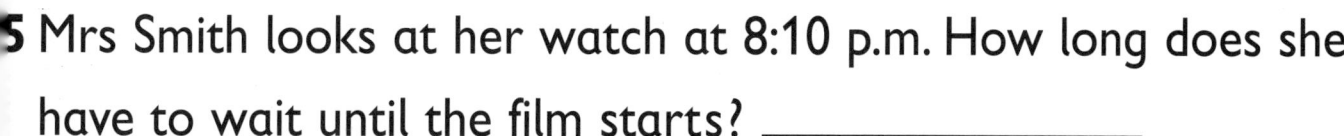

NOW TRY THIS!

• **Write** 3 **questions of your own about the TV times for a partner to solve.**

eachers' note Read through the TV times together and revise the meaning of p.m. Encourage
hildren to describe their decision making when choosing how to work the answer out. Provide them
vith geared clocks if necessary. The times can be altered to provide differentiation and variety.

A Lesson for Every Day
Maths
7-8 Years
© A&C Black

Record breakers

• **Read the world records and fill in the missing numbers.**

> The world's longest goldfish measured 47 cm
> from mouth to tail
>
> The longest rabbit ears measured 79 cm
> in a complete span
>
> The world's longest human hair measured 563 cm
>
> The world record for the highest jump by a dog is 173 cm

1 The length of the world's largest goldfish is:

_____ mm

_____ cm less than half a metre.

2 The longest rabbit ears are:

_____ mm

_____ cm less than 1 metre.

3 The world's longest human hair is:

_____ cm longer than 5 metres

_____ cm shorter than 6 metres.

4 The highest jump by a dog is:

_____ cm higher than a metre and a half

_____ cm less than 2 metres.

NOW TRY THIS!

• **Imagine each world record was broken by 4½ cm. Write each new record.**

Teachers' note Remind the children of the equivalents 10 mm = 1 cm and 100 cm = 1 m. Read through the world records together and encourage the children to visualise (or measure out) each length and consider the size in the context given.

A Lesson for Every Day
Maths
7–8 Years
© A&C Black

Weekend bedtime

Coco the clown's weekend show lasts [half an hour]. **He has been told that all 7-year-olds go to bed at 7:00.**

- **Should Coco's show start at 6:30?** _____
- **Put the information about the children into the** [table] **to help you.**

8:00 — Anil

7:30 — Susie

8:15 — Amy

6:45 — Tim

6:50 — Ruby

8:45 — Ben

8:30 — Josh

6:45 — Leah

8:30 — Ella

8:00 — Peter

9:00 — Tony

7:15 — Leela

8:30 — Lily

7:10 — Kate

7:10 — Tom

1 What should Coco do? _____

2 Why? _____

Teachers' note The children should consider the questions and information carefully and decide for themselves the headings for the columns on the table. If any have difficulty doing this, suggest they write 'before 7 o'clock' at the top of one column and 'after 7 o'clock' at the top of the other because this will be the time his show ends and the time Coco thinks 7-year-olds will be in bed.

A Lesson for Every Day
Maths
7–8 Years
© A&C Black

Racing cars

- **Tick to show whether each number is a multiple of 2, 5 or 10. Some numbers may be multiples of more than one of them.**

1. 125
2 ☐ 5 ☐ 10 ☐

2. 350
2 ☐ 5 ☐ 10 ☐

3. 124
2 ☐ 5 ☐ 10 ☐

4. 475
2 ☐ 5 ☐ 10 ☐

5. 292
2 ☐ 5 ☐ 10 ☐

6. 776
2 ☐ 5 ☐ 10 ☐

7. 400
2 ☐ 5 ☐ 10 ☐

8. 938
2 ☐ 5 ☐ 10 ☐

9. 177
2 ☐ 5 ☐ 10 ☐

10. 804
2 ☐ 5 ☐ 10 ☐

11. 705
2 ☐ 5 ☐ 10 ☐

12. 270
2 ☐ 5 ☐ 10 ☐

NOW TRY THIS!

- **Write 6 three-digit numbers that are multiples of 2, 5 and 10.**

☐☐☐ ☐☐☐ ☐☐☐

☐☐☐ ☐☐☐ ☐☐☐

Teachers' note At the start of the lesson remind children how to recognise numbers that are multiples of 2 (even), multiples of 5 (ending with the units digit 0 or 5) or multiples of 10 (ending with the units digit 0). Encourage them to describe what they notice about the multiples once they have completed the activity, for example that multiples of 10 are always multiples of 2 but not vice versa.

A Lesson for Every Day
Maths
7-8 Years
© A&C Black

Strawberry picking

• **Play this game with a partner.**

☆ Take turns to pick two strawberries. Decide whether to add them or to find the difference.

☆ Your partner should check your answer. If your answer is correct and it is on the grid, place one of your counters on it.

☆ Get four counters in a line to win the game.

You need one copy of this sheet.

...and counters in two colours.

Strawberries: 42, 58, 24, 71, 36, 93

35	6	29	78	100	51
117	12	16	135	129	13
113	18	94	95	47	60
22	66	129	151	57	22
164	35	107	34	82	69

Teachers' note Discuss appropriate strategies for finding sums and differences of pairs of two-digit numbers, for example using informal written approaches such as drawing number lines, or using partitioning to help in the calculation. Encourage the children to check each other's answers by using the inverse operation, for example adding 24 to 12 to check that 36 – 24 equals 12.

A Lesson for Every Day
Maths
7-8 Years
© A&C Black

A knight's challenge

- **Answer the questions on the shields and find the answers in the grid.**

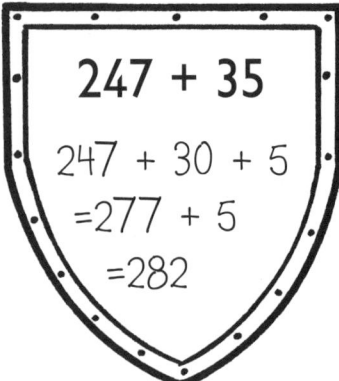

247 + 35

247 + 30 + 5
=277 + 5
=282

186 + 73

118 + 39

289 + 86

385 + 29

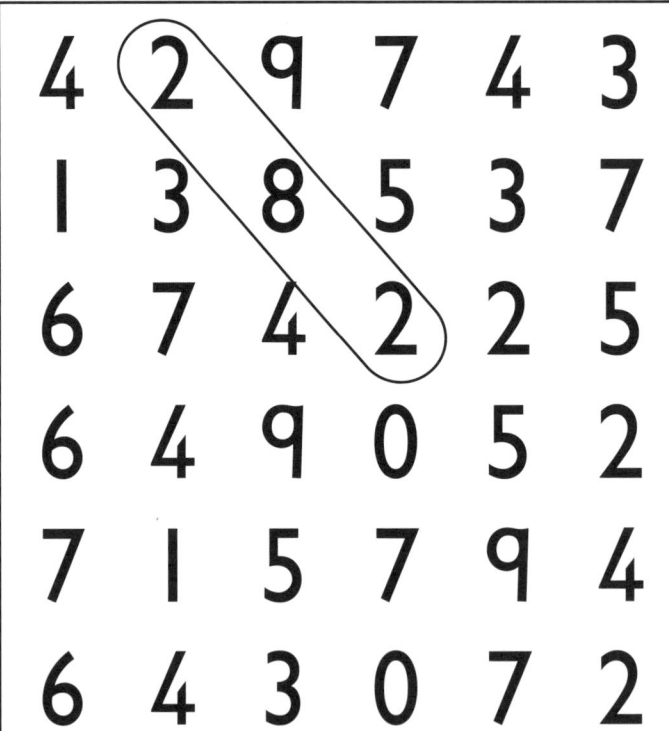

4	2	9	7	4	3
1	3	8	5	3	7
6	7	4	2	2	5
6	4	9	0	5	2
7	1	5	7	9	4
6	4	3	0	7	2

555 + 84

842 + 63

639 + 37

689 + 54

318 + 56

567 + 76

463 + 59

A Lesson for Every Day
Maths
7–8 Years
© A&C Black

Circuit training

☆ Place a counter on each circuit.

☆ Roll the dice and move each counter that number of places.

☆ Multiply the two numbers together. Show your workings.

☆ Repeat ten times. What is the **highest** answer you get?

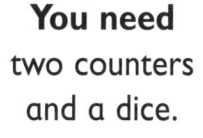

You need
two counters
and a dice.

59 81 63 47 29 58 36 44 32 38 74 61

3 4 5 6 2 2 3 4

Show your workings here.

Teachers' note Encourage the children to use an appropriate method of multiplication, such as partitioning the number into parts (for example 38 = 10 + 10 + 10 + 8) and multiplying to find each part separately before adding them together. As an extension, encourage the children to find the highest answer possible.

A Lesson for Every Day
Maths
7–8 Years
© A&C Black

Triangular tiles

The numbers on each tile can be used to write some multiplication and division facts.

• **Write four number facts for each tile.**

1.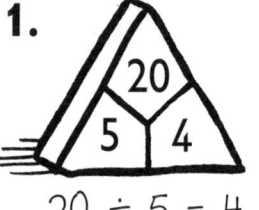

20 ÷ 5 = 4

_____

_____

_____

2.

_____

_____

_____

_____

3.

_____

_____

_____

_____

4.

_____

_____

_____

_____

5.

_____

_____

_____

_____

6.

_____

_____

_____

_____

7.

_____

_____

_____

_____

8.

_____

_____

_____

_____

NOW TRY THIS!

• **This time fill in the missing numbers first.**

(a)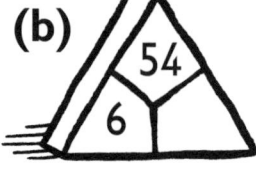

_____

_____

_____

_____

(b)

_____

_____

_____

_____

(c)

_____

_____

_____

_____

Teachers' note This activity can help children begin to appreciate that division is the inverse of multiplication, and vice versa. For the last question in the extension activity, the children should make up their own tile.

A Lesson for Every Day
Maths
7–8 Years
© A&C Black

It's your turn!

The first tile in the row is turned.

- Tick ✔ the picture which shows the correct turn.

1. One right angle turn clockwise

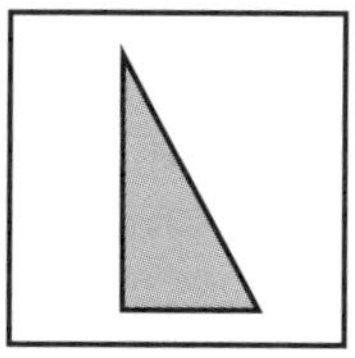

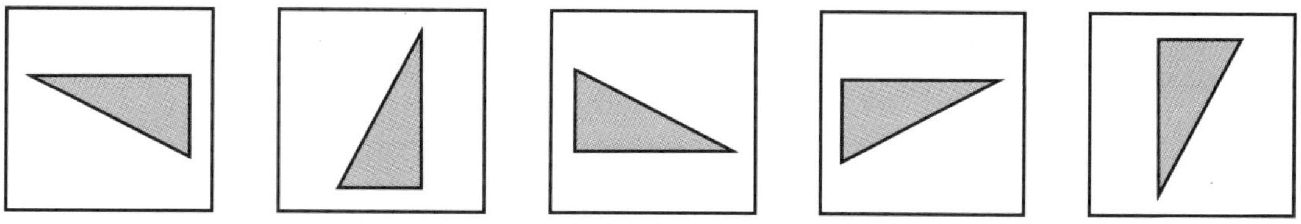

2. One half turn clockwise

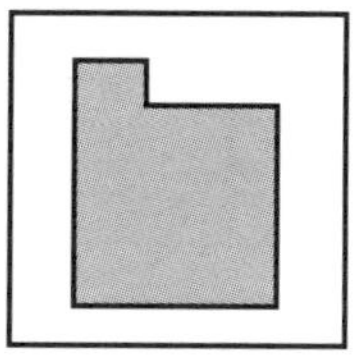

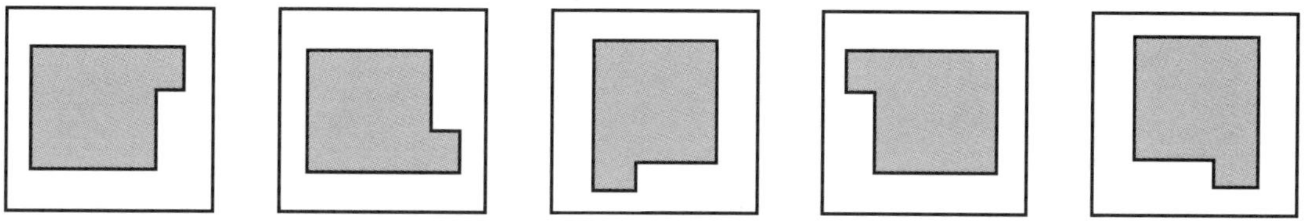

3. One right angle turn anticlockwise

4. Two right angle turns clockwise

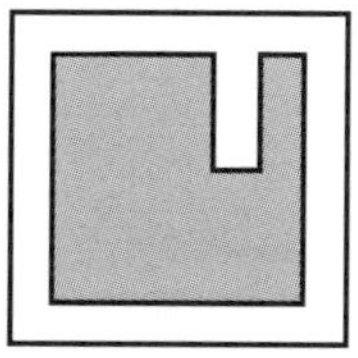

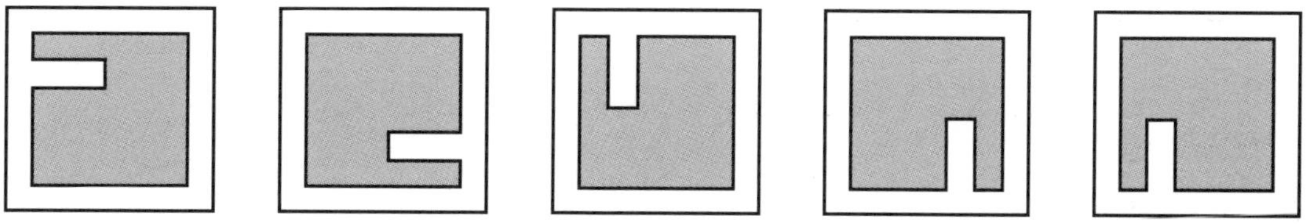

- **Draw your own tile pattern for a partner to solve.**

One right angle turn clockwise

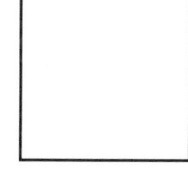  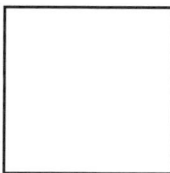  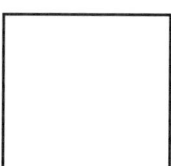

Teachers' note At the start of the lesson, demonstrate turning clockwise and anticlockwise through a number of right angles (see the notes on the activity on page 19). If necessary, the children could cut out the first tile in each row and turn it to match the description to see which picture it matches. Alternatively they could trace the tile.

A Lesson for Every Day
Maths
7-8 Years
© A&C Black

Birds' beaks

• Work with a partner.

☆ Look at the angle of each beak.

☆ Say what size you think it is.

☆ Use the right angle gobbler to check.

It looks about one-third of a right angle.

Mmm.

NOW TRY THIS!

• **Cut out the birds.**
• **Put the angles of the beaks in order, smallest to largest.**

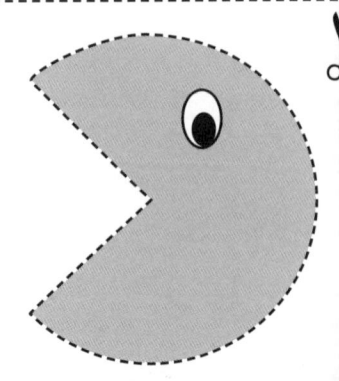

Teachers' note Children find the concept of angle very difficult and can wrongly confuse angle with the length of the beak or the distance between the two end-points of the line. Encourage them to describe the size of the angles in relation to a right angle, for example 'I think this looks about one-third of a right angle'.

A Lesson for Every Day
Maths
7–8 Years
© A&C Black

You need Crack the code: 2.

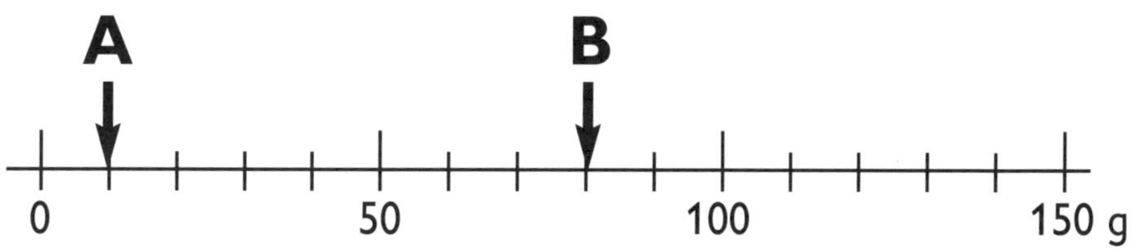

A   B

0   50   100   150 g

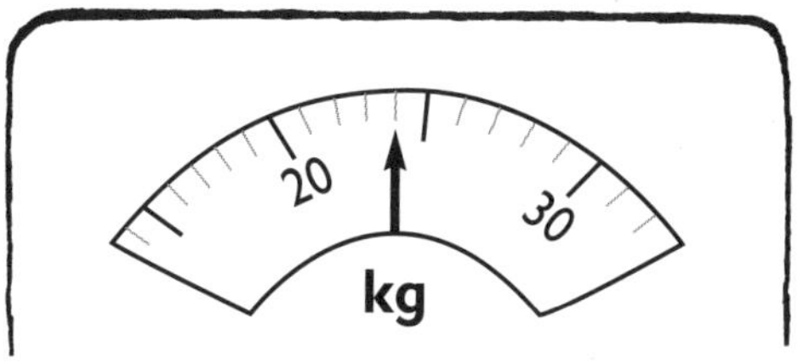

C   20   30   **kg**

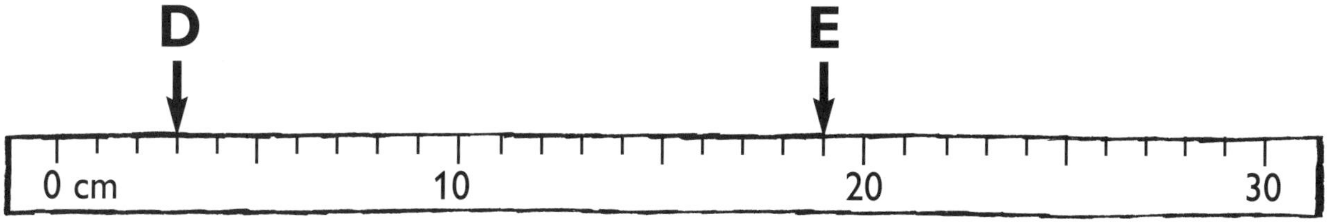

D   E

0 cm   10   20   30

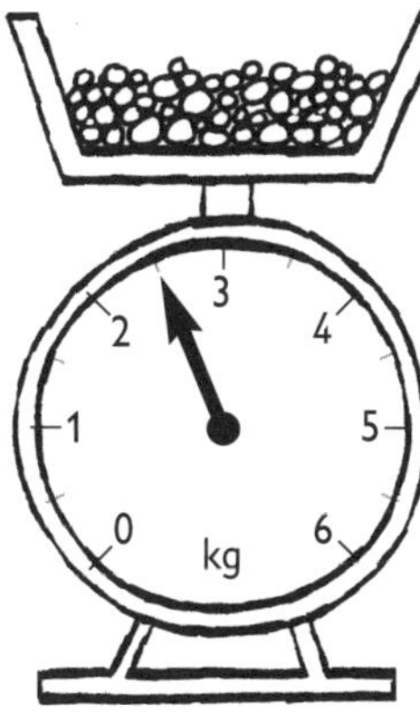

F   0 1 2 3 4 5 6 **kg**

G   700 ml 600 500 400 300 200 100

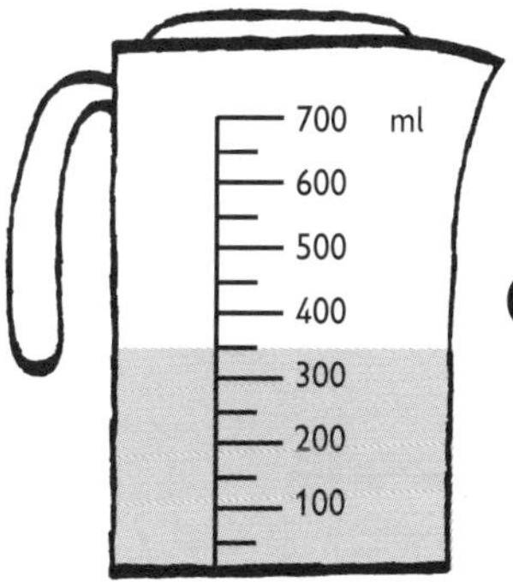

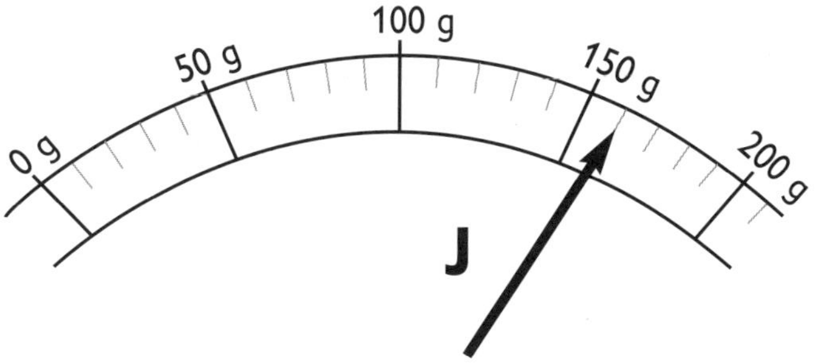

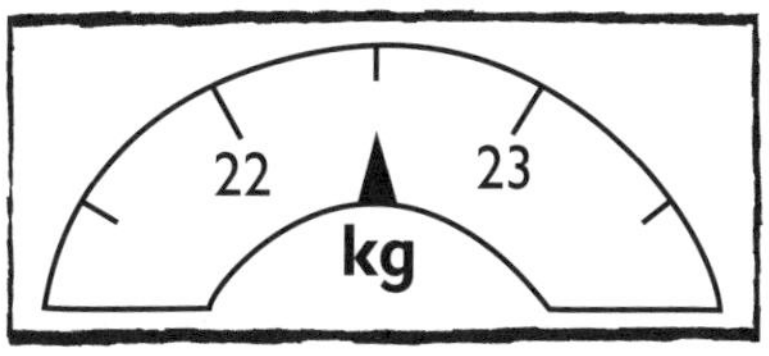

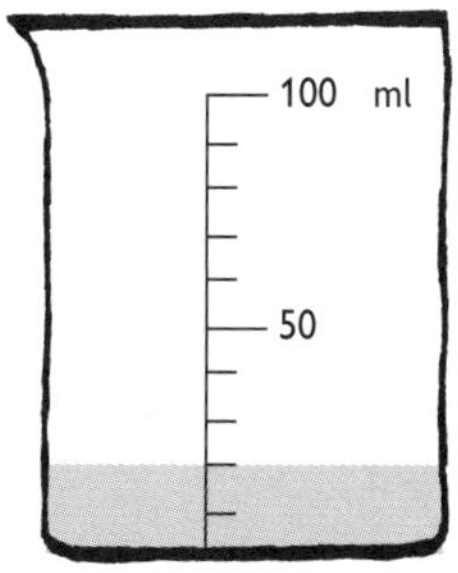

H   0 grams 50 100 150 200 250 300 350

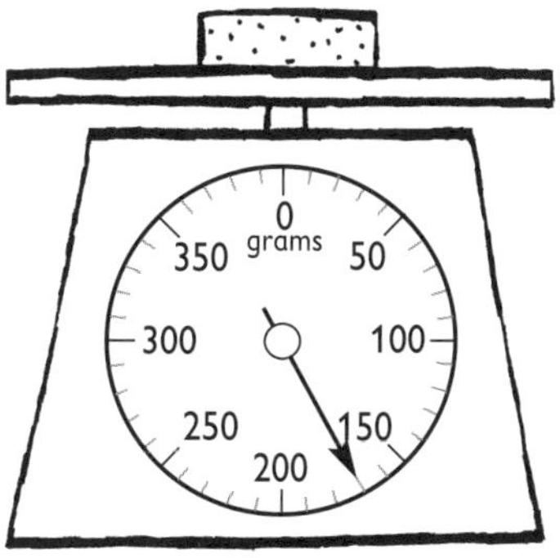

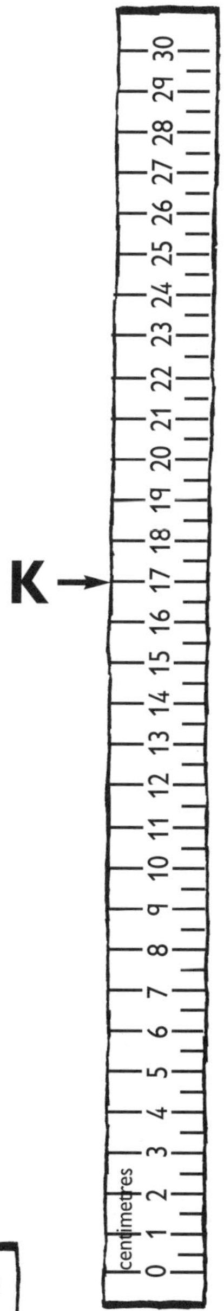

K

I   kg 0   10   20   30   40

J   0 g   50 g   100 g   150 g   200 g

L   1400 ml 1200 1000 800 600 400 200

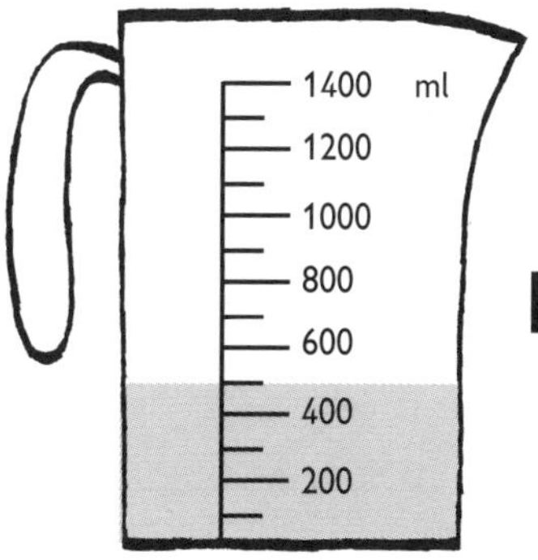

M   22   23   **kg**

N   100 ml 50

centimetres 0 1 2 3 4 5 6 7 8 9 10 11 12 13 14 15 16 17 18 19 20 21 22 23 24 25 26 27 28 29 30

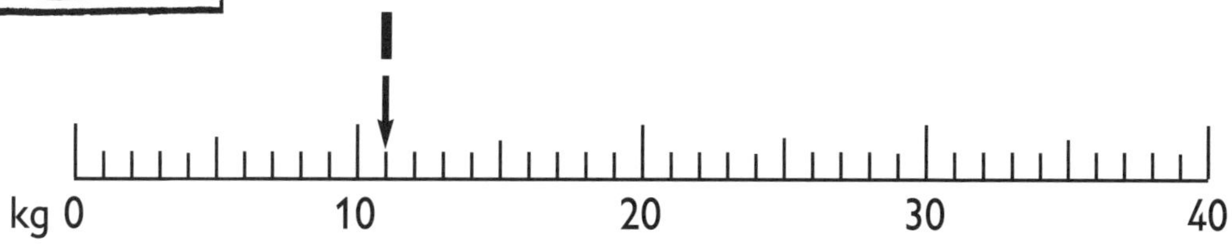

Teachers' note Use this sheet in conjunction with 'Crack the code: 2'. Some children might benefit from this sheet being enlarged to A3 size so that they can number the intermediate, unnumbered divisions.

• You need Crack the code: 1.

☆ Read the scales and record the answers below.

☆ Find the answers in the key and copy out the matching letter pairs on scrap paper.

☆ When you have worked out what the sentence says, copy it out neatly at the bottom of this sheet.

A [10g]   **B** [   ]   **C** [   ]

D [   ]   **E** [   ]   **F** [   ]

G [   ]   **H** [   ]   **I** [   ]

J [   ]   **K** [   ]   **L** [   ]

M [   ]   **N** [   ]

Key

500 ml	10g	24 kg	160 g	19 cm	350 ml	20 ml
ea	be	gc	yo	er	lk	hy

3 cm	11 kg	80 g	$2\frac{1}{2}$ kg	$22\frac{1}{2}$ kg	17 cm	170 g
he	ps	in	fu	lt	uh	ee

• Copy the sentence here.

be

Teachers' note Use this sheet in conjunction with 'Crack the code: 1'. Encourage the children to cross off each answer as they write the letters in order. If the children have written 2.5 kg rather than $2\frac{1}{2}$ kg, ensure they realise that this is the same measurement.

A Lesson for Every Day
Maths
7–8 Years
© A&C Black

At the airport

• **Write how long it is before each plane leaves.**

1. Flight B253a to Berlin
Leaving at **11:20**

| 15 | minutes

2. Flight B192a to Paris
Leaving at **7:05**

| | minutes

3. Flight B124b to Lisbon
Leaving at **6:50**

| | minutes

4. Flight B457a to Oslo
Leaving at **3:15**

| | minutes

5. Flight B444a to Munich
Leaving at **6:05**

| | minutes

6. Flight B945b to Nice
Leaving at **1:25**

| | minutes

7. Flight B111b to Malaga
Leaving at **2:35**

| | minutes

8. Flight B754c to Athens
Leaving at **11:10**

| | minutes

Teachers' note As an extension, the children could be given the lengths of the flights and asked to work out the arrival times in each of the destinations, for example the Nice flight is 2 hours and 20 minutes, the Athens flight is 3 hours 10 minutes, etc.

A Lesson for Every Day
Maths
7–8 Years
© A&C Black

The TV race

• Play this game with a partner.

You need one counter and a dice.

☆ Start by placing the counter anywhere on the trail.

☆ Take turns to roll the dice and move the counter forward.

☆ Answer the question and cross off the time on your time strip.

☆ Cross off five times in a row on your strip to win the game.

A TV show starts at 3:30. It lasts for three-quarters of an hour. What time does it end?	Half an hour ago, a TV show started at 3:55. What time is it now?	A TV show has been on for quarter of an hour. The time now is 5:10. What time did it start?
A TV show starts at quarter to four. It lasts for one hour. What time does it end?		A film lasts for $1\frac{1}{2}$ hours. It will end at twenty past six. What time did it start?
A film finishes at five past six. If it has been on for 2 hours, what time did it start?		A TV show finishes at five past five. If it has been on for 25 minutes, what time did it start?
A quarter of an hour ago, a TV show started at five to four. What time is it now?		Three-quarters of an hour ago, a TV show started at 3:35. What time is it now?
A TV show has been on for three-quarters of an hour. It is now 5.20. What time did it start?		A film lasts for $1\frac{1}{4}$ hours. It began at 3:15. What time does it end?
A TV show starts at twenty to four. It lasts for 45 minutes. What time does it end?	A TV show finishes at half past five. It has been on for 55 minutes. What time did it start?	A TV show starts at quarter past three. It lasts for 45 minutes. What time does it end?

Player 1's time strip

4:00	4:05	4:10	4:15	4:20	4:25	4:30	4:35	4:40	4:45	4:50	4:55

Player 2's time strip

4:00	4:05	4:10	4:15	4:20	4:25	4:30	4:35	4:40	4:45	4:50	4:55

Teachers' note The children should move the counter in a clockwise direction.

A Lesson for Every Day
Maths
7–8 Years
© A&C Black

Centi-pods

A centi-pod is a strange creature that grows 1 cm each year of its life. Each section of its body is a straight line that is 1 cm long.

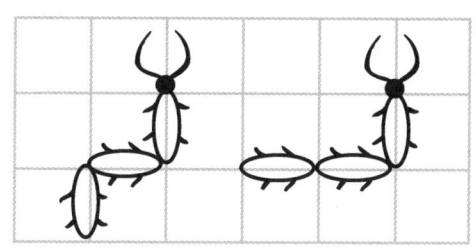

These are 3 years old

Investigate different aged centi-pods.

- How many different 2-year-old centi-pods can you draw? Then try 3-year-old ones and so on.

NOW TRY THIS!

- Make a poster about all the things you have discovered about the centi-pods.
- Organise the poster clearly so that others can see what you found out.

Teachers' note Explain that the bodies of centi-pods hinge at the end of each straight section and can bend to 90° (i.e. they can only be drawn along the grid lines of the squared paper). Urge children to observe when centi-pods are the same but rotated or reflected. Provide plain and squared paper for the extension activity. Ask the children to present their findings clearly using diagrams and words.

A Lesson for Every Day
Maths
7–8 Years
© A&C Black

The $\boxed{\text{total}}$ of the petal numbers must make the centre number.

These two flowers are the **same**...

- **Can you see why?**

Every petal must show a whole number greater than zero.

- **How many** $\boxed{\text{different}}$ **possible ways are there to make the total** $\boxed{8}$ **?**

NOW TRY THIS!

- **What about the total** $\boxed{9}$ **?**

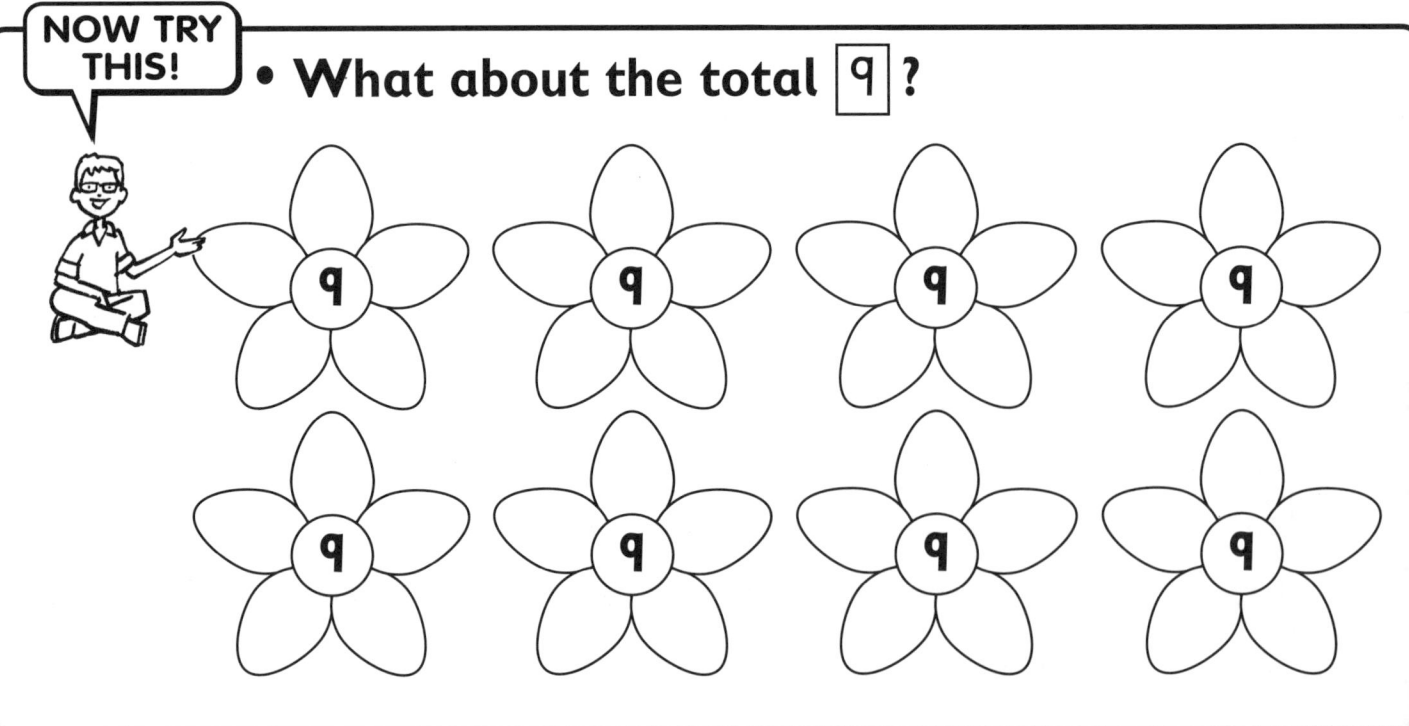

Teachers' note Stress that the number zero cannot be used. The following sheet can be used to investigate other totals between 5 and 12. Encourage the children to generalise and look for patterns in the numbers of possible different ways there are for each number. See notes to the activity on page 19 for more information about the patterns.

A Lesson for Every Day
Maths
7-8 Years
© A&C Black

Teachers' note Use this sheet in conjunction with the previous page for investigating different possible totals. See notes on the activity on page 19 for more information. Numbers can be written into the centres of the flowers before copying or given blank for children to investigate their own numbers.

A Lesson for Every Day
Maths
7–8 Years
© A&C Black

Ways to pay

- **Write different ways to pay each amount below.**
- **Then write the | fewest | number of coins needed to pay.**

		Fewest number of coins needed
1p	1p	1 coin
2p	2p or 1p + 1p	1 coin
3p	2p + 1p or 1p + 1p + 1p	2 coins
4p		
5p		
6p		
7p		
8p		
9p		
10p		
11p		
12p		
13p		
14p		
15p		
16p		
17p		
18p		
19p		
20p		

NOW TRY THIS!

- **Which amounts between | 20p | and | 40p | cannot be bought with 3 or fewer coins?**

Teachers' note Encourage children to look for patterns in the numbers and to make predictions about larger amounts. They could group the amounts between 1p and 20p into groups according to the fewest coins needed. See notes on the activity on page 20 for more information. Children could ask their own questions like that in the extension activity and investigate amounts further.

A Lesson for Every Day
Maths
7-8 Years
© A&C Black

Patterns

• **Fill in the missing digits to continue the patterns.**

4 7 + [ ] 8 = 5 5	1 5 + 1 9 = 3 4
3 7 + 1 8 = 5 5	1 5 + 2 9 = 4 4
[ ] [ ] + 2 8 = 5 5	1 5 + [ ] [ ] = 5 4
[ ] [ ] + [ ] [ ] = 5 5	[ ] [ ] + [ ] [ ] = [ ] [ ]
[ ] [ ] + [ ] [ ] = [ ] [ ]	[ ] [ ] + [ ] [ ] = [ ] [ ]

[ ] 7 + 3 5 = 4 2	3 0 + 5 2 = 8 2
1 7 + 3 5 = 5 2	2 9 + 5 2 = 8 1
2 7 + 3 5 = 6 2	2 8 + 5 2 = 8 0
[ ] [ ] + [ ] [ ] = [ ] [ ]	[ ] [ ] + [ ] [ ] = [ ] [ ]
[ ] [ ] + [ ] [ ] = [ ] [ ]	[ ] [ ] + [ ] [ ] = [ ] [ ]

8 5 + [ ] 8 = 9 3	[ ] 7 + [ ] 7 = 1 4
7 5 + 1 8 = 9 3	1 7 + 1 7 = 3 4
6 5 + 2 8 = 9 3	2 7 + 2 7 = 5 4
[ ] [ ] + [ ] [ ] = 9 3	[ ] [ ] + [ ] [ ] = [ ] [ ]
[ ] [ ] + [ ] [ ] = [ ] [ ]	[ ] [ ] + [ ] [ ] = [ ] [ ]

NOW TRY THIS!

• **Talk to a partner about the patterns above.**

Teachers' note Encourage children to discuss the patterns in the numbers and to say whether it is the tens or units digit changing each time and which numbers in the calculations are increasing or decreasing.

A Lesson for Every Day
Maths
7-8 Years
© A&C Black

Snail trail

• Play this game with a partner.

☆ Take turns to roll the dice and move your counter round the trail.

☆ Answer the question and find the answer on a snail. If it is not coloured, shade it in your colour.

☆ The first player to colour four snails in a line is the winner.

> **You need** a dice and a different-coloured pencil and counter each.

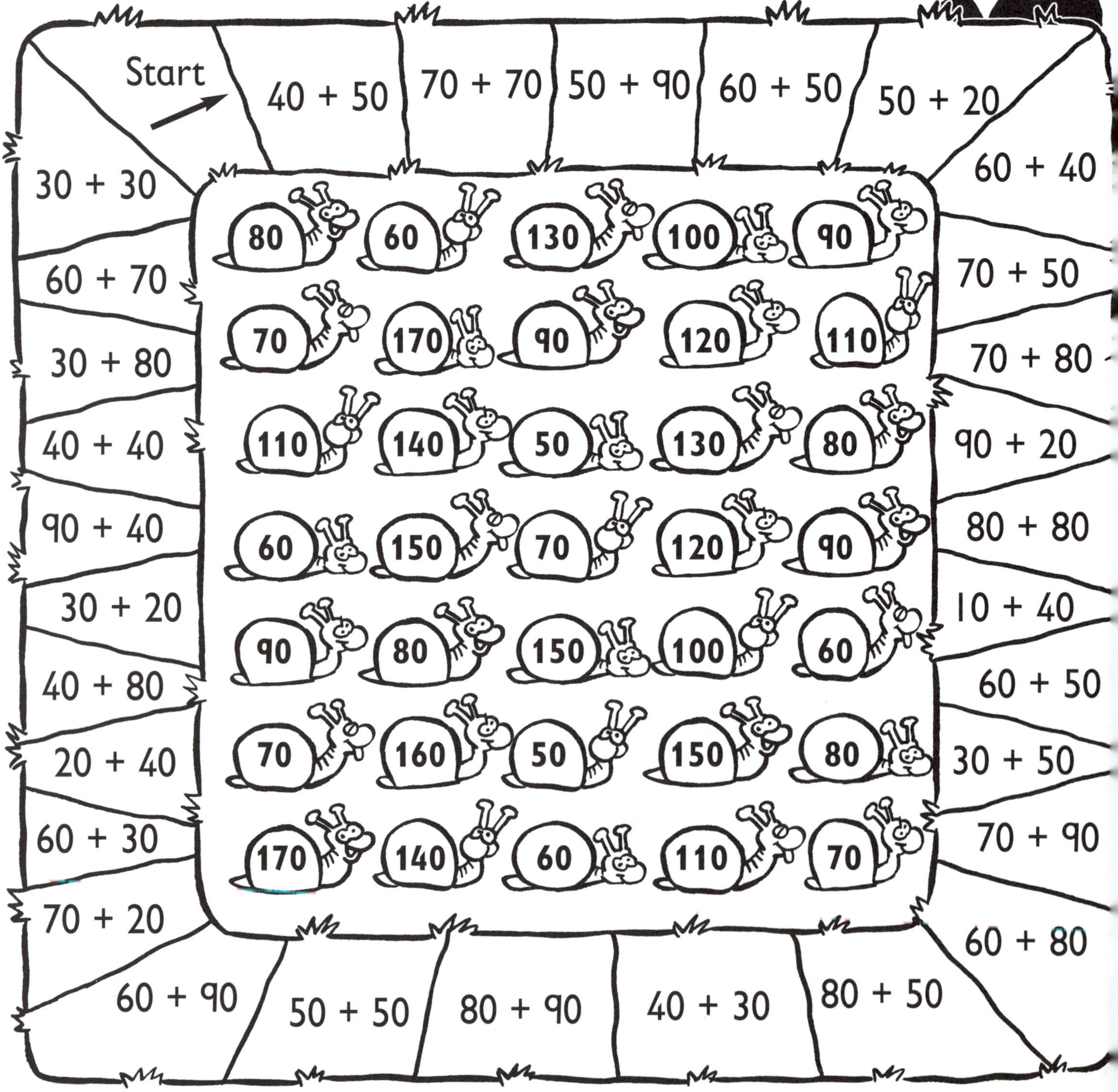

Start →

40 + 50 | 70 + 70 | 50 + 90 | 60 + 50 | 50 + 20

30 + 30

60 + 40

60 + 70

70 + 50

30 + 80

70 + 80

40 + 40

90 + 20

90 + 40

80 + 80

30 + 20

10 + 40

40 + 80

60 + 50

20 + 40

30 + 50

60 + 30

70 + 90

70 + 20

60 + 80

60 + 90 | 50 + 50 | 80 + 90 | 40 + 30 | 80 + 50

Snails:
80 · 60 · 130 · 100 · 90
70 · 170 · 90 · 120 · 110
110 · 140 · 50 · 130 · 80
60 · 150 · 70 · 120 · 90
90 · 80 · 150 · 100 · 60
70 · 160 · 50 · 150 · 80
170 · 140 · 60 · 110 · 70

Teachers' note At the start of the lesson, demonstrate the link between adding pairs of single-digit numbers and adding multiples of ten, for example 3 + 8 = 11 and 30 + 80 = 110. Show how the multiples of ten can be written as 3 tens + 8 tens = 11 tens. As an extension activity, ask the children to write ten facts with the answer 130, using multiples of ten.

A Lesson for Every Day
Maths
7–8 Years
© A&C Black

The great escape

Answers $\boxed{50}$ **or** $\boxed{60}$ **show the route from the dungeon to the only door that is unlocked.**

1. Answer the questions as quickly as you can.
2. Draw the route from the dungeon to the unlocked door.

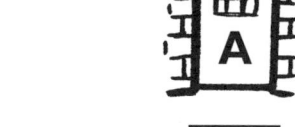 **A**  **B** **C** **D**

A	B	C	D
100 – 40 = ☐	120 – 70 = ☐	90 – 40 = ☐	100 – 30 = ☐
140 – 80 = ☐	140 – 70 = ☐	70 – 20 = ☐	150 – 80 = ☐
110 – 50 = ☐	180 – 80 = ☐	180 – 120 = ☐	160 – 90 = ☐
140 – 90 = ☐	160 – 80 = ☐		140 – 50 = ☐
80 – 30 = ☐	130 – 60 = ☐		120 – 80 = ☐
130 – 70 = ☐	170 – 90 = ☐	150 – 50 = ☐	170 – 30 = ☐
120 – 60 = ☐	130 – 80 = ☐	100 – 50 = ☐	130 – 60 = ☐
130 – 40 = ☐	100 – 80 = ☐	90 – 30 = ☐	160 – 60 = ☐
90 – 70 = ☐	110 – 60 = ☐	150 – 90 = ☐	110 – 70 = ☐
110 – 80 = ☐	80 – 20 = ☐	130 – 50 = ☐	190 – 60 = ☐

E **F** **G** **H**

Teachers' note The numbers on this sheet could be altered to provide more of a challenge to some children, for example where each three-digit number is changed from one hundred and something to two hundred and something (130 becomes 230). As an extension activity, the children could make a dungeon puzzle where all the answers are 80.

A Lesson for Every Day
Maths
7-8 Years
© A&C Black

Cracking times

- **Look, cover, write and then check.**

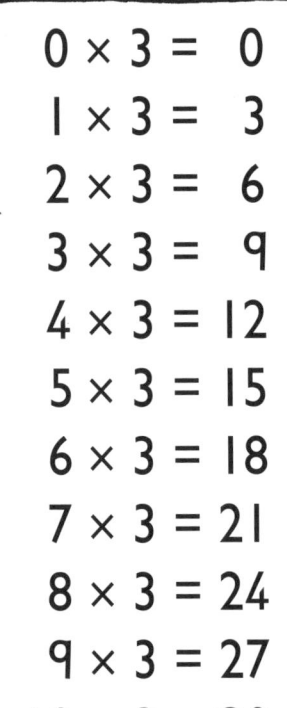

0 × 3 =	0
1 × 3 =	3
2 × 3 =	6
3 × 3 =	9
4 × 3 =	12
5 × 3 =	15
6 × 3 =	18
7 × 3 =	21
8 × 3 =	24
9 × 3 =	27
10 × 3 =	30

0 × 3 =
1 × 3 =
2 × 3 =
3 × 3 =
4 × 3 =
5 × 3 =
6 × 3 =
7 × 3 =
8 × 3 =
9 × 3 =
10 × 3 =

0 × 3 =
1 × 3 =
2 × 3 =
3 × 3 =
4 × 3 =
5 × 3 =
6 × 3 =
7 × 3 =
8 × 3 =
9 × 3 =
10 × 3 =

0 × 3 =
1 × 3 =
2 × 3 =
3 × 3 =
4 × 3 =
5 × 3 =
6 × 3 =
7 × 3 =
8 × 3 =
9 × 3 =
10 × 3 =

NOW TRY THIS!

- **Fold the sheet so you cannot see the main activity. Time yourself for these tests.**

10 × 3 =	3 × 9 =	6 × 3 =
1 × 3 =	10 × 3 =	3 × 0 =
3 × 9 =	3 × 3 =	10 × 3 =
8 × 3 =	3 × 4 =	3 × 1 =
3 × 6 =	3 × 5 =	2 × 3 =
3 × 3 =	8 × 3 =	3 × 7 =

Time:

Teachers' note Introduce the 'Look, cover, write and check' approach where children should examine the first list of answers, then cover them, then write answers for the other three lists and finally check. Provide timers for the extension activity and ensure that children understand the commutative nature of multiplication, for example that 4 × 3 has the same answer as 3 × 4.

A Lesson for Every Day
Maths
7–8 Years
© A&C Black

Tractor times

- ## Use your own methods to answer these multiplications.
- ## Talk to a partner about what you are going to do.

1.

× 5 = _____

× 3 = _____

× 4 = _____

2.

× 2 = _____

× 4 = _____

× 3 = _____

3.

× 5 = _____

× 2 = _____

× 4 = _____

4.

× 3 = _____

× 4 = _____

× 6 = _____

5.

× 5 = _____

× 3 = _____

× 6 = _____

6.

× 4 = _____

× 5 = _____

× 6 = _____

NOW TRY THIS!

- ## Ring the question which you __think__ has the largest answer.
- ## Answer the questions to check.

$23 × 6 =$ _____ $27 × 5 =$ _____ $29 × 4 =$ _____ $43 × 3 =$ _____

Teachers' note Discuss methods that could be used to answer these questions. For example, for 13 × 4 the children could find 10 × 4 and 3 × 4 and add the answers, or they could use a double, double approach (double 13, double 26). The children could use practical apparatus such as base 10 materials. Provide scrap paper for the children's workings.

A Lesson for Every Day
Maths
7-8 Years
© A&C Black

Fraction stations

On each platform there are some people.

- Use the fractions to help you fill in the missing numbers.

On Platform A there are **12** people.

$\frac{1}{4}$	are children	3
$\frac{1}{2}$	are females	
$\frac{1}{6}$	are wearing jeans	
$\frac{1}{3}$	are carrying a bag	

On Platform B there are **20** people.

$\frac{1}{20}$	are children	
$\frac{1}{2}$	are males	
$\frac{1}{10}$	are wearing hats	
$\frac{1}{5}$	are on their mobile	

On Platform C there are **30** people.

$\frac{1}{3}$	are adults	
$\frac{1}{6}$	are boys	
$\frac{1}{5}$	are chatting	
$\frac{1}{15}$	are yawning	
$\frac{1}{10}$	have a dog	
$\frac{1}{30}$	have a suitcase	

On Platform D there are **36** people.

$\frac{1}{4}$	are girls	
$\frac{1}{2}$	are adults	
$\frac{1}{9}$	are wearing boots	
$\frac{1}{6}$	are reading	
$\frac{1}{3}$	are eating	
$\frac{1}{12}$	are drinking	

NOW TRY THIS!

- **Write eight different fraction statements about the 24 people on Platform E.**

PLATFORM E

Teachers' note At the start of the lesson, demonstrate how unit fractions of numbers can be found by dividing the number by the denominator (bottom number). Encourage the children to use the fraction statements above to give them ideas for statements to use in the extension activity.

A Lesson for Every Day
Maths
7-8 Years
© A&C Black

The Street

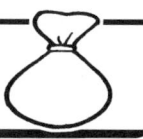

- **Talk to a partner about how to solve each problem.**

1 36 people live in the street. 4 people live in each house. How many houses are there?

$$36 \div 4 = 9$$

2 On Monday the postman delivers 3 letters to each house. How many letters does he deliver?

3 Of the 36 people in the street, 17 are children. How many are adults?

4 The houses are numbered 1 to 9. What is the total of all the house numbers?

5 3 houses have 5 windows and 6 houses have 4 windows. How many windows in total?

6 There are 7 lamp-posts on one side of the street and twice as many on the other side. How many lamp-posts altogether?

7 The street lights come on at 7 in the evening and go off at 6 in the morning. How many hours is this?

8 4 houses have 2 cars each and 5 houses have 1 car each. How many cars altogether?

NOW TRY THIS!

- **Make up** $\boxed{2}$ **of your own street questions for a partner to solve.**

Teachers' note Encourage the children to use number sentences to show what they have decided to do for each calculation and ask them to describe their methods for answering each question. They could record their strategies on the back of the sheet.

A Lesson for Every Day
Maths
7–8 Years
© A&C Black

Pick 3 cards

- **Cut out the cards.**
- **Pick ☐2☐ small cards and a question card.**
- **Solve the problem.**

Work with a partner.

How much does it cost for both items?	How much more to buy the more expensive item than the cheaper one?
If you bought the cheaper item, how much change from £5?	If you bought the more expensive item, how much change from £10?
Which is more expensive, 4 of the cheaper item or 2 of the more expensive item?	How much more to buy the more expensive item than the cheaper one?
If you bought both items, how much change from £10?	How much to buy 10 of the cheaper item?
How much to buy 2 of the more expensive item?	How much change from £10 if you buy 2 of the cheaper item?

48p 	90p 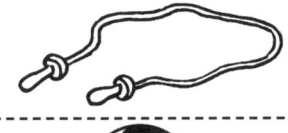	£2.55 
£3.50 	£2.99 	45p 
£2.75 	£4.99 	£2.45 
65p 	40p 	£1.25 
37p	£1.30 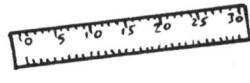	£4.50 

Teachers' note The cards could be copied onto thin card and laminated as a more practical and durable classroom resource. The prices could be changed before copying to provide differentiated sheets.

A Lesson for Every Day
Maths
7–8 Years
© A&C Black

Tile teasers

Eden has made some patterns and shapes with triangular tiles.

• Count the tiles and write what fraction of each shape is shaded.

1 $\dfrac{1}{6}$

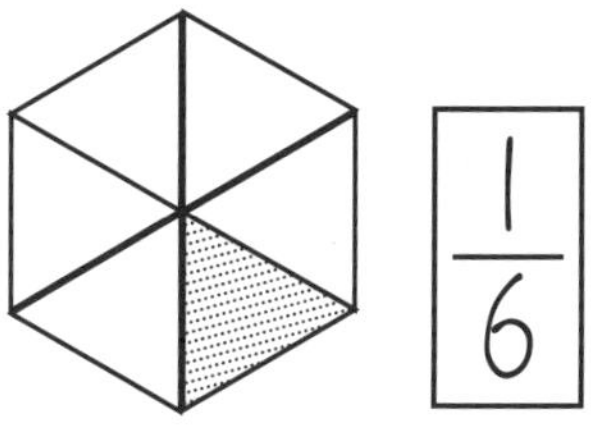

2

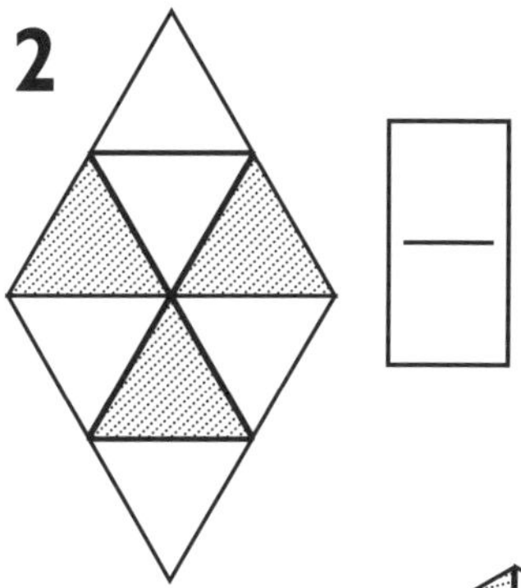

3

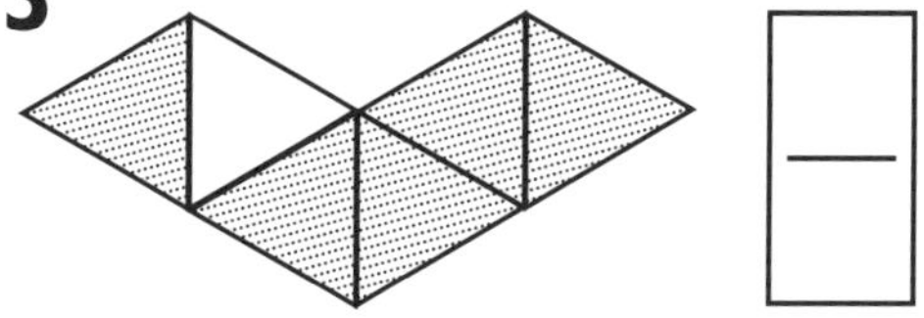

4

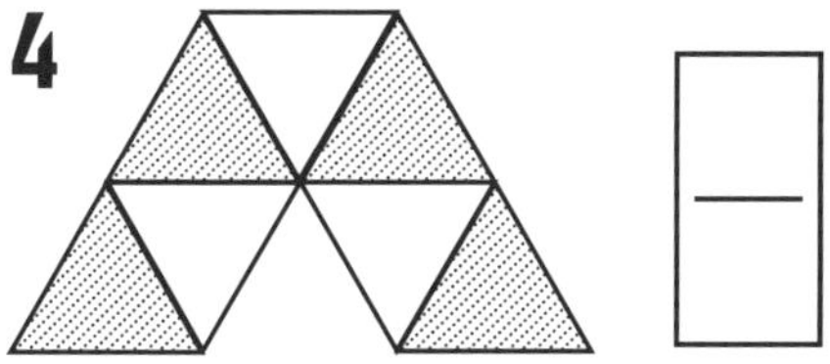

5

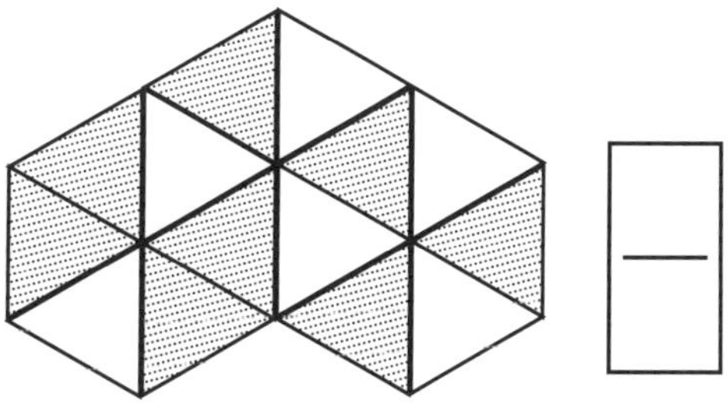

6

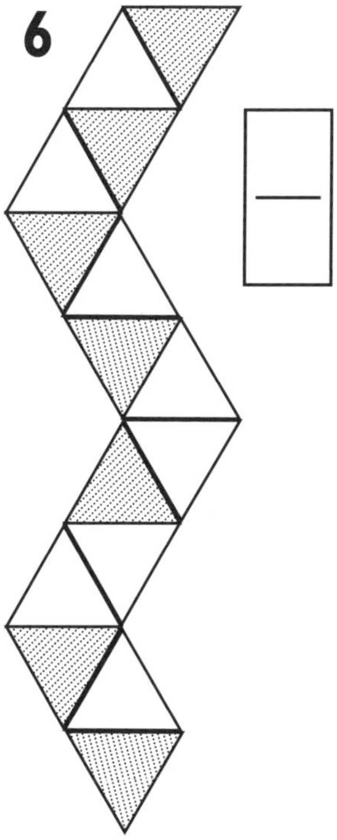

7

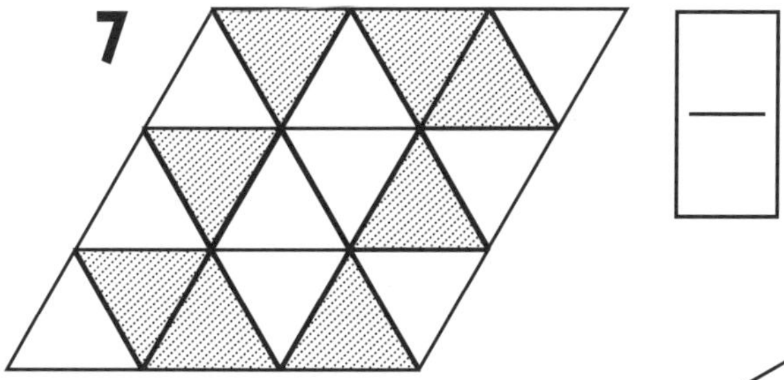

8

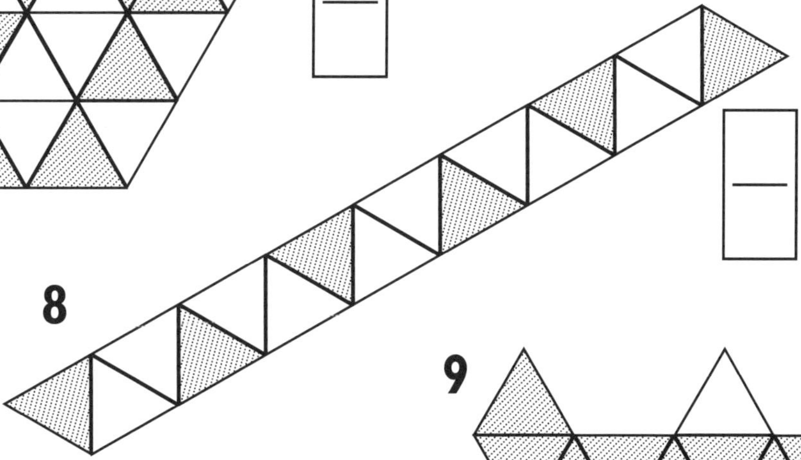

9

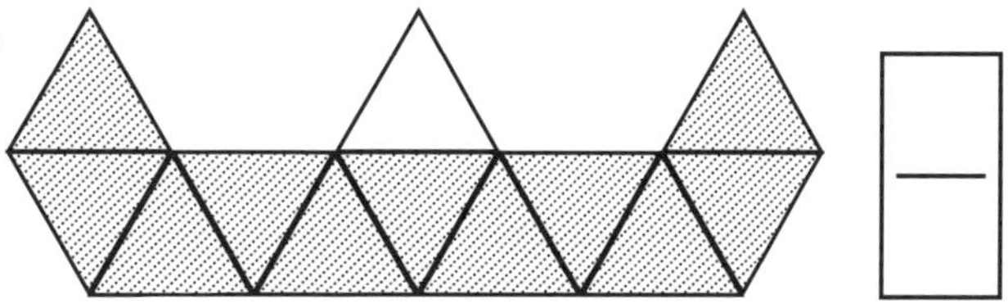

NOW TRY THIS!

• **Make some triangular tile puzzles of your own.**

• **Write what fraction of each shape is shaded.**

Teachers' note Watch out for the common error of writing the number of unshaded tiles as the denominator rather than the total number of tiles altogether, for example where 3 out of 7 tiles are shaded the children incorrectly write $\frac{3}{4}$ instead of $\frac{3}{7}$. The children will need isometric paper for the extension activity.

A Lesson for Every Day
Maths
7-8 Years
© A&C Black

Yo-ho-ho!

• Play this game with a partner.

☆ Each pick a treasure chest.

☆ Take turns to roll the dice and move
your counter around the map.

☆ Work out the answer to the question, and if
you can, cross off the answer in your treasure chest.

☆ The winner is the first player to cross off all their coins.

You need
a counter each
and a dice.

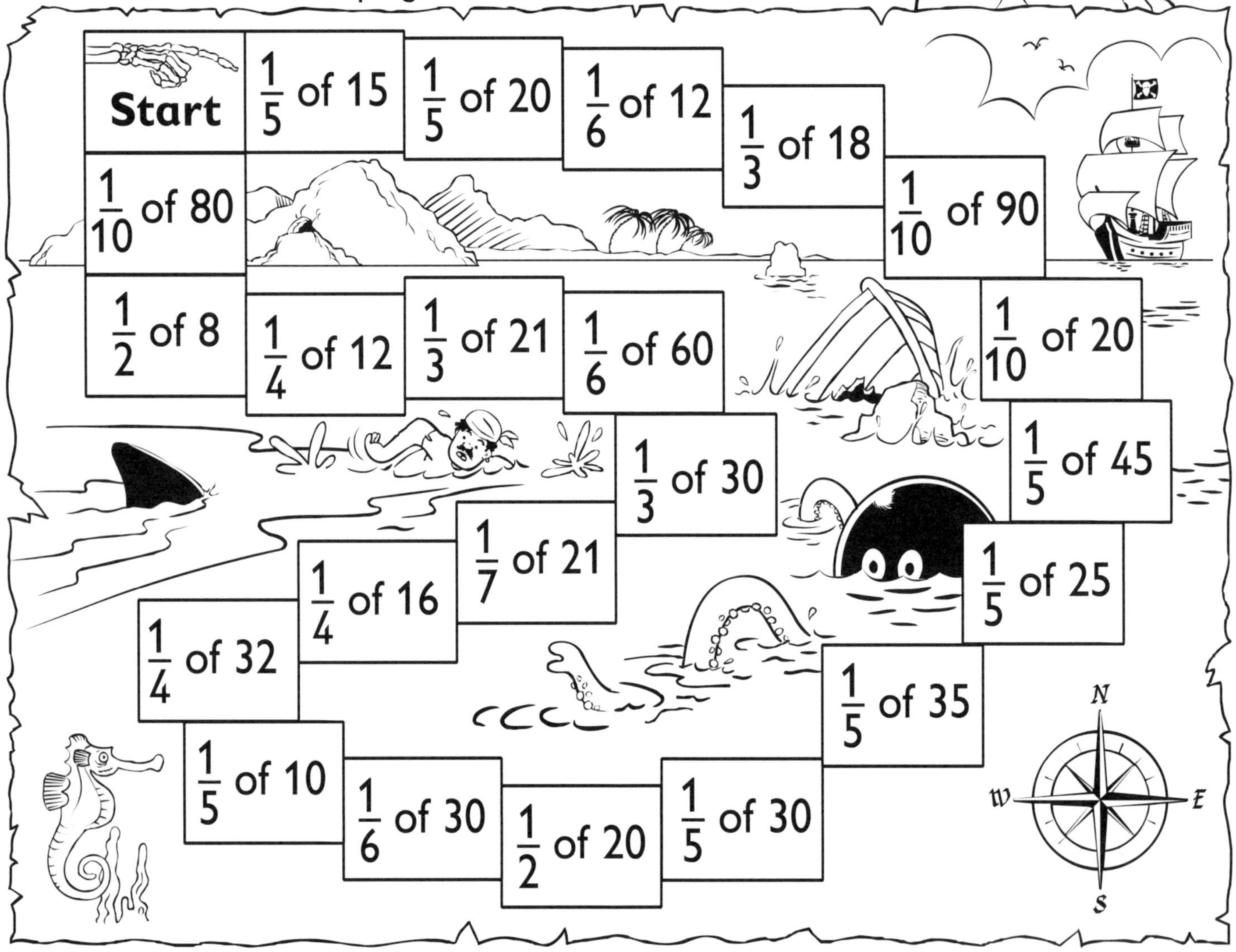

| Start | $\frac{1}{5}$ of 15 | $\frac{1}{5}$ of 20 | $\frac{1}{6}$ of 12 | $\frac{1}{3}$ of 18 | |
| $\frac{1}{10}$ of 80 | | | | $\frac{1}{10}$ of 90 | |

$\frac{1}{2}$ of 8 $\frac{1}{4}$ of 12 $\frac{1}{3}$ of 21 $\frac{1}{6}$ of 60 $\frac{1}{10}$ of 20

$\frac{1}{3}$ of 30 $\frac{1}{5}$ of 45

$\frac{1}{7}$ of 21 $\frac{1}{5}$ of 25

$\frac{1}{4}$ of 16

$\frac{1}{4}$ of 32

$\frac{1}{5}$ of 35

$\frac{1}{5}$ of 10 $\frac{1}{6}$ of 30 $\frac{1}{2}$ of 20 $\frac{1}{5}$ of 30

N *W* *E* *S*

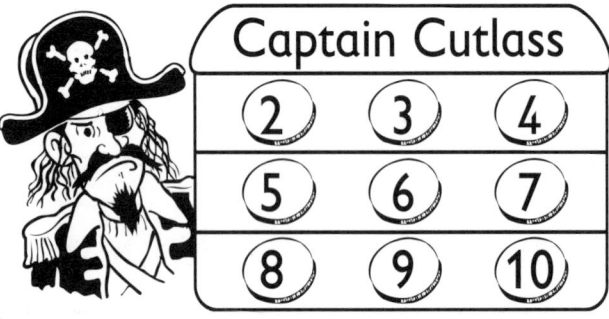

Captain Cutlass

2	3	4
5	6	7
8	9	10

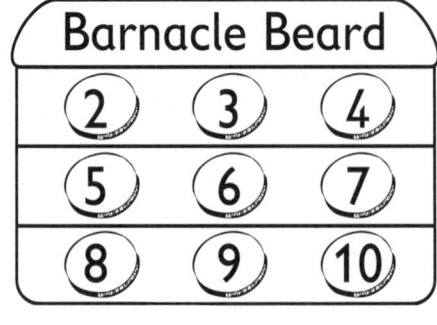

Barnacle Beard

2	3	4
5	6	7
8	9	10

Teachers' note Ensure the children understand that when finding a unit fraction of a number, they should divide the number into equal parts, according to the denominator, for example, $\frac{1}{5}$ of 20 is 20 divided by 5.

A Lesson for Every Day
Maths
7–8 Years
© A&C Black

Colourful kaleidoscopes

- **Colour the kaleidoscope to match the description.**

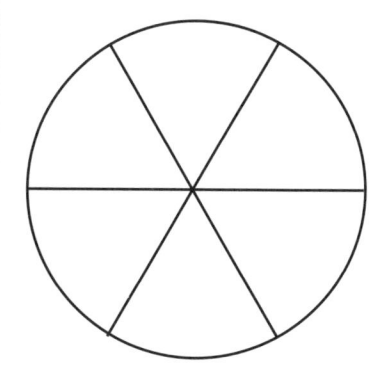

$\frac{1}{6}$ is red

$\frac{1}{2}$ is blue

$\frac{1}{3}$ is yellow

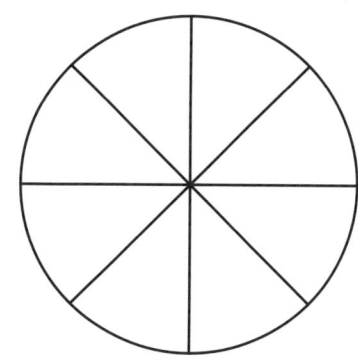

$\frac{1}{8}$ is red

$\frac{3}{8}$ is blue

$\frac{1}{2}$ is yellow

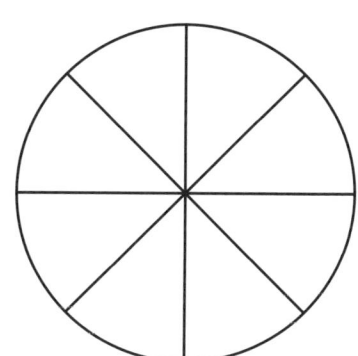

$\frac{2}{8}$ is red

$\frac{1}{2}$ is blue

$\frac{1}{4}$ is yellow

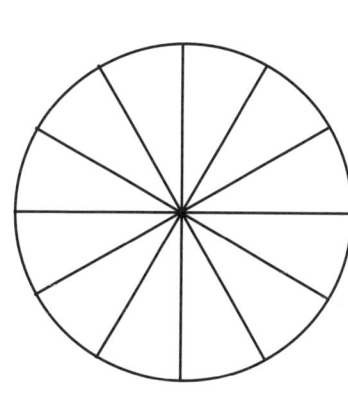

$\frac{1}{12}$ is red

$\frac{1}{2}$ is blue

$\frac{1}{6}$ is yellow

$\frac{1}{4}$ is orange

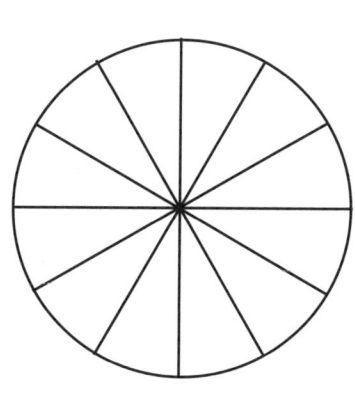

$\frac{5}{12}$ is red

$\frac{1}{6}$ is blue

$\frac{1}{4}$ is yellow

$\frac{2}{12}$ is orange

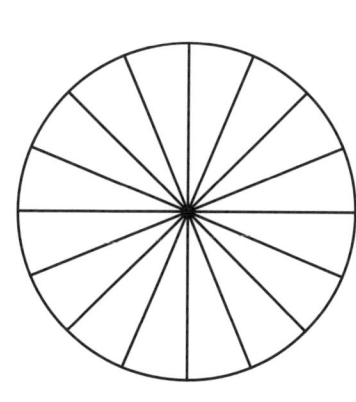

$\frac{2}{16}$ is red

$\frac{1}{8}$ is blue

$\frac{1}{4}$ is yellow

$\frac{1}{2}$ is orange

NOW TRY THIS!

- **Make some more kaleidoscope patterns and describe them using fractions.**

Teachers' note This activity can really test a child's understanding of fractions. There are a variety of ways in which children can work out how many sections to shade in each colour. One way is to ask the children to find fractions of number, for example by finding $\frac{1}{4}$ of 8 or $\frac{1}{6}$ of 12. For more information, see the notes on the activity on page 21.

A Lesson for Every Day
Maths
7–8 Years
© A&C Black

Motorcycle race

- **Play this game with a partner.**
  You need a counter each and a dice.

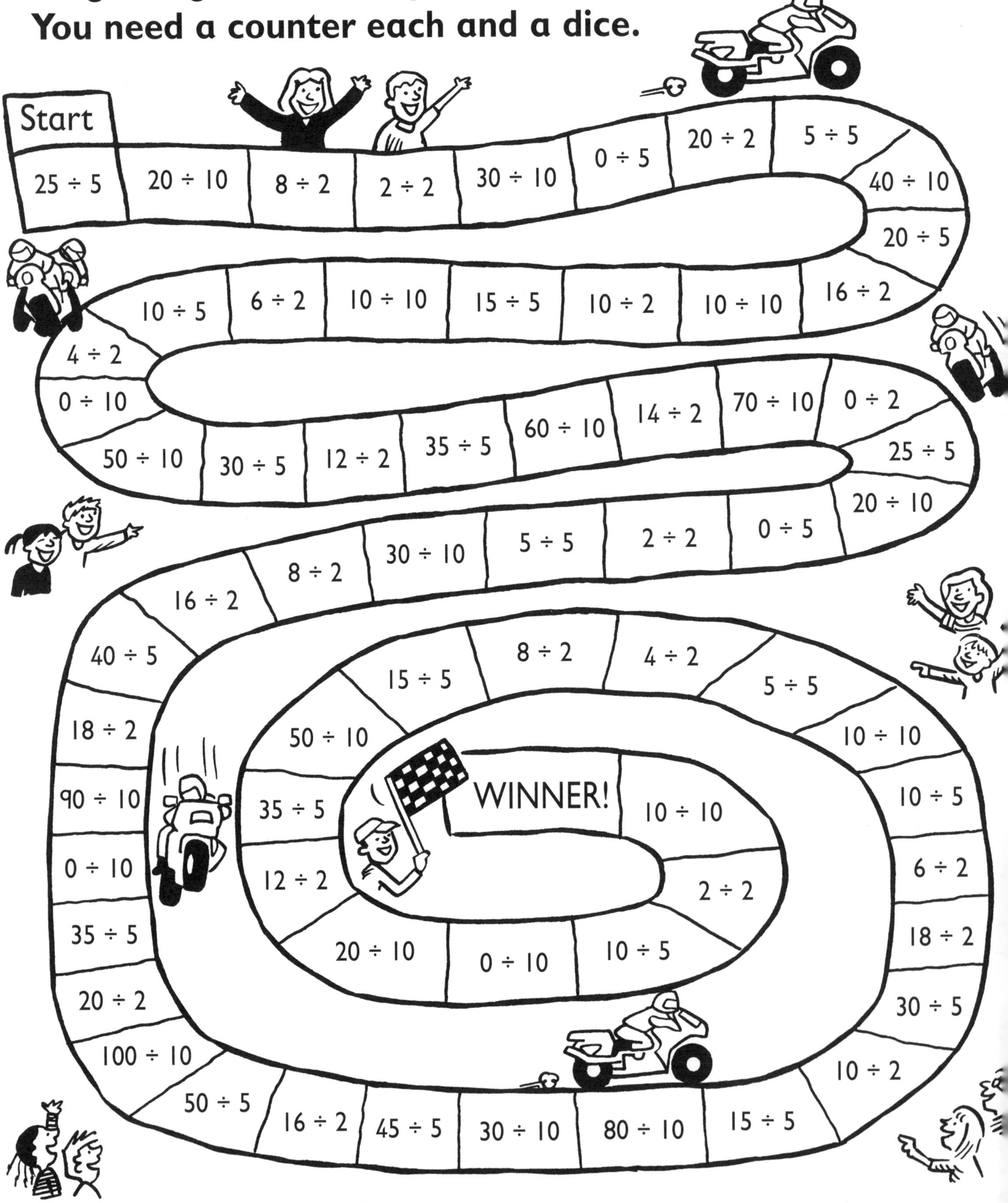

Start

| 25 ÷ 5 | 20 ÷ 10 | 8 ÷ 2 | 2 ÷ 2 | 30 ÷ 10 | 0 ÷ 5 | 20 ÷ 2 | 5 ÷ 5 |

40 ÷ 10

20 ÷ 5

| 10 ÷ 5 | 6 ÷ 2 | 10 ÷ 10 | 15 ÷ 5 | 10 ÷ 2 | 10 ÷ 10 | 16 ÷ 2 |

4 ÷ 2

0 ÷ 10

| 50 ÷ 10 | 30 ÷ 5 | 12 ÷ 2 | 35 ÷ 5 | 60 ÷ 10 | 14 ÷ 2 | 70 ÷ 10 | 0 ÷ 2 |

25 ÷ 5

20 ÷ 10

| 8 ÷ 2 | 30 ÷ 10 | 5 ÷ 5 | 2 ÷ 2 | 0 ÷ 5 |

16 ÷ 2

40 ÷ 5   15 ÷ 5   8 ÷ 2   4 ÷ 2   5 ÷ 5

18 ÷ 2   50 ÷ 10   10 ÷ 10

90 ÷ 10   35 ÷ 5   **WINNER!**   10 ÷ 10   10 ÷ 5

0 ÷ 10   12 ÷ 2   2 ÷ 2   6 ÷ 2

35 ÷ 5   20 ÷ 10   0 ÷ 10   10 ÷ 5   18 ÷ 2

20 ÷ 2   30 ÷ 5

100 ÷ 10   10 ÷ 2

50 ÷ 5   16 ÷ 2   45 ÷ 5   30 ÷ 10   80 ÷ 10   15 ÷ 5

Teachers' note As players take turns to roll the dice and move forward they answer the question and then move forward the number of places in the answer, for example if they land on 4 ÷ 2 they move forward an extra two places. Play then moves to the next player. This sheet can be copied onto A3 and laminated for a more permanent resource.

190

A Lesson for Every Day
Maths
7–8 Years
© A&C Black

The Meddler

The Meddler likes to multiply by 100, but he also loves to meddle with the answers!

- ✓ or ✗ to show whether these facts are true or false, and write the correct answers.

1.
$9 \times 100 = 9000$

900

☒

2.
45 multiplied by 100 is 4500

☐

3.
86 times 100 is 8600

☐

4.
63 multiplied by 100 is 630

☐

5.
$52 \times 100 = 520$

☐

6.
10 multiplied by 100 is 1000

☐

7.
30 multiplied by 100 is 300

☐

8.
17 times 100 is 1700

☐

9.
$78 \times 100 = 780$

☐

10.
7 lots of 100 is 700

☐

11.
124 times 100 is 124 000

☐

12.
350 multiplied by 100 is 3500

☐

NOW TRY THIS!

- **Answer these questions.**

(a) ☐ × 100 = 700 (b) ☐ × 100 = 8000

(c) ☐ × 100 = 1800 (d) ☐ × 100 = 36 000

Teachers' note Use a strip of paper to illustrate the effect of multiplying by 100, showing how the digits move two places to the left and zeros are used to show the empty columns. Encourage the children to appreciate the movement of the digits rather than focusing on 'putting two zeros on the end', as this will cause them difficulties when multiplying decimals in the future.

A Lesson for Every Day
Maths
7–8 Years
© A&C Black

Cruncher: 1

When the handle is pulled, the number is divided by $\boxed{10}$.

• **Write the digits of the answer in the correct columns.**

1.

H	T	U
	4	0
		4

2.

H	T	U
	7	0

3.

H	T	U
2	8	0

4.

H	T	U
5	1	0

5.

H	T	U
3	3	0

6.

H	T	U
6	9	0

7.

H	T	U
1	4	0

8.

H	T	U
4	0	0

9.

H	T	U
7	0	0

NOW TRY THIS!

• **Divide these numbers by 10 in the same way.**

(a)

Th	H	T	U
2	8	4	0

(b)

Th	H	T	U
7	5	3	0

(c)

Th	H	T	U
1	9	0	0

Talk to a partner about how you divide a number by 10.

Teachers' note Encourage the children to appreciate the movement of the digits rather than focusing on 'getting rid of the zero from the end', as this will cause them difficulties when dividing numbers that do not have a zero in the units column, for example 35 ÷ 10 = 3.5, not 3.

A Lesson for Every Day
Maths
7–8 Years
© A&C Black

Cruncher: 2

When the handle is pulled, the number is divided by | 100 |.
- Write the digits of the answer in the correct columns.

1.

Th	H	T	U
	5	0	0
			5

2.

Th	H	T	U
4	2	0	0

3.

Th	H	T	U
2	9	0	0

4.

Th	H	T	U
1	8	0	0

5.

Th	H	T	U
	7	0	0

6.

Th	H	T	U
6	0	0	0

7.

Th	H	T	U
3	3	0	0

8.

Th	H	T	U
	2	0	0	0

9.

Th	H	T	U
7	5	0	0

NOW TRY THIS!

- Divide these numbers by 100 in the same way.

(a)

TTh	Th	H	T	U
2	4	5	0	0

(b)

TTh	Th	H	T	U
4	0	7	0	0

(c)

TTh	Th	H	T	U
1	9	0	0	0

Talk to a partner about how you divide a number by 100.

Teachers' note Encourage the children to appreciate the movement of the digits rather than focusing on 'getting rid of two zeros from the end', as this will cause them difficulties when dividing numbers that do not have zeros in both the units and tens columns, for example 350 ÷ 100 = 3.5, not 35 or 3.

A Lesson for Every Day
Maths
7–8 Years
© A&C Black

Lost and found

Alfie has lost something.

- **First answer the questions.**
- **Then use the key to spell out what Alfie is looking for.**

125 O	164 E	336 T	288 S
64 R	192 U	185 D	375 N
184 P	415 A	348 S	234 N

1. There are 64 chocolates in a box. How many chocolates are in 3 boxes?

`192`

2. I have 39 boxes, each holding 6 eggs. How many eggs do I have altogether?

3. Kieran has 37 toy cars. Kai has 5 times as many. How many does he have?

4. A sheep has 4 legs. How many legs do 41 sheep have?

5. A box holds 16 pencils. How many pencils are in 4 boxes?

6. An octopus has 8 legs. How many legs do 23 octopuses have?

7. 83 people pay £5 each to go to the cinema. How many pounds are spent in total?

8. Ice-creams cost 75p. If I buy 5 ice-creams, how many pence do I spend?

9. A coach holds 56 people. 6 full coaches go to the football match. How many people go by coach?

10. 72 people each win £4. How many pounds are won in total?

Alfie is looking for his _ _ _ _ _ _ _ _ _ _ _ _ !

Teachers' note The children could use any appropriate multiplication method for these questions. Encourage them to use scrap paper for their workings.

A Lesson for Every Day
Maths
7–8 Years
© A&C Black

Help! Mummy!

The engraving on each stone shows a fact.
- **Write three related multiplication or division facts on the mummy's bandages.**

1.

$18 \times 5 = 90$

$5 \times 18 = 90$ $90 \div 18 = 5$ $90 \div 5 = 18$

2.

$26 \times 3 = 78$

3.

$23 \times 4 = 92$

4.

$13 \times 5 = 65$

5.

$27 \times 6 = 162$

NOW TRY THIS!

- **Write two related number facts.**

(a)

$81 \div 3 = 27$

(b)

$145 \div 5 = 29$

Teachers' note Encourage the children to appreciate that multiplication and division are inverse operations. This can be illustrated by showing an array, such as 3 rows of 4. Demonstrate that the multiplication facts $3 \times 4 = 12$ (3 rows of 4) or $4 \times 3 = 12$ (4 columns of 3) can be written, together with $12 \div 4 = 3$ (12 split into 4 columns) and $12 \div 3 = 4$ (12 split into 3 rows).

A Lesson for Every Day
Maths
7–8 Years
© A&C Black

Teddy and Eddy

Teddy is very strong. He can lift heavy weights.

Eddy is not as strong. He can only lift a fraction of the weight that Eddy can.

- **Write the weight that Eddy is able to lift.**

1.  30 kg   Eddy lifts $\frac{1}{3}$ of this   Eddy lifts $\boxed{10}$ kg

2. 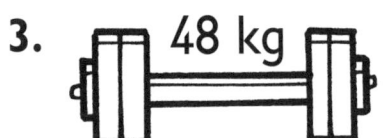 45 kg   Eddy lifts $\frac{1}{5}$ of this   Eddy lifts $\boxed{}$ kg

3.  48 kg   Eddy lifts $\frac{1}{2}$ of this   Eddy lifts $\boxed{}$ kg

4.  36 kg   Eddy lifts $\frac{1}{4}$ of this   Eddy lifts $\boxed{}$ kg

5. 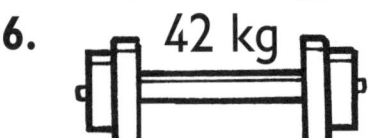 18 kg   Eddy lifts $\frac{1}{3}$ of this   Eddy lifts $\boxed{}$ kg

6. 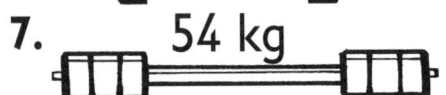 42 kg   Eddy lifts $\frac{1}{6}$ of this   Eddy lifts $\boxed{}$ kg

7. 54 kg   Eddy lifts $\frac{1}{6}$ of this   Eddy lifts $\boxed{}$ kg

---

NOW TRY THIS!

- **Write what fraction of the weight Eddy is able to lift.**

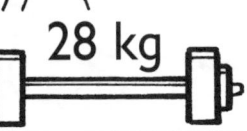 28 kg   Eddy lifts $\boxed{\frac{}{}}$ of this   Eddy lifts 7 kg

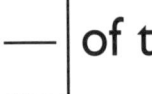

Teachers' note This activity encourages the children to see the relationship between division and finding unit fractions of numbers. At the start of the lesson, discuss how a unit fraction can be found by dividing the number by the denominator (bottom number) of the fraction. As a further extension, ask the children to write three more questions for a partner to solve.

A Lesson for Every Day
Maths
7–8 Years
© A&C Black

- **For each question, write a calculation and work out the answer.**

1

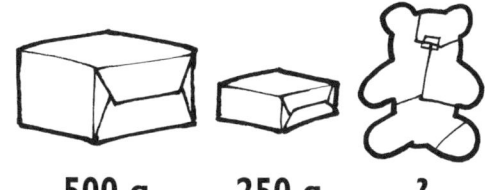

500 g   **250 g**   **?**

The total mass of these three parcels is 1 kg. What is the mass of the third parcel?

2

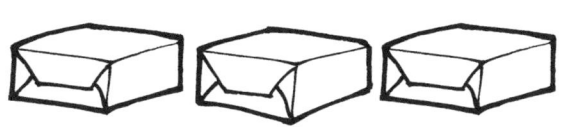

The total mass of these three identical parcels is 900 g. What is the mass of each parcel?

3

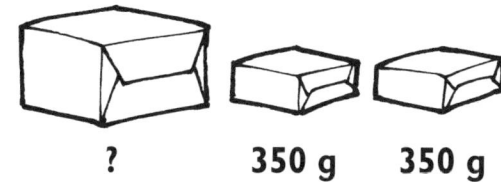

?   **350 g**   **350 g**

The total mass of these three parcels is 2 kg. What is the mass of the largest parcel?

4

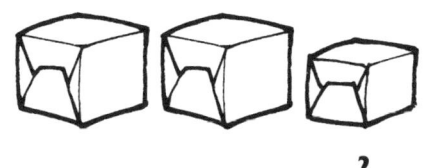

?

Two identical parcels together weigh 900 g. A smaller parcel weighs 100 g less than one of them. What is its mass?

5

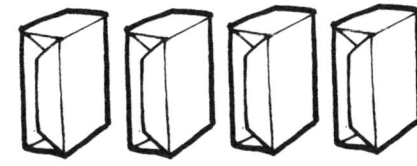

Four identical parcels each weigh 125 g. What is the total mass of the parcels?

6

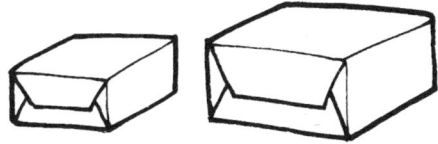

The larger parcel is 3 times heavier than the smaller one. The smaller one weighs 200 g. What is the total mass of the parcels?

Teachers' note As an extension activity, ask the children to make up 2 parcel questions for a partner to solve. The sheets can be given for children to write on in a standard way or alternatively the children could cut out the questions and use as question cards, writing the answers on the back.

A Lesson for Every Day
Maths
7–8 Years
© A&C Black

Parcel problems: 2

- **For each question, write a calculation and work out the answer.**

1

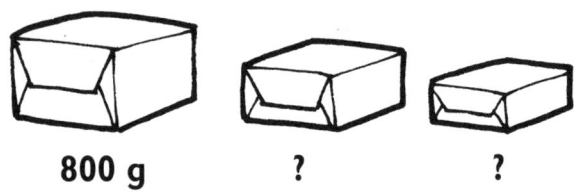

800 g   **?**   **?**

The medium parcel is half the mass of the large one. The smallest is half the mass of the medium one. What is the total mass of the parcels?

2

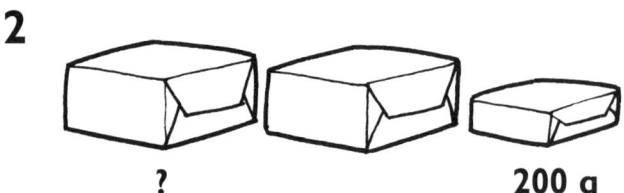

?   **200 g**

The total mass of the parcels is 2 kg. Two have the same mass and the smaller one weighs 200 g. What is the mass of one of the larger ones?

3

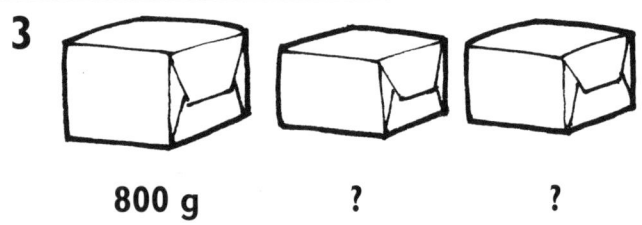

800 g   **?**   **?**

The total mass of the parcels is 2 kg. Two have the same mass and the larger one weighs 800 g. What is the mass of one of the smaller ones?

4

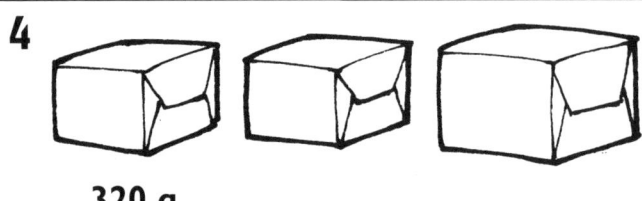

320 g

Two identical parcels each weigh 320 g. A larger parcel weighs 180 g more than one of them. What is the total mass of the parcels?

5

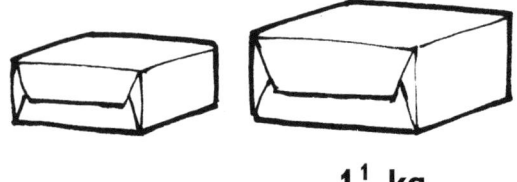

1½ kg

The larger parcel is 3 times heavier than the smaller one. The larger one weighs 1½ kg. What is the total mass of the parcels?

6

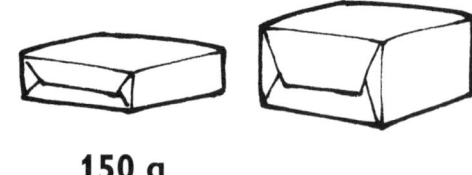

150 g

The larger parcel is 4 times heavier than the smaller one. The smaller one weighs 150 g. What is the mass of the larger parcel?

198

Teachers' note As an extension activity, ask the children to make up 2 parcel questions for a partner to solve. The sheets can be given for children to write on in a standard way or alternatively the children could cut out the questions and use as question cards, writing the answers on the back.

A Lesson for Every Day
Maths
7–8 Years
© A&C Black

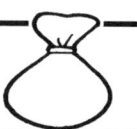

• **You need the nets on 'Dice: 2' to make 3 dice.**

☆ Roll the 3 dice and find the total.

☆ Repeat this 20 times, recording the totals.

☆ What do you notice?

• **What are all the possible │totals│ that can be made with the 3 dice labelled 0, 1 and 2?**

[0] + [0] + [0] = 0		[0] + [0] + [1] = 1
[ ] + [ ] + [ ] =		[ ] + [ ] + [ ] =
[ ] + [ ] + [ ] =		[ ] + [ ] + [ ] =
[ ] + [ ] + [ ] =		[ ] + [ ] + [ ] =
[ ] + [ ] + [ ] =		[ ] + [ ] + [ ] =
[ ] + [ ] + [ ] =		[ ] + [ ] + [ ] =
[ ] + [ ] + [ ] =		[ ] + [ ] + [ ] =
[ ] + [ ] + [ ] =		[ ] + [ ] + [ ] =
[ ] + [ ] + [ ] =		[ ] + [ ] + [ ] =
[ ] + [ ] + [ ] =		[ ] + [ ] + [ ] =
[ ] + [ ] + [ ] =		[ ] + [ ] + [ ] =
[ ] + [ ] + [ ] =		[ ] + [ ] + [ ] =

NOW TRY THIS!

• **Use 2 real dice. Write all the possible totals that can be made. Draw a table to help you find all the totals.**

Teachers' note When the children are writing the possible totals, encourage them to work systematically. Discuss whether 0+1+0 is classed as the same as 1+0+0 or 0+0+1 and encourage children to reason for themselves. For the extension activity demonstrate how a table can be used to find the 36 different totals. See the note on the activity on page 22 for more information.

A Lesson for Every Day
Maths
7–8 Years
© A&C Black

• **Cut out the dice nets and make 3 dice.**

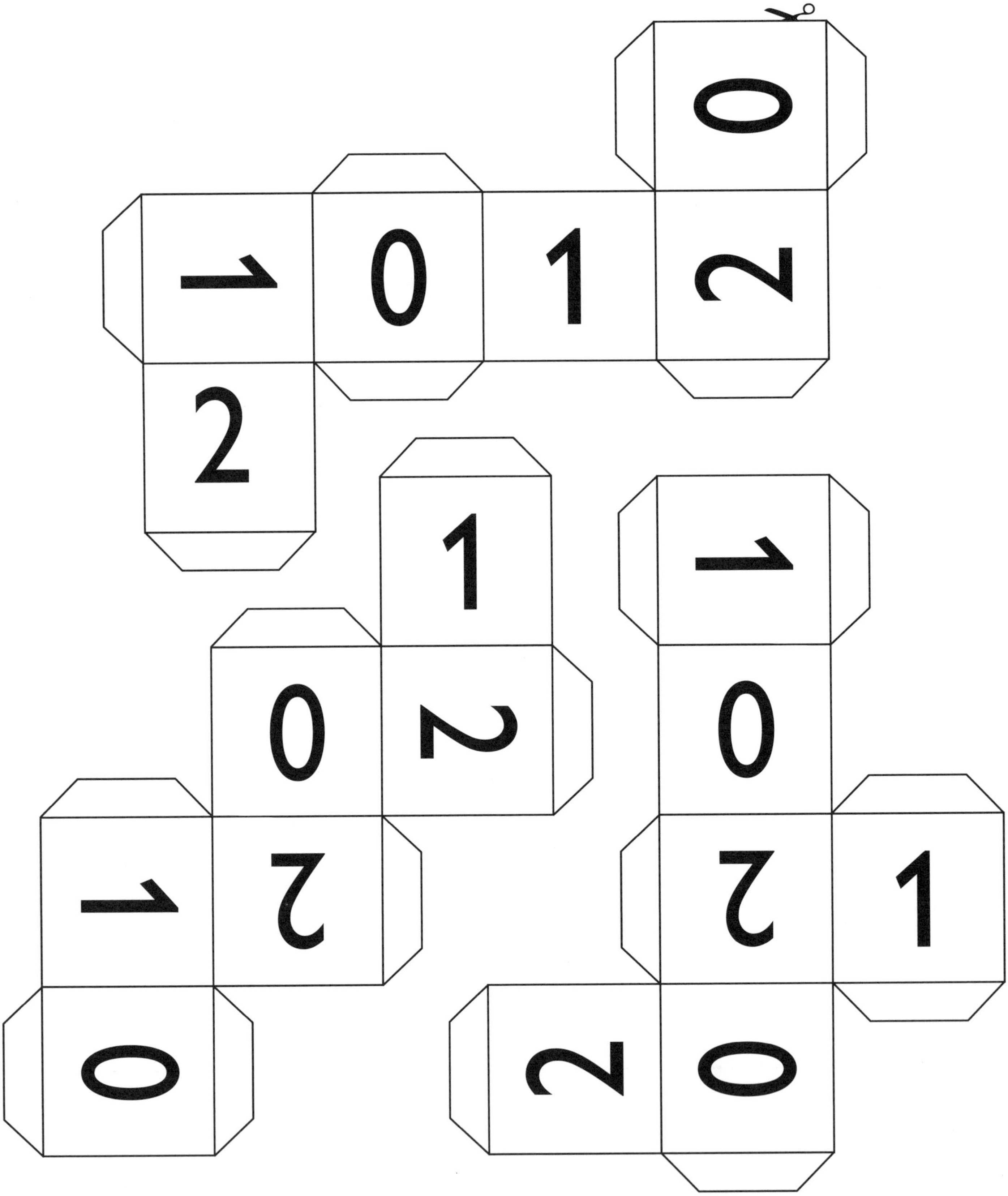

Teachers' note Use this sheet in conjunction with 'Dice: 1'. The sheet should be copied onto card, and the children will need scissors and glue or sticky tape.

A Lesson for Every Day
Maths
7–8 Years
© **A&C Black**

True or false?

- **Is the statement** ☐true☐ **or** ☐false☐ **?**
- **Colour the correct answer.**
- **Write examples to show whether it is true or false.**

---

1 There are exactly 5 multiples of 3 between 20 and 30.

_____

_____

☐ true ☐

☐ false ☐

2 There are exactly 6 multiples of 4 between 30 and 59.

_____

_____

☐ true ☐

☐ false ☐

---

3 If you divide any even number by an even number the answer is always even.

_____

_____

☐ true ☐

☐ false ☐

4 If you double any odd number the answer is always even.

_____

_____

☐ true ☐

☐ false ☐

---

5 There are exactly 11 multiples of 5 between 43 and 97.

_____

_____

☐ true ☐

☐ false ☐

6 There are exactly 5 multiples of 3 between 26 and 40.

_____

_____

☐ true ☐

☐ false ☐

NOW TRY THIS!

- **Write two statements of your own and find out whether they are** ☐true☐ **or** ☐false☐ **.**

Teachers' note Ask the children to make predictions before checking and finding examples to show whether the statement is true or false. As a further extension activity, the children could amend the statements to make them true.

A Lesson for Every Day
Maths
7–8 Years
© A&C Black

Partition patterns

- **Continue each partition pattern.**

467

400	+	60	+	7
400	+	50	+	17
400	+	40	+	27
400	+	☐	+	☐
400	+	☐	+	☐
400	+	☐	+	☐

952

900	+	50	+	2
900	+	☐	+	12
900	+	☐	+	22
900	+	☐	+	☐
900	+	☐	+	☐
900	+	☐	+	☐

648

600	+	40	+	8
600	+	☐	+	☐
600	+	☐	+	☐
600	+	☐	+	☐

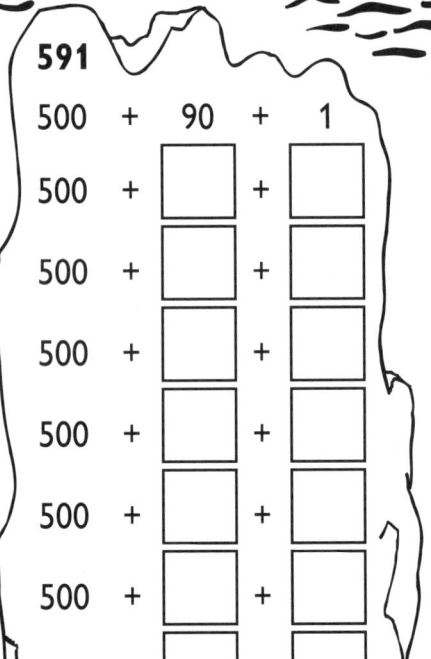

591

500	+	90	+	1
500	+	☐	+	☐
500	+	☐	+	☐
500	+	☐	+	☐
500	+	☐	+	☐
500	+	☐	+	☐
500	+	☐	+	☐
500	+	☐	+	☐

800

800	+	0	+	0
700	+	100	+	0
700	+	90	+	10
700	+	80	+	☐
700	+	☐	+	☐
700	+	☐	+	☐
700	+	☐	+	☐
700	+	☐	+	☐
700	+	☐	+	☐

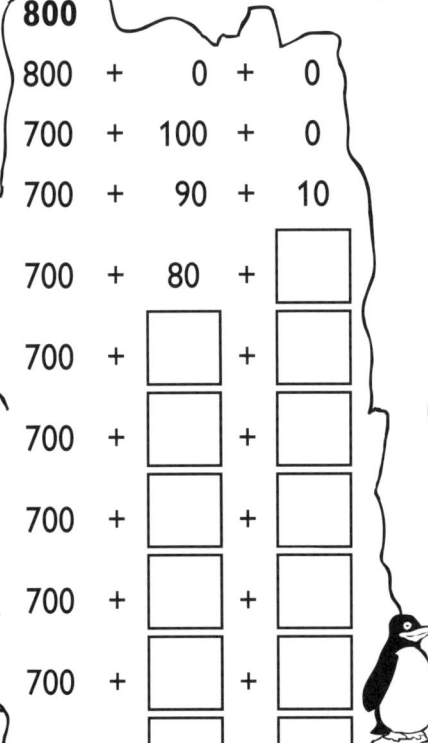

308

300	+	0	+	8
300	+	100	+	8
300	+	90	+	18
200	+	☐	+	☐
200	+	☐	+	☐
200	+	☐	+	☐
200	+	☐	+	☐
200	+	☐	+	☐
200	+	☐	+	☐

NOW TRY THIS!

- **Write a three-digit number on the back of this sheet. Make your own partition pattern.**

Teachers' note This skill is valuable for helping children to understand written methods of addition and subtraction. It is particularly useful as a way to begin subtracting, leading towards the decomposition method.

A Lesson for Every Day
Maths
7–8 Years
© A&C Black

Hedgehog numbers

• Fill in the numbers hidden by the hedgehogs.

452 = 400 + 50 + **2**

354 = 300 + 50 +

507 = 400 + 100 +

275 = 200 + + 5

596 = 500 + + 6

467 = 400 + + 7

751 = 600 + 150 +

863 = 700 + 160 +

394 = 300 + 90 +

354 = 300 + 40 +

452 = 400 + 40 +

692 = 600 + + 2

596 = 500 + + 16

467 = 400 + + 17

874 = 700 + 170 +

784 = 600 + 170 +

NOW TRY THIS!

• Now try these.

881 = 700 + + 1

738 = + 30 + 8

697 = + 190 + 7

881 = 700 + + 11

738 = + 130 + 8

697 = 500 + 180 +

Teachers' note This skill is valuable for helping children to understand written methods of addition and subtraction. It is particularly useful as a way to begin subtracting, leading towards the decomposition method. Ensure the children notice that the last four questions of the main activity involve more complex partitioning.

A Lesson for Every Day
Maths
7-8 Years
© A&C Black

Going crackers!

• **Write three-digit numbers on the crackers to make the statement** | true | .

is 100 more than

is 100 more than

is 10 more than

is 10 more than

is 100 less than

is 100 less than

is 10 less than

is 10 less than

NOW TRY THIS!

• **Write numbers on the crackers to make these statements** | true | .

is 200 more than

is 30 less than

is 6 more than

is 400 less than

is 300 less than

is 50 more than

is 90 less than

is 500 more than

Teachers' note This activity can be used as an open activity where children choose their own numbers to make the statements true. It encourages children to observe patterns, for example that when adding 100 to 321 only the hundreds digit changes. Alternatively, for some children specific numbers could be written onto one end of the cracker.

A Lesson for Every Day
Maths
7–8 Years
© A&C Black

Fraction wall

- **Write** > **or** < **between each pair of fractions to show which is** more **or** less.

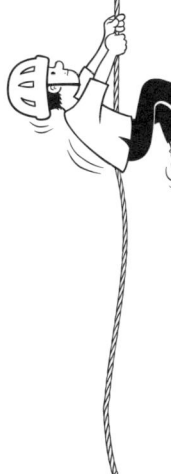

Example: $\frac{3}{4}$ > $\frac{1}{2}$

1 whole							
$\frac{1}{2}$				$\frac{1}{2}$			
$\frac{1}{3}$		$\frac{1}{3}$			$\frac{1}{3}$		
$\frac{1}{4}$		$\frac{1}{4}$		$\frac{1}{4}$		$\frac{1}{4}$	
$\frac{1}{5}$		$\frac{1}{5}$	$\frac{1}{5}$		$\frac{1}{5}$		$\frac{1}{5}$
$\frac{1}{6}$	$\frac{1}{6}$	$\frac{1}{6}$		$\frac{1}{6}$	$\frac{1}{6}$		$\frac{1}{6}$
$\frac{1}{7}$	$\frac{1}{7}$	$\frac{1}{7}$	$\frac{1}{7}$	$\frac{1}{7}$	$\frac{1}{7}$		$\frac{1}{7}$
$\frac{1}{8}$	$\frac{1}{8}$	$\frac{1}{8}$	$\frac{1}{8}$	$\frac{1}{8}$	$\frac{1}{8}$	$\frac{1}{8}$	$\frac{1}{8}$

1 $\frac{1}{2}$ ☐ $\frac{1}{4}$

2 $\frac{3}{8}$ ☐ $\frac{1}{4}$

3 $\frac{9}{10}$ ☐ $\frac{7}{8}$

4 $\frac{2}{5}$ ☐ $\frac{1}{3}$

5 $\frac{2}{3}$ ☐ $\frac{3}{4}$

6 $\frac{3}{10}$ ☐ $\frac{2}{5}$

7 $\frac{5}{6}$ ☐ $\frac{4}{5}$

8 $\frac{4}{8}$ ☐ $\frac{2}{5}$

9 $\frac{6}{10}$ ☐ $\frac{2}{3}$

10 $\frac{5}{8}$ ☐ $\frac{3}{4}$

11 $\frac{1}{6}$ ☐ $\frac{1}{5}$

12 $\frac{1}{8}$ ☐ $\frac{1}{10}$

13 $\frac{4}{6}$ ☐ $\frac{5}{8}$

14 $\frac{2}{3}$ ☐ $\frac{2}{5}$

15 $\frac{3}{5}$ ☐ $\frac{7}{10}$

16 $\frac{7}{8}$ ☐ $\frac{5}{6}$

17 $\frac{5}{8}$ ☐ $\frac{3}{5}$

18 $\frac{7}{10}$ ☐ $\frac{2}{3}$

NOW TRY THIS!

- **Write four other fractions** equivalent **to** $\frac{1}{2}$.

☐/☐ ☐/☐ ☐/☐ ☐/☐

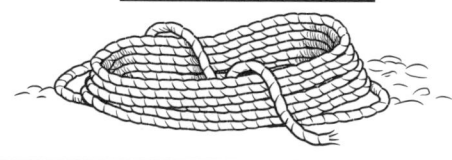

Teachers' note This page can be used in conjunction with coloured rods, such as Cuisenaire rods, so that the children can physically manipulate the fractional parts of a whole. If necessary, explain the term 'equivalent' as meaning 'worth the same'.

A Lesson for Every Day
Maths
7-8 Years
© A&C Black

Fit and tidy

The Smothers family are trying to decide who is the fittest and tidiest person in their house.

- Sort the information into the ⎡Carroll⎤ diagram for them.

Eddie — Fit $\frac{9}{10}$ Tidy $\frac{8}{10}$

Lisa — Fit $\frac{3}{10}$ Tidy $\frac{4}{10}$

George — Fit $\frac{9}{10}$ Tidy $\frac{2}{10}$

Sadie — Fit $\frac{9}{10}$ Tidy $\frac{9}{10}$

Hugh — Fit $\frac{9}{10}$ Tidy $\frac{2}{10}$

Tina — Fit $\frac{1}{10}$ Tidy $\frac{8}{10}$

Mum — Fit $\frac{6}{10}$ Tidy $\frac{9}{10}$

Liam — Fit $\frac{9}{10}$ Tidy $\frac{4}{10}$

Dad — Fit $\frac{3}{10}$ Tidy $\frac{7}{10}$

	Fit	Not fit
Tidy		
Not tidy		

1 Who is fit? _____

2 Who is not fit? _____

3 Who is tidy and fit? _____

4 Who is not tidy? _____

5 Who is the fittest and tidiest member of the family? _____

NOW TRY THIS!

- Make a ⎡Venn⎤ diagram to show this information. Now add your name and some of your friends to your diagram.

206

Teachers' note Discuss the information about the Smothers family and decide with the children what number out of ten should be the division between fit/not fit and tidy/not tidy. If the children don't, suggest it should be 5/10. They then put the family members in the correct places.

A Lesson for Every Day
Maths
7–8 Years
© A&C Black

Clever cylinders

These cylinders help you to find | equivalent | fractions.

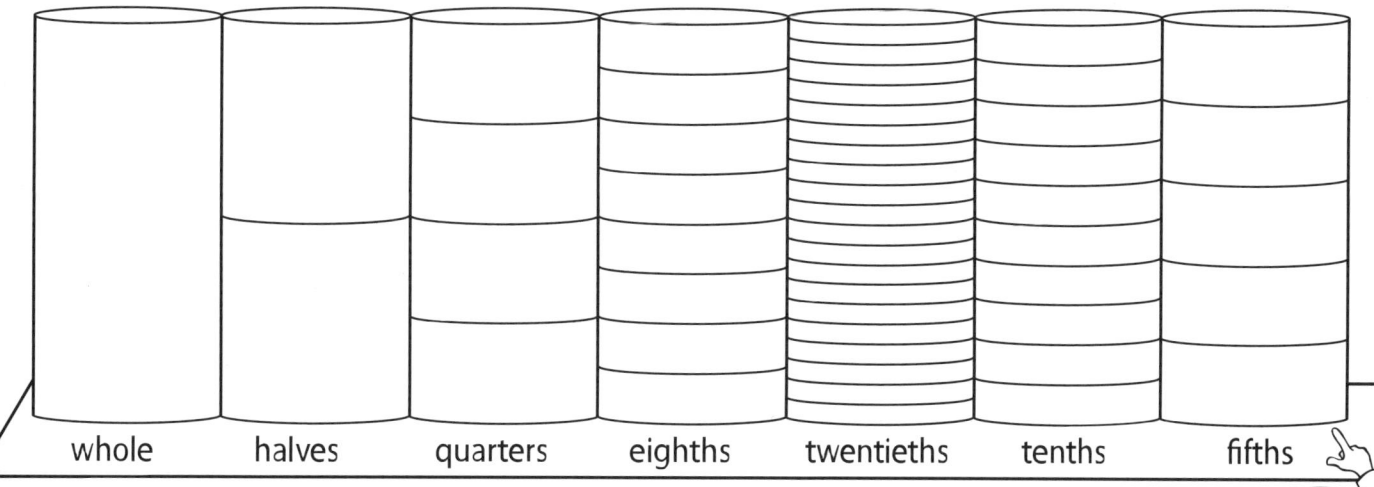

whole   halves   quarters   eighths   twentieths   tenths   fifths

1 Use the cylinders to help you fill in the missing numbers.

a 1 whole = ☐2☐ halves   **b** 3 quarters = ☐ eighths

c 1 quarter = ☐ eighths   **d** 2 eighths = ☐ twentieths

e 4 twentieths = ☐ tenths   **f** 4 tenths = ☐ fifths

g 3 fifths = ☐ tenths   **h** 4 fifths = ☐ tenths

i 9 tenths = ☐ twentieths   **j** 7 tenths = ☐ twentieths

2. Write four fractions equivalent to 1 half.

_____ = 1 half   _____= 1 half

_____= 1 half   _____= 1 half

NOW TRY THIS!

• **On a separate piece of paper, rewrite all the equivalent statements above, like this:**

$$1a \quad 1 = \frac{2}{2}$$

Teachers' note Demonstrate how the diagram can be used to compare fractions, working from the bottom of each cylinder and looking across to find matching levels. If necessary, explain the term 'equivalent' as meaning 'worth the same'.

A Lesson for Every Day
Maths
7-8 Years
© A&C Black

Equivalent cards

- **Cut out the cards.**
- **Match** equivalent **pairs.**

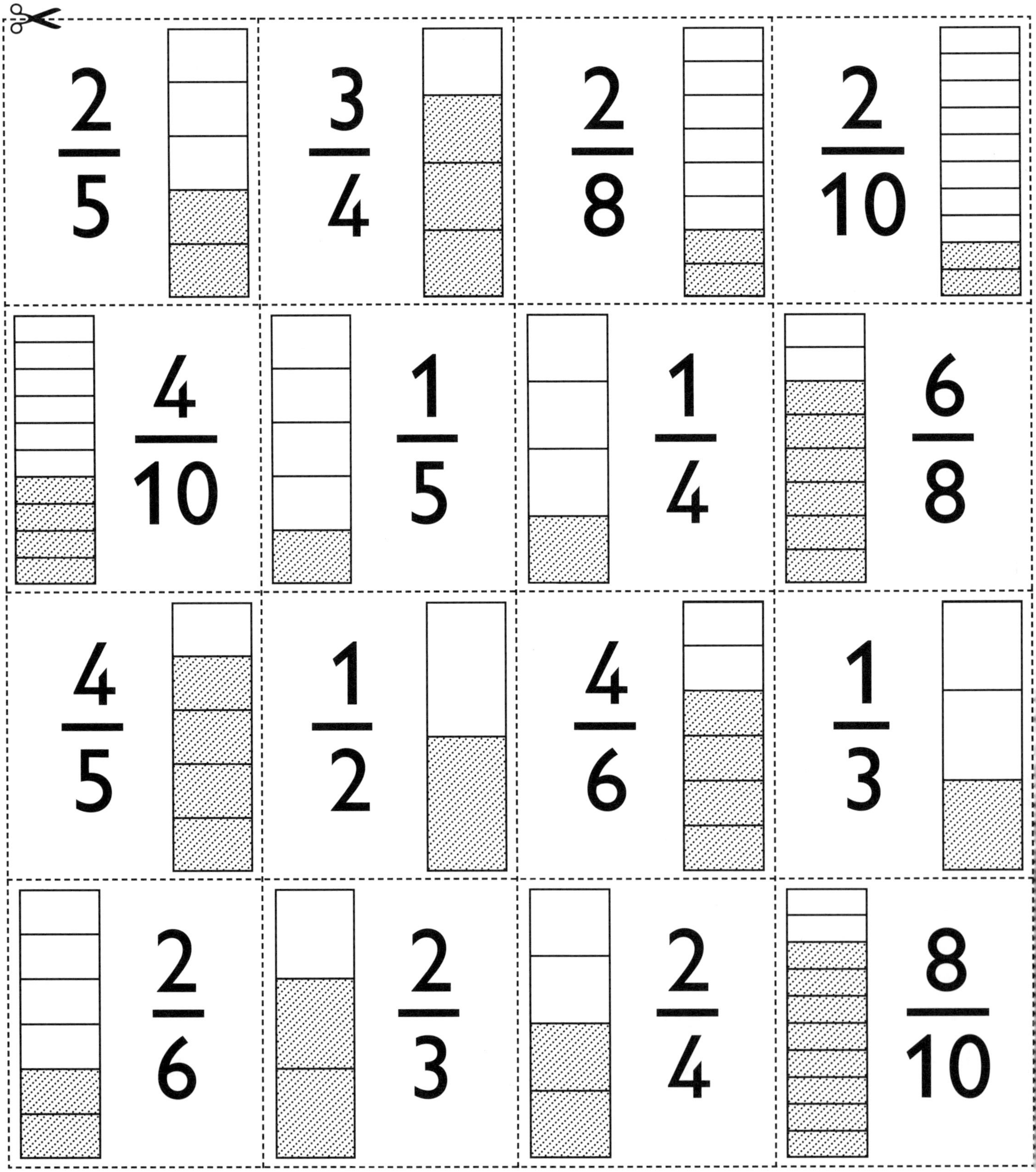

$\dfrac{2}{5}$		$\dfrac{3}{4}$		$\dfrac{2}{8}$		$\dfrac{2}{10}$	
	$\dfrac{4}{10}$		$\dfrac{1}{5}$		$\dfrac{1}{4}$		$\dfrac{6}{8}$
$\dfrac{4}{5}$		$\dfrac{1}{2}$		$\dfrac{4}{6}$		$\dfrac{1}{3}$	
	$\dfrac{2}{6}$		$\dfrac{2}{3}$		$\dfrac{2}{4}$		$\dfrac{8}{10}$

Teachers' note These cards can be used in a variety of ways, with children working individually or in pairs/groups (see the notes on the activity on page 22 for more information).

A Lesson for Every Day
Maths
7–8 Years
© A&C Black

Difference search

☆ Choose pairs of touching numbers from the grid. Find the **difference** between them.

☆ If the difference is **28**, draw a **red** loop around the numbers.

☆ If the difference is **37**, draw a **blue** loop around the numbers.

Numbers can touch vertically or horizontally.

93	130	158	121	115	152	189	217
56	92	112	84	78	124	96	180
182	71	99	136	106	79	115	143
145	108	80	108	69	107	87	124

Show your workings here.

Teachers' note Here, the children are subtracting two- and three-digit numbers to find the difference. Remind them to put the larger number first and subtract the smaller number from it. Discuss appropriate strategies at the start of the lesson, including those outlined in the Primary National Strategy Guidance Paper on Calculation.

A Lesson for Every Day
Maths
7-8 Years
© A&C Black

Wind farm

- Next to each arrow, write the difference between the two numbers either side of it.
- Show your workings on a separate piece of paper.

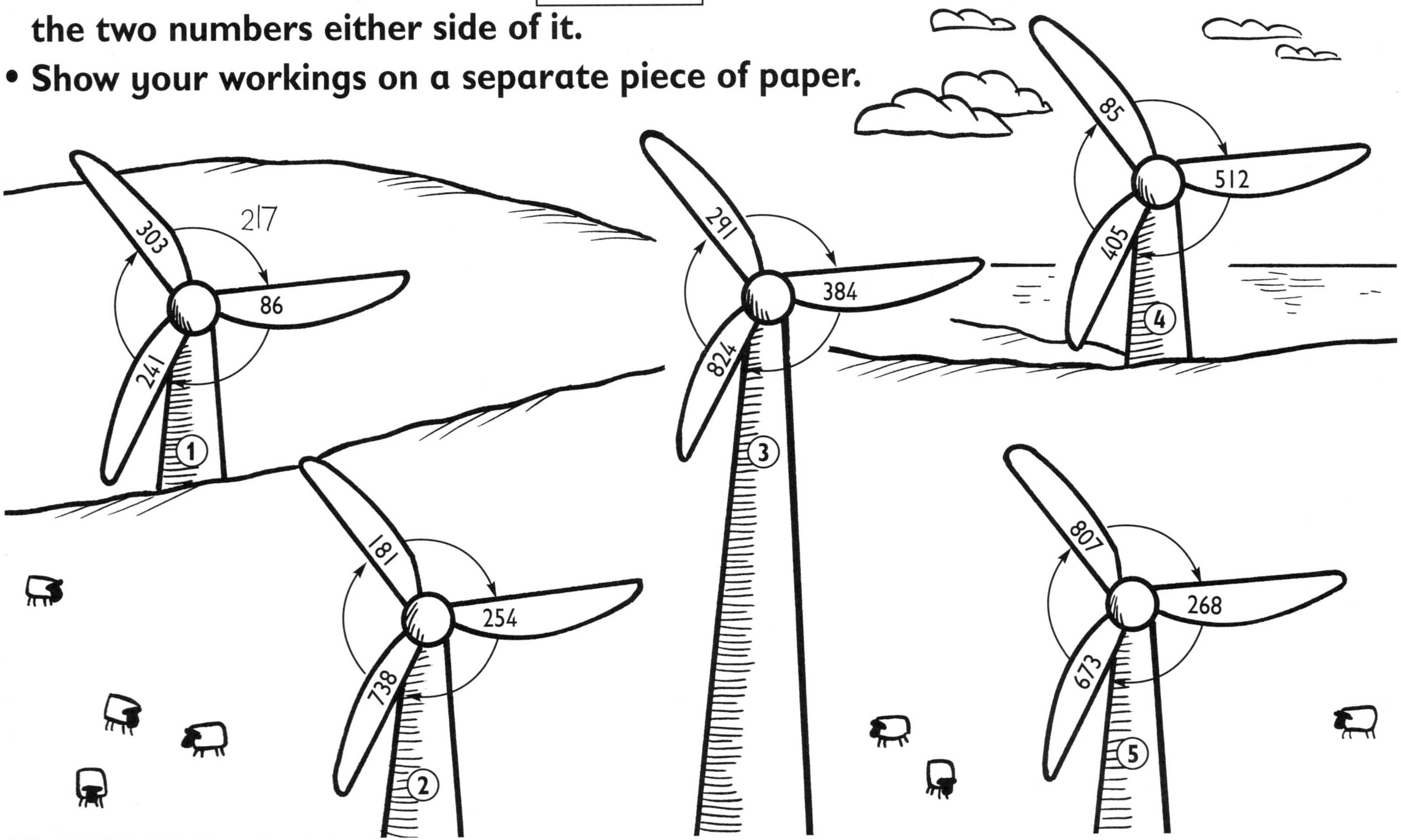

512 85 405 ④

268 807 673 ⑤

384 291 824 ③

254 181 738 ②

217 86 303 241 ①

Teachers' note Remind the children to put the larger number first and subtract the smaller number from it. Any suitable written or informal method could be used for these questions. As an extension, ask the children to write three pairs of numbers that have a difference of 174.

A Lesson for Every Day
Maths
7–8 Years
© A&C Black

Peas please, Louise

Louise shares out her peas between her imaginary friends.

- **How many peas will each friend get and what is the** remainder **?**

1.

26 peas ÷ 3 friends

| | peas each |
| | remainder |

2.

17 peas ÷ 4 friends

| | peas each |
| | remainder |

3.

38 peas ÷ 5 friends

| | peas each |
| | remainder |

4.

37 peas ÷ 3 friends

| | peas each |
| | remainder |

5.

30 peas ÷ 4 friends

| | peas each |
| | remainder |

6.

41 peas ÷ 5 friends

| | peas each |
| | remainder |

NOW TRY THIS!

- **Write four questions with the answer** 5 remainder 1 **.**

☐ ÷ ☐ = 5 r 1   ☐ ÷ ☐ = 5 r 1

☐ ÷ ☐ = 5 r 1   ☐ ÷ ☐ = 5 r 1

Teachers' note *Discuss suitable ways in which the children could find the remainder when dividing, for example by using a number line and counting in threes, fours or fives, or by using their knowledge of tables facts to find the difference between the number and the next lowest multiple of 3, 4 or 5.*

A Lesson for Every Day
Maths
7-8 Years
© A&C Black

Post Office Pam

Customers are always asking Pam questions.

• **Cut out the cards.**

• **Work with a partner to help Pam solve each problem.**

Write the answers on the back of the cards.

How many 5p stamps can I buy with 42p?

I need 25 envelopes. How many packs of 4 must I buy?

How many 3p stamps can I buy with 29p?

I need 14 envelopes. How many packs of 4 must I buy?

I need 33 envelopes. How many packs of 4 must I buy?

How many 5p stamps can I buy with 53p?

How many 4p stamps can I buy with 39p?

I need 27 pencils. How many packs of 10 must I buy?

How many 3p stamps can I buy with 32p?

I need 27 envelopes. How many packs of 4 must I buy?

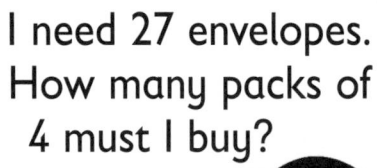

How many 6p stamps can I buy with 46p?

I need 84 pencils. How many packs of 10 must I buy?

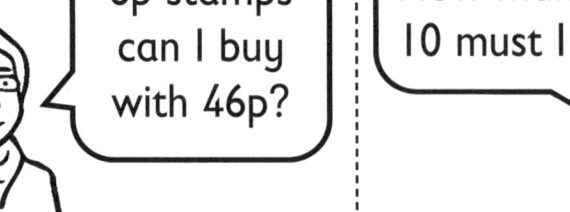

Teachers' note These problems require the children to make decisions about whether to round up or down, depending on the context. Encourage the children to work in pairs and to discuss each situation. The questions and answers could be read out as a role-play by the children in each pair, one being the customer and the other being Pam.

A Lesson for Every Day
Maths
7–8 Years
© A&C Black

Smoothies

Lauren is making smoothies with different types of fruit pulp and a secret ingredient.

- **Write how much of each type of fruit pulp is used.**

Amount   Different types of fruit used

100 ml Zesty	$\frac{1}{2}$ is orange 50 ml	$\frac{1}{5}$ is grape ☐ ml	$\frac{1}{4}$ is apple ☐ ml
60 ml Refresher	$\frac{1}{3}$ is mango ☐ ml	$\frac{1}{10}$ is pineapple ☐ ml	$\frac{1}{4}$ is lemon ☐ ml
60 ml Tutti Frutti	$\frac{1}{6}$ is passion fruit ☐ ml	$\frac{1}{2}$ is grapefruit ☐ ml	$\frac{1}{5}$ is kiwi fruit ☐ ml
150 ml Fruit Kick	$\frac{1}{5}$ is pear ☐ ml	$\frac{1}{10}$ is mandarin ☐ ml	$\frac{1}{3}$ is banana ☐ ml
36 ml Very Berry	$\frac{1}{4}$ is strawberry ☐ ml	$\frac{1}{6}$ is raspberry ☐ ml	$\frac{1}{3}$ is lime ☐ ml

NOW TRY THIS!

- **Use your answers to find out how much of the secret ingredient is in each smoothie.**

Teachers' note If necessary, explain the term 'pulp' to the children. The children could make up their own smoothies, name them and say what fraction of each smoothie different fruits could be.

A Lesson for Every Day
Maths
7-8 Years
© A&C Black

Code breaker – page 27
SOLUTION

8	7	0	6	1	5	8
5	2	9	4	1	0	9
0		9	4	1		0
		7	0	9		0
6	9	9	9			6
9	4	1	7	0		7
9	7	9	0	5	5	5

NTT 'One fine day a fat rat sat on a gnat'

More or less – page 28

Monkey puzzles – page 30
SOLUTIONS
325, 352, 456, 635, 652, 808, 910, 981, 1001, 1010,
1011, 1020, 1050, 1120, 1210
1542, 1190, 1001, 987, 897, 1600, 1060, 1016,
1006, 610, 8342, 8243, 4283, 2843, 2463

Mixed up, missed out! – page 33
SOLUTIONS
1 60, 70   400, 450   140, 160   270, 300   200, 240
2 70, 40   250, 200   140, 60   180, 90   360, 320
NTT When counting on from zero in 40s the
numbers are double the numbers in the 20s. The
numbers are all multiples of 10 and all have
even digits (apart from zero).

Multiple octopus – page 34
NTT
	in 9s	in 2s, 3s and 6s
in 5s		
in 2s, 4s and 8s	in 3s and 9s	in 7s
	in 4s and 7s	in 4s, 6s and 9s

Changing the guard – page 35
SOLUTIONS
1 14, 12, 10, 8, 6, 4, 2,
2 28, 24, 20, 16, 12, 8, 4
3 21, 18, 15, 12, 9, 6, 3
4 42, 36, 30, 24, 18, 12, 6
5 56, 48, 40, 32, 24, 16, 8
6 49, 42, 35, 28, 21, 14, 7
NTT 90, 81, 72, 63, 54, 45, 36, 27, 18, 9

Superheroes – page 36
SOLUTIONS
1 200 + 60 + 2   2 400 + 50 + 7
3 900 + 30 + 1   4 800 + 40 + 4
5 600 + 0 + 5   6 200 + 70 + 8
7 100 + 30 + 7   8 500 + 0 + 9
9 800 + 80 + 8
NTT
931 and 137   262 and 278
457 and 137   605 and 509

Bows and arrows – page 38
1 Miss 12   2 Hit 13   3 Miss 17   4 Hit 15
5 Miss 11   6 Hit 16   7 Miss 18   8 Miss 18

Pigs on parade – page 47
1 65   2 30   3 55   4 25
5 95   6 6   7 16   8 49
9 85   10 98   11 43   12 81
13 66   14 28   15 37   16 71
NTT 24 and 76   26 and 74

Genius gerbil – page 49
SOLUTIONS
1 350   2 90   3 780   4 590   5 80
6 300   7 600   8 470   9 990

NTT (a) 7   (b) 52   (c) 80   (d) 18   (e) 487   (f) 360

At the ice rink – page 50
SOLUTIONS
1 26 + 7 = 33   2 8 + 13 = 21   3 3 × 7 = 21
£5.80 + £13.20
4 £3.70 × 2 + £5.80 = £13.20 or £3.70 + £3.70 +
£5.80 = £13.20
5 £2.10 × 5 = £10.50
6 £23.20 ÷ £5.80 = 4 or £5.80 × [4] = £23.20
7 £23.70 ÷ £7.90 = 3 or £7.90 × [3] = £23.70
8 34 − 26 + 17 = 25
9 27 + 12 − 15 = 24
10 45 + 8 = 53

Have a good trip! – page 53
SOLUTIONS
1 500   2 500   3 600   4 900   5 900   6 800
7 900   8 800   9 800
NTT 1000   1200

Jack-in-the-box – page 54
SOLUTIONS
Numbers in each pair could be in any order.
1 4, 5   2 3, 5   3 3, 4   4 4, 6   5 3, 6   6 3, 7
7 4, 7   8 5, 7   9 5, 8   10 3, 8   11 4, 9   12 3, 9
13 5, 9   14 4, 8

The value of words – page 55
SOLUTIONS

he 70	so 33	be 17	ox 90
to 33	ma 43	at 37	us 43
up 97	pa 99	is 46	we 59
it 38	as 45	of 66	am 43
am 74	by 29	or 52	my 40

NTT
he 84	so 41	be 31	ox 98
to 25	ma 27	at 21	us 31
up 85	pa 83	is 28	we 45
it 20	as 29	of 58	am 27
am 58	by 19	or 44	my 30

Katie's kittens: 1 – page 56
1 80 + 13 = 93   2 80 + 15 = 95
3 60 + 16 = 76   4 110 + 14 = 124
5 110 + 12 = 122   6 90 + 13 = 103
NTT (a) 106   (b) 113   (c) 122   (d) 124

Katie's kittens: 2 – page 57
1 10 + 3 = 13   2 40 + 7 = 47
3 20 + 7 = 27   4 30 + 9 = 39
5 50 + 6 = 56   6 50 + 7 = 57
NTT (a) 46   (b) 49   (c) 18   (d) 38

Triangle tricks – page 58
SOLUTIONS
This is one possible solution
(all rotations of this solution
are also possible)

Question time – page 59
[16] + 12 = 28   40 − [23] = 17
[6] × 3 = 18   50 − 24 = [26]
[50] ÷ 5 = 10   [90] − 30 = 60
17 + 24 = [41]   24 + 4 = [6]

Problem page – page 60
SOLUTIONS
16p   16
£1.05   25p

Bing, Bong, Bang – page 61
SOLUTIONS

Bong, Bing, Bang	Bing, Bong, Bang
Bong, Bing, Bang	Bang, Bong, Bong
Bong, Bang, Bong	Bang, Bing, Bong

1
Bong, Bing, Bung, Bong	Bong, Bong, Bung, Bong
	Bung, Bong, Bong
	Bung, Bong, Bong, Bang

2
Bong, Bung, Bong, Bing	Bong, Bing, Bung, Bong
Bong, Bang, Bing	Bang
	Bong, Bong, Bang

3
Bang, Bong, Bong, Bing	Bang, Bung, Bong, Bing
Bong	Bung
	Bong, Bong, Bong, Bong

4
Bang, Bong, Bong, Bing	Bung, Bong, Bing
Bung, Bong, Bong, Bung	Bung, Bong, Bong
Bung, Bong, Bong, Bung	Bung, Bang, Bong, Bong

Chair challenge – page 63
SOLUTIONS
3 × 4 = 6 = 6   5 × 3 − 6 = 9   6 × 3 − 5 = 13
4 × 3 = 8 = 4   3 × 5 − 6 = 9   3 × 6 − 5 = 13
3 × 4 = 5 = 7   5 × 3 − 4 = 11   6 × 3 − 4 = 14
4 × 3 − 5 = 7   3 × 5 − 4 = 11   3 × 6 − 4 = 14
5 × 4 − 6 = 14   6 × 4 − 5 = 19   5 × 6 − 4 = 26
4 × 5 − 6 = 14   4 × 6 − 5 = 19   6 × 5 − 4 = 26
5 × 4 − 3 = 17   6 × 4 − 3 = 21   5 × 6 − 3 = 27
4 × 5 − 3 = 17   4 × 6 − 3 = 21   6 × 5 − 3 = 27

Easter-egg hunt – page 64
SOLUTIONS
9	4	7	7	11	9	8
1	12	3	4	8	6	7
6	8	4	4	8	9	

The egg with 2 on is uncoloured.

Brain box – page 65
SOLUTIONS
Questions 4 to 8 have two possible answers

Permission to land – page 68
SOLUTIONS
Example answers:
1 537 + 162 = 699   2 162 + 218 = 380
3 127 + 162 = 289   4 696 + 218 = 914
5 479 + 358 = 837   6 479 + 127 = 606

A sticky situation – page 70
SOLUTIONS
Possible answers:
1 triangle

---

2 (a) 4 (b) quadrilateral (rhombus)
3 (a) 4 (b) quadrilateral (trapezium)
4 (a) 3, 4 or 6 (b) triangle, quadrilateral
(parallelogram) or hexagon
5 (a) 4, 5, 6 or 7 (b) quadrilateral (trapezium),
pentagon, hexagon, heptagon

Building work – page 71
SOLUTIONS
1 3   2 4   3 4   4 4   5 4   6 4   7 4   8 4
NTT
The shapes in questions 3, 4 and 5 are the same.
The shapes in questions 6 and 8 are the same.

Traffic lights – page 72
SOLUTIONS
1 red: square-based pyramid   orange:
triangular prism   green: cylinder
2 red: cone   orange: cube   green: triangular
prism
3 red: cylinder   orange: cone   green: sphere

Two numbers – page 73
SOLUTIONS
2, 5   3, 2
10, 4   5, 5
10, 2   10, 1
7, 5   10, 9

Match it: 1 – page 75
SOLUTIONS TO SHEET 1
90 ÷ 15 = 6, [ ] × 15 = 90, 90 ÷ 15 = [ ], (15 × 25) +
8 = [ ], 90 − [ ] = 15, [ ] × 15 = 90, 90 ÷ 15 = [ ], 15
+ [ ] = 90

Match it: 2 – page 76
SOLUTIONS
100 − 25 − [ ] = 8, 1 × 8 + [ ] = [ ], 90 − 25 − [ ] = 8,
100 × 8 − [ ] = [ ], 100 − 25 = [ ], 8, (1
× 8) = [ ], 90 − [ ], [ ] × [ ] 15 = 90, 90 ÷ 15 = [ ], 15
+ [ ] = 90

Sweet talk – page 77
SOLUTIONS
40 sweets
NTT 16

Toy scale – page 80
SOLUTIONS
1 92p   2 5p   3 20p   4 79p   5 85p   6 60p
7 55p   8 23p   9 45p   10 18p   11 37p   12 26p
13 84p   14 68p   15 53p   16 34   17 73p
18 81p

Shape all-sorts – page 85
SOLUTIONS

	At least one circular face		No circular faces	
	cone	cuboid	cube prism (triangular)	cuboid pyramid (square-based)
At least one vertex			cube prism (triangular)	sphere
No vertices	cylinder			
NTT

	No rectangular face		No rectangular faces	
Prism		cylinder	cube cylinder	
Not a prism			pyramid (square-based)	cone

Symmetry Cemetery – page 86
SOLUTIONS
✓ ✓ ✗ ✓ ✓
✓ ✓ ✗ ✗ ✓
✗ ✗ ✓ ✓ ✓
✓ ✗ ✗ ✓ ✓

NTT
Line 2 shape 3 should be coloured green.
Line 3 shape 5 should be coloured blue.
Line 1 shape 1 should be coloured yellow.

Shape symmetry – page 87
SOLUTIONS
NTT
1 square   2 square   3 rectangle   4 triangle
5 hexagon   6 octagon   7 quadrilateral (kite)

Mosaic patterns – page 88
SOLUTIONS

Express pizza – page 89
SOLUTIONS
1 (a) £9.98   b) £32.97   c) £27.98   d) £15.48
e) £45.46   f) £34.96
2 a) £2.03   b) £9.51   c) £2.02   d) £0.04 or 4p
NTT Yes (£19.47)

Loop the loop – page 90
SOLUTIONS
The phrase from start to finish is TRY TO DANCE

Sheep solutions – page 91
SOLUTIONS
17 sheep, 10 lambs, 7 ewes

Sensible statements – page 92
SOLUTIONS
1 40 − [ ] = 15, 2 42 ÷ 14 = [ ], 3 24 × 3 = [ ],
4 [ ] − 14 = 11

Coin quiz – page 93
SOLUTIONS
The words spell:
CAP, BIN, GET, ROD

Right-angle wrangle and Right-angle tangle
– page 94–5
SOLUTIONS
Right-angle wrangle
1 triangle 1 right angle
2 triangle 1 right angle
3 pentagon 2 right angles
4 square 4 right angles
5 pentagon 3 right angles
6 pentagon 3 right angles
7 pentagon 3 right angles
8 square 4 right angles
Right-angle tangle
1 5 sides 3 right angles
2 7 sides 4 right angles
3 11 sides 4 right angles
4 12 sides 8 right angles
5 12 sides 7 right angles

6 12 sides 6 right angles
7 12 sides 3 right angles
8 12 sides 4 right angles

Clock angles – page 96
SOLUTIONS
1 6 2 7 3 9 4 6 5 5 6 11 7 10 8 11

Gee-up horsel – page 98
SOLUTIONS
1 1/6 2 3/8 3 5/6 4 4/7 5 8/14 6 7/15
7 8/18 8 6/16 9 11/12

Musical mental maths – page 99
SOLUTIONS
1 15 2 7 3 8 4 13 5 9 6 12 7 50
8 60 9 110 10 40 11 55 12 84

Snap – page 100
SOLUTIONS

2	8	4	4
Not snap	3	7	Snap
3	2	1	10
6	6	8	9
6	Not snap	9	10
Snap	0	1	5
0	1	5	9
	Snap	Not snap	8

The dabble birds – page 101
SOLUTIONS
1 ÷ 8 13 2 − 37 18 3 × 9 54 4 + 16 75
5 ÷ 6 16 6 × 5 34 7 + 39 54 8 − 16 84
9 ÷ 4 23 10 × 4 60
NTT 100

Learning about turning – page 103
SOLUTIONS

Less than	Right angle	More than
AM	AN	AS
GO	ME	HE
BE	IS	TO
ON	BY	IT
MY		AT
IN		OH
HI		
SO		

Sorting coins – page 105
SOLUTIONS

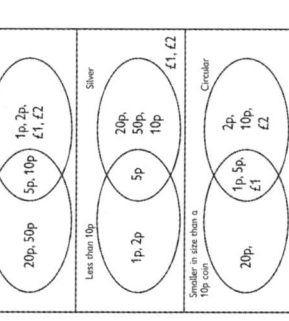

Stream scheme – page 106
SOLUTIONS
1 400 2 700 3 200 4 300 5 100 6 50
7 10 8 650 9 2500 10 1000 11 25 12 75

NTT (a) 5m 18 cm (b) 9m 0 cm (c) 1m 50 cm
(d) 3m 50cm (e) 1m 25 cm (f) 0m 75cm
(g) 1m 20 cm (h) 0m 75cm

Rulers rule – page 108
SOLUTIONS
1 17 cm 2 25 cm 3 12cm 4 29 cm
5 21 cm 6 26cm

Newspaper sales – page 110
SOLUTIONS
1 The Comet 2 The Galaxy
3 The Comet 2500 Daily Moon 2300, The Star 2000, The Comet 1550, Daily Planet 1350, The Galaxy 750
4 The Comet, Daily Moon, The Star, The Meteor because they are the most popular.

Berries – page 111
SOLUTIONS
1 a Blackberries: 13 b Strawberries: 16
c Both: 4 d Only blackberries: 9
e Only strawberries: 12 f Neither: 2
2 Number of friends: 27

Multiples – page 112
SOLUTIONS
2a Any four of the following: 9, 18, 27, 51, 21, 12, 24, 36. The multiple: 3
2b Any six of the following: 16, 32, 44, 80, 8, 56, 20, 53, 5, 26, 17, are not multiples of 3.
2c 53, 5, 26, 17
2d 36, 24, 12
NTT Numbers that are not multiples of 3 or 4

Party food: 1 and 2 – page 113–4
SOLUTIONS
1 pizza, pies, baguette, nuts, mini quiches, green salad, juice, crisps, carrot sticks, dips, samosas, satay sticks
2 arteau, mini burgers
3 pizza, baguette, juice, carrot sticks, dips
4 Check that the children's choices total exactly £2.
NTT Children should notice that the ring for 'More than £1' is inside the ring for 'More than £2'.

How far? – page 117
SOLUTIONS
1 true 2 false 3 true 4 true 5 true 6 true
NTT Caz lives about 2000 m from school.
Ella lives about 1500 m from school.

Woolly jumpers – page 118
SOLUTIONS
1 14 cm 2 12½ cm 3 22 cm 4 40 cm 5 29 cm

At the laundry – page 121
SOLUTIONS
Shirts: 1 more bubble; trousers: 7 more bubbles; dresses: 1 bubble crossed off; skirts: 3 more bubbles; shorts: 2 bubbles crossed off; jumpers: 3 more bubbles.
Skirts 9, jumpers 6, dresses 5, shirts 7, shorts 4, trousers 12
NTT 43 items

Birthday presents – page 122
SOLUTIONS
Table football 15, Remote control car 16, Skateboard 11, Magic set 13, Keyboard 20, Painting set 16, Puzzles 9
Most popular three: keyboard, remote control car, painting set

---

Oranges and lemons – page 123
SOLUTIONS
1 Oranges and lemons: 15 2 Neither: 6
3 Lemons: 19 4 Oranges only: 23
5 100 oranges

Monkey business – page 124
SOLUTIONS
Bananas/apples: Eli, Flo, Bob
No bananas/apples: Paul, Ella
Bananas/no apples: Sam, Jon, Ann, Rosa
No apples/no bananas: Sara, Ian, Dan
1 Bananas: 7 2 Apples: 5
3 Bob: 3 4 Raisins: 3

Symmetry: 1 and 2 – page 125–6
SOLUTIONS
4 sides/symmetrical: rectangle, square, trapezium
4 sides/not symmetrical: the two irregular quadrilaterals
Not 4 sides/symmetrical: circle, equilateral triangle, regular pentagon, regular hexagon
Not 4 sides/not symmetrical: scalene triangle, irregular pentagon, irregular hexagon
1 5 2 5 3 3 4 7 5 Symmetrical and does not have 4 sides

Lines of enquiry – page 127
SOLUTIONS
25, 3, 45, 30, 2, 20, 60, 35, 17, 8

Share and share alike – page 128
SOLUTIONS
7p 6p 7p
9p 8p 7p

Broken keys – page 129
SOLUTIONS
Possible calculations:
11 + 10 = [21] × 60 ÷ 3
100 ÷ 12 − 12
333 × 2 + 111
400 − 134 − 1
104 ÷ 2 ÷ 2 − 2

Milkshake mistakes – page 130
SOLUTIONS
1 second child 2 first child 3 first child
4 first child 5 second child 6 second child

Pyramid picture – page 131
SOLUTIONS
No. (Total is about 53 cm to the nearest half-centimetre.)

Game show – page 132
SOLUTIONS
1 100 g 2 30m 3 3001 4 25cm
5 500 g 6 400ml 7 40 cm 8 70cm

Measuring jugs – page 133
NTT
400 ml 950 ml 750 ml
450 ml 350 ml 925 ml
975 ml 825 ml 575 ml

Hobbies: 1 and 2 – page 135–6
SOLUTIONS
1 6 reading, 9 sport, 4 making models, 8 music, 2 watching TV, 3 playing computer games
2 sport, music, reading, making models, playing computer games, watching TV
3 Check children's answers are reasonable.

The Basketeers – page 137
SOLUTIONS
Tally in this order to show:

Jan	卌 卌	
Jack	卌 卌 卌	
Jade	卌 卌 卌	
Jon	卌 卌	
Jim	卌 卌 卌	|||
Jill	卌 卌	||||

Jack and Jade should both win the cup because they scored the most baskets.

Email – page 138
SOLUTIONS
Check that children have correctly labelled the bar chart and that the bars are at correct heights

The great library sort out: 1 and 2 – page 139–40
SOLUTIONS
1 Comedy: 28, History: 29, Geography: 22, Music: 30, Art: 28
Check that children have drawn and labelled the bar chart correctly.
2 137

Chocolate matters – page 141
SOLUTIONS
1 13 2 7 3 108 4 27 5 4 6 21

Fruit corner – page 142
SOLUTIONS
1 8 2 9 3 6 4 10 5 6 6 8 7 40 8 4

What's the difference? – page 143
SOLUTIONS
Clockwise around each diagram:
1 6, 13, 7
2 22, 31, 9
3 20, 25, 40, 15, 10 with central numbers 45 and 55
4 8, 21, 15, 8, 18 with central numbers 13, 23, 10
5 27, 21, 11, 21, 5, 11, 34, 14, with central numbers 13, 76, 55, 44, 26, 18, 29, 63
6 31, 15, 21, 12, 11, with central numbers 58, 27, 12, 33, 45, 76

Counter tracker – page 144
SOLUTIONS
1 F7 2 F2 3 F7 4 A3 5 B5

Ribbons – page 145
SOLUTIONS
1 50 2 30 3 95 4 83 5 76 6 33 7 72
8 65 9 41

Cookery class – page 147
SOLUTIONS
NTT 1 54 minutes 2 15 minutes
3 39 minutes 4 23 minutes 5 2 minutes
6 37 minutes 7 43 minutes 8 6 minutes
9 21 minutes

Digital puzzles – page 149
SOLUTIONS
1 1:50 2 5:10 3 3:45 4 8:40
5 7:15 6 2:35 7 10:50 8 9:25

TV times: 1 and 2 – page 150–1
SOLUTIONS
40 mins = Cartoons 20 mins = Y Factor
15 mins = The News 25 mins = Football
45 mins = Art-magic 35 mins = Em Street

---

5 mins = Now-a-story 30 mins = Dino World
50 mins = Dino Warrior 55 mins = Westenders

Campsite capers – page 152
SOLUTIONS
20 children (A = 3, B = 6, C = 1, D = 7, E = 3)

Ship ahoy! – page 153
SOLUTIONS
1 4 cm 2 2 cm 3 33 cm
5 23 cm 6 11 cm 7 31 cm
NTT (a) 92 cm (b) 67 cm (c) 55 cm

Odd one out – page 154
SOLUTIONS
1 40 × 2 2 three-quarters of thirty
3 5 ÷ 20 4 6 5 7 6 24 ÷ 6

Dotty symmetry – page 156
SOLUTIONS

Map work – page 157
SOLUTIONS
1 8 cm East 2 12 cm West 3 2½ cm South
4 4 cm North 5 3½ cm South 6 10 cm West

Weight lifters – page 159
SOLUTIONS
Questions 1, 3, 4, 5, 7, 8, 10, 11 and 12 should be coloured.

Time for TV – page 161
SOLUTIONS
1 1:25 p.m. 2 2 hours 45 minutes
3 3:15 p.m. 4 25 minutes
5 40 minutes 6 10:35 p.m.

Record breakers – page 162
SOLUTIONS
1 470 mm 2 790 mm 3 63 cm 4 23 cm
3 cm 21 cm 37 cm 27 cm

Weekend bedtime – page 163
Child-initiated but suggested:
Table: Before 7pm: Tim, Ruby, Leah
After 7pm: Anil, Susie, Ben, Amy, Ella, Peter, Leela, Josh, Tony, Tom, Kate, Lily
1 Coco shouldn't cancel his show.
2 Because at the weekend, most 7-year-olds go to bed after 7 o'clock.

Racing cars – page 164
SOLUTIONS
1 5 2 2, 5, 10 3 2 4 5 5 2 6 2 7 2, 5, 10
8 2 9 none 10 2 11 5 12 2, 5, 10
NTT All numbers should end in 0.

A knight's challenge – page 166
SOLUTIONS
282 259 157 375
414   639
905   676
743 374 643 522

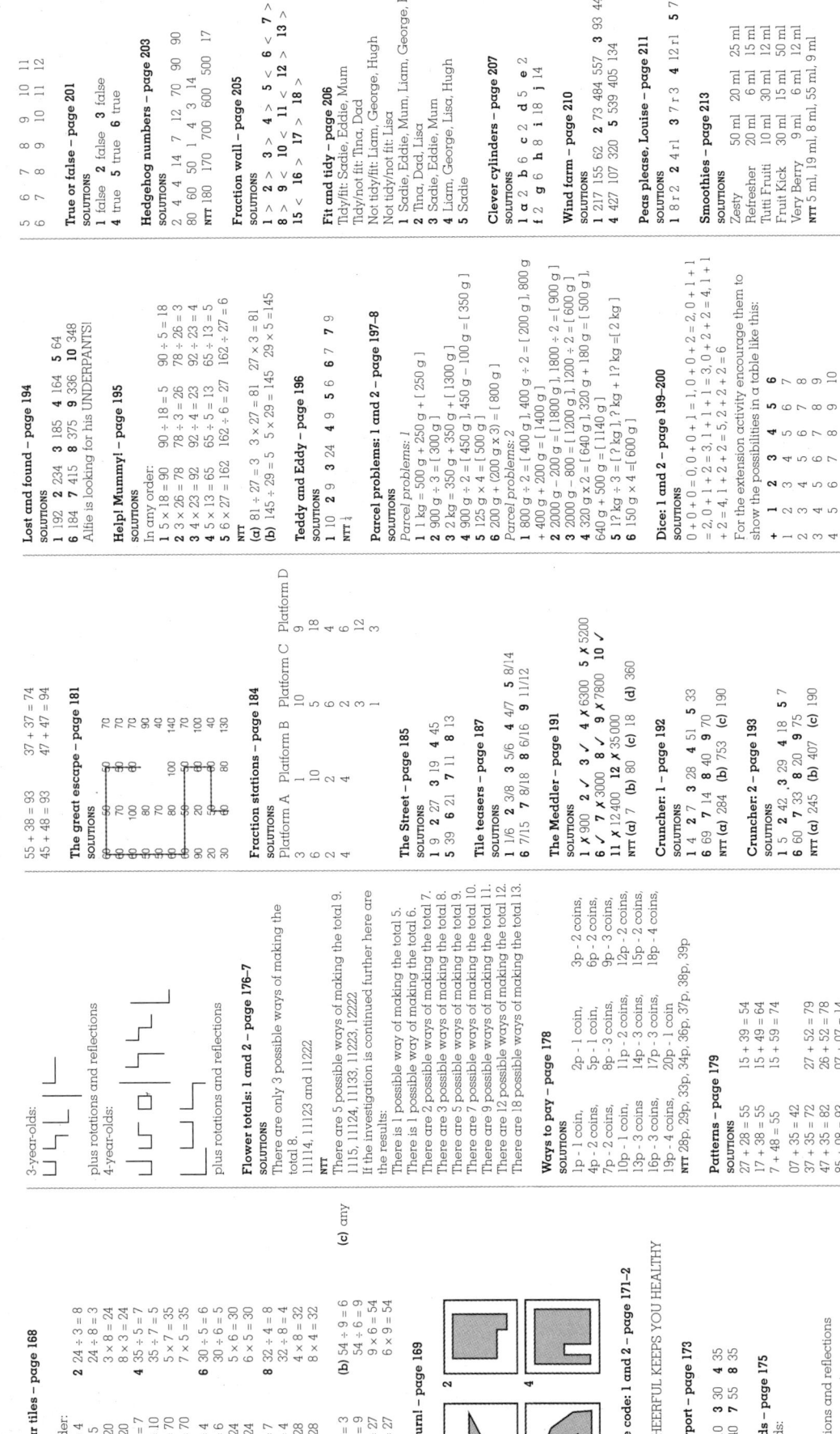

Triangular tiles – page 168
SOLUTIONS
In any order:
1 20 ÷ 5 = 4
   20 ÷ 4 = 5
   4 × 5 = 20
   5 × 4 = 20

2 24 ÷ 3 = 8
   24 ÷ 8 = 3
   3 × 8 = 24
   8 × 3 = 24

3 70 ÷ 10 = 7
   70 ÷ 7 = 10
   7 × 10 = 70
   10 × 7 = 70

4 35 ÷ 5 = 7
   35 ÷ 7 = 5
   5 × 7 = 35
   7 × 5 = 35

5 24 ÷ 6 = 4
   24 ÷ 4 = 6
   4 × 6 = 24
   6 × 4 = 24

6 30 ÷ 6 = 5
   30 ÷ 5 = 6
   5 × 6 = 30
   6 × 5 = 30

7 28 ÷ 4 = 7
   28 ÷ 7 = 4
   7 × 4 = 28
   4 × 7 = 28

8 32 ÷ 4 = 8
   32 ÷ 8 = 4
   4 × 8 = 32
   8 × 4 = 32

NTT
(a) 27 ÷ 9 = 3   (b) 54 ÷ 9 = 6
    27 ÷ 3 = 9   54 ÷ 6 = 9
    3 × 9 = 27   9 × 6 = 54
    9 × 3 = 27   6 × 9 = 54

(c) any

It's your turn! – page 169
SOLUTIONS
1 2
3 4

Crack the code: 1 and 2 – page 171-2
SOLUTIONS
BEING CHEERFUL KEEPS YOU HEALTHY

At the airport – page 173
SOLUTIONS
1 15 2 10 3 30 4 35
5 55 6 40 7 55 8 35

Centi-pods – page 175
SOLUTIONS
2-year-olds:

plus rotations and reflections

3-year-olds:

plus rotations and reflections

4-year-olds:

plus rotations and reflections

Flower totals: 1 and 2 – page 176-7
SOLUTIONS
There are only 3 possible ways of making the total 8.
11114, 11123 and 11222
NTT
There are 5 possible ways of making the total 5.
11115, 11124, 11133, 11223, 12222
If the investigation is continued further here are the results:
There is 1 possible way of making the total 5.
There is 1 possible way of making the total 6.
There are 2 possible ways of making the total 7.
There are 3 possible ways of making the total 8.
There are 5 possible ways of making the total 9.
There are 7 possible ways of making the total 10.
There are 9 possible ways of making the total 11.
There are 12 possible ways of making the total 12.
There are 18 possible ways of making the total 13.

Ways to pay – page 178
SOLUTIONS
1p - 1 coin,   2p - 1 coin,   3p - 2 coins,
4p - 2 coins,   5p - 1 coin,   6p - 2 coins,
7p - 2 coins,   8p - 3 coins,   9p - 3 coins,
10p - 1 coin,   11p - 2 coins,   12p - 2 coins,
13p - 3 coins   14p - 3 coins,   15p - 2 coins,
16p - 3 coins,   17p - 3 coins,   18p - 4 coins.
19p - 4 coins,   20p - 1 coin

Patterns – page 179
SOLUTIONS
27 + 28 = 55   15 + 39 = 54
17 + 38 = 55   15 + 49 = 64
7 + 48 = 55   15 + 59 = 74

07 + 35 = 42   27 + 52 = 79
37 + 35 = 72   26 + 52 = 78
47 + 35 = 82   07 + 07 = 14
85 + 08 = 93

55 + 38 = 93   37 + 37 = 74
45 + 48 = 93   47 + 47 = 94

NTT 28p, 29p, 33p, 34p, 36p, 37p, 38p, 39p

The great escape – page 181
SOLUTIONS
(grid of numbers)

Fraction stations – page 184
SOLUTIONS

Platform A	Platform B	Platform C	Platform D
3	1	10	9
6	5	5	18
2	6	6	4
4	2	3	12
	4	1	3

The Street – page 185
SOLUTIONS
1 9 2 27 3 19 4 45
5 39 6 21 7 11 8 13

Tile teasers – page 187
SOLUTIONS
1 1/6 2 3/8 3 5/6 4 4/7 5 8/14
6 7/15 7 8/18 8 6/16 9 11/12

The Meddler – page 191
SOLUTIONS
1 ✗ 900 2 ✓ 3 ✓ 4 ✗ 6300 5 ✗ 5200
6 ✓ 7 ✗ 3000 8 ✓ 9 ✗ 7800 10 ✓
11 ✗ 12 400 12 ✗ 35 000
NTT (a) 7 (b) 80 (c) 18 (d) 360

Cruncher: 1 – page 192
SOLUTIONS
1 4 2 7 3 28 4 51 5 33
6 69 7 14 8 40 9 70
NTT (a) 284 (b) 753 (c) 190

Cruncher: 2 – page 193
SOLUTIONS
1 5 2 42 3 29 4 18 5 7
6 60 7 33 8 20 9 75
NTT (a) 245 (b) 407 (c) 190

Lost and found – page 194
SOLUTIONS
1 192 2 234 3 185 4 164 5 64
6 184 7 415 8 375 9 336 10 348
Allie is looking for his UNDERPANTS!

Help! Mummy! – page 195
SOLUTIONS
In any order:
1 5 × 18 = 90   90 ÷ 18 = 5
2 3 × 26 = 78   78 ÷ 3 = 26   78 ÷ 26 = 3
3 4 × 23 = 92   92 ÷ 4 = 23   92 ÷ 23 = 4
4 5 × 13 = 65   65 ÷ 5 = 13   65 ÷ 13 = 5
5 6 × 27 = 162   162 ÷ 6 = 27   162 ÷ 27 = 6

NTT
(a) 81 ÷ 27 = 3   3 × 27 = 81   27 × 3 = 81
(b) 145 ÷ 29 = 5   5 × 29 = 145   29 × 5 = 145

Teddy and Eddy – page 196
SOLUTIONS
1 10 2 9 3 24 4 9 5 6 6 7 7 9
NTT ⅓

Parcel problems: 1 and 2 – page 197-8
SOLUTIONS
Parcel problems: 1
1 1 kg = 500 g + 250 g + [250 g]
2 900 g ÷ 3 = [300 g]
3 2 kg = 350 g + 350 g + [1300 g]
4 900 g ÷ 2 = [450 g], 450 g − 100 g = [350 g]
5 125 g × 4 = [500 g]
6 200 g ÷ (200 g × 3) = [800 g]
Parcel problems: 2
1 800 g ÷ 2 = [400 g], 400 g ÷ 2 = [200 g], 800 g
  + 400 g + 200 g = [1400 g]
2 2000 g − 200 g = [1800 g], 1800 g ÷ 2 = [900 g]
3 2000 g − 800 = [1200 g], 1200 g ÷ 2 = [600 g]
4 320 g × 2 = [640 g], 320 g + 180 g = [500 g],
  640 g + 500 g = [1140 g]
5 [? kg] ÷ 3 = [? kg], ? kg + 1? kg = [2 kg]
6 150 g × 4 = [600 g]

Dice: 1 and 2 – page 199-200
SOLUTIONS
0 + 0 = 0, 0 + 0 + 1 = 1, 0 + 0 + 2 = 2, 0 + 1 + 1
= 2, 0 + 1 + 2 = 3, 1 + 1 + 1 = 3, 0 + 2 + 2 = 4, 1 + 1
+ 2 = 4, 1 + 2 + 2 = 5, 2 + 2 + 2 = 6
For the extension activity encourage them to
show the possibilities in a table like this:

+	1	2	3	4	5	6
1	2	3	4	5	6	7
2	3	4	5	6	7	8
3	4	5	6	7	8	9
4	5	6	7	8	9	10
5	6	7	8	9	10	11
6	7	8	9	10	11	12

True or false – page 201
SOLUTIONS
1 false 2 false 3 false
4 true 5 true 6 true

Hedgehog numbers – page 203
SOLUTIONS
2 4 4 14 7 12 70 90 90
80 60 50 1 4 3 14
NTT 180 170 700 600 500 17

Fraction wall – page 205
SOLUTIONS
1 > 2 > 3 > 4 > 5 < 6 < 7 >
8 > 9 < 10 < 11 < 12 > 13 > 14 >
15 < 16 > 17 > 18 >

Fit and tidy – page 206
SOLUTIONS
Tidy/fit: Sadie, Eddie, Mum
Tidy/not fit: Tina, Dad
Not tidy/fit: Liam, George, Hugh
Not tidy/not fit: Lisa
1 Sadie, Eddie, Mum, Liam, George, Hugh
2 Tina, Dad, Lisa
3 Sadie, Eddie, Mum
4 Liam, George, Lisa, Hugh
5 Sadie

Clever cylinders – page 207
SOLUTIONS
1 a 2 b 6 c 2 d 5 e 2
  f 2 g 8 h 8 i 18 j 14

Wind farm – page 210
SOLUTIONS
1 217 155 62 2 73 484 557 3 93 440 533
4 427 107 320 5 539 405 134

Peas please, Louise – page 211
SOLUTIONS
1 8 r 2 2 4 r 1 3 7 r 3 4 12 r 1 5 7 r 2 6 8 r 1

Smoothies – page 213
SOLUTIONS
Zesty   50 ml   20 ml   25 ml
Refresher   20 ml   6 ml   15 ml
Tutti Fruiti   10 ml   30 ml   12 ml
Fruit Kick   30 ml   15 ml   50 ml
Very Berry   9 ml   6 ml   12 ml
NTT 5 ml, 19 ml, 8 ml, 55 ml, 9 ml